Praise for *The Add*

"I've often searched for the right words and advice when I see addiction destroying great lawyers. *The Addicted Lawyer* is filled with the right words and advice, for all lawyers."

—BRIAN TANNEBAUM, Ethics Lawyer and Author of
The Practice; Brutal Truths About Lawyers and Lawyering

"Brian Cuban's book *The Addicted Lawyer* is a courageous account of his personal battle with addiction and how it impacted his life as a law student and lawyer. As a law school dean, I have seen first-hand the devastating impact of substance abuse on students' paths to achieve their goals and on lawyers' ability to thrive in the profession. It is more important now than ever to provide law students and lawyers with the tools they need to recognize the problem in themselves and others and move toward resolving it. Brian's book is a page-turner and reads like an exciting novel. But, rather than fiction, it portrays the harsh realities for so many in our profession who are struggling with addiction. The book's message is one of hope—the hope that it is possible for those struggling with addiction to regain control of their lives and move forward for the benefit of themselves and their clients. This book is a must-read for all law students and lawyers."

—CYNTHIA L. FOUNTAINE, Dean and Professor of Law,
Southern Illinois University School of Law

"If you want information beyond data and citations, communicated in a way that will resonate with you, look no further than *The Addicted Lawyer*. You will find stories at your level, as well as advice on what to do next."

—DAVID JAFFE, Associate Dean for Student Affairs,
American University Washington College of Law

"Brian Cuban has done something very important with *The Addicted Lawyer*—taken the subject of a widespread problem that most lawyers and law firms would rather ignore and made it accessible, personal, and above all, real. Without question, this book is going to help people."

—PATRICK R. KRILL, Attorney, addiction counselor, and leading expert on addiction in the legal profession. Co-author of *The Prevalence of Substance Use and Other Mental Health Concerns Among American Attorneys*

"Brian Cuban gives us a crash course in the brutal realities of alcoholism and addiction among lawyers. He spares no painful detail in recounting the many challenges he overcame to build a new and purposeful life. Incorporating the stories of other lawyers who struggle with addiction, this book will be of great service to those in the profession in need of inspiration. Many lawyers are reluctant to admit they have a problem and reach out for help. Brian makes clear that the only way to tackle this issue among attorneys is to speak up and extend a hand to the next person who is suffering."

–LISA F. SMITH, author of *Girl Walks Out of a Bar*

THE
ADDICTED
LAWYER

TALES OF THE BAR, BOOZE, BLOW, AND REDEMPTION

BRIAN CUBAN

Post Hill Press
posthillpress.com

Printed in the United States of America

DEDICATION

I dedicate this book first and foremost to my wife Amanda,
who has seen me at my pre-sobriety worst and in my daily,
ever-going process of becoming my post-sobriety best.
Without her love and support,
this book would still be just an idea.

ACKNOWLEDGMENTS

In addition to the contributors, I would like to acknowledge and thank those who listened to my ideas, pointed out my mistakes, and told me what I did not want to hear in helping make this the best work possible including, but not limited to, my wonderful literary agent Jennifer Cohen and the great people at Post Hill Press: Anthony Ziccardi, Michael Wilson, and Billie Brownell. I would also like to thank Luke Gerwe, Bonnie Hearn Hill, Joe Moran Esq., Mark Haak Esq., Miriam Seddiq Esq., Eric Mayer Esq., Kent Krabill Esq., and Kathy Kinser Esq., Lee Barrett Esq.

TABLE OF CONTENTS

PREFACE

By Patrick Krill

As attorneys, judges, and even law students, those in the legal profession play a uniquely pivotal role in the proper functioning of society, the economy, and government. Simply put, we've got an important job to do. For that one practical reason—though there are indeed many others—we really shouldn't be drunk or high. Given the nature and importance of our work, it doesn't require complex analysis to arrive at that conclusion.

Unfortunately, as new research has confirmed, staggeringly large numbers of us *are* engaged in problematic substance use, and we're struggling with significant levels of mental health problems, too. It had long been suspected that attorneys experience considerable levels of substance use disorders and mental health concerns. But sufficient actionable data on legal professionals and substance use has been sorely and inexcusably lacking until 2016. That data is a fundamental predicate to effectively tackling the problem and to providing attorneys with the resources and support they need in order to effectively serve the public.

Published in the January/February 2016 issue of *The Journal of Addiction Medicine*, a new, landmark study[1] conducted by the Hazelden Betty Ford Foundation and the American Bar Association's Commission on Lawyer Assistance Programs (CoLAP) legal career is strongly correlated with a high risk of developing an alcohol use disorder.

- Of those attorneys who think that alcohol or other drugs have been a problem at some point in their life, the majority say the problem started within the first fifteen years after entering the profession.

- Lawyers don't seek help for their behavioral health problems most often because they fear someone will find out and it will discredit them and possibly affect their license.

This research is a call for action. The numbers we uncovered are incompatible with a sustainable professional culture. Too many individuals are struggling and suffering, and the impact on the public is too great for the profession to allow.

So how did we get here? That's a complicated story. While attempting to understand why so many lawyers and judges struggle with problem drinking and depression, clinicians, researchers, and members of the legal profession themselves have written, theorized, and debated about whether it's the culture and structure of the profession that is more to blame, or whether it's the personality types of people who are drawn to law school in the first place that make them more susceptible to developing these problems. In reality, it's a combination of both, and more. Not only does the culture of the legal profession encourage and foster some very unhealthy behaviors—beginning with law school when those behaviors are deeply ingrained in the psyches of would-be attorneys—but the personalities and priorities of those attracted to the law as a career often provide fertile ground in which those behaviors can take root.

Where do we go from here? For a systemic problem, a systemic response is warranted. All members of the profession have a part to play in righting the ship. We *must* challenge prevailing attitudes and behaviors that simultaneously encourage unhealthy lifestyles while discouraging help-seeking—we must disrupt the sick and dysfunctional status quo. From law schools to Bar admission agencies, Bar associations, legal regulators, lawyer assistance programs, private firms, and beyond, it is time for *all* stakeholders to step up and get actively involved. The list of possible solutions is long, but it might include an emphasis on early referral to behavioral health services at the first signs of a problem, encouraging and de-stigmatizing help-seeking behavior, establishing and supporting policies and procedures that de-emphasize the use of alcohol within work settings and at work events, and promoting overall wellness and balance. The common denominator in all of these ideas? Change. The old ways of thinking and acting just won't cut it anymore.

INTRODUCTION

Meet the Addicted Lawyer

Despite my hangover, June 7, 2006, was a good day. An all-night cocaine-and-Jack-Daniel's-rager was not going to dampen my excitement for my older brother. Mark had purchased an NBA team six years earlier—the Dallas Mavericks. Now, for the first time, the Mavs were going for the championship, playing against the Miami Heat the next day, June 8. Excitement within the city of Dallas reached an all-time high. The Mavs had improved significantly under Mark's ownership, going from the laughing stock of the league to making the playoffs in each full season since he had taken over. A championship series, however, was uncharted territory.

Even before buying the club, Mark had pretty decent seats down by the floor when they played at Reunion Arena. When he was not using the seats, I'd often get to use them. I may not have cared about the game of basketball, but I did care about the opportunity to party, and sporting events are a great place for that.

For the 2006 NBA Finals, I planned to be sitting in a suite Mark provided for family and friends with my new girlfriend of fewer than four months. I also had the opportunity to obtain hard-to-get tickets for friends in first-level seats just off the floor. I purchased two for game one of the championship series and considered giving them to a good friend and his wife. I also thought about selling them on eBay for drug and alcohol money. Ultimately, I decided that scalping the tickets would be disrespectful to Mark and the team.

Then I picked up the phone. My call was not to my friend and his wife. The call was to my cocaine dealer. Hey, he was like a friend, I reasoned. I'd trade the two tickets to him for as much cocaine as I could get at scalpers' prices. Selling them on eBay was disrespectful in my mind, but trading them to my drug dealer "friend" was perfectly acceptable.

My dealer, eager to see the team play in their first championship series in team history, showed up at my door in record time. I handed him the two coveted tickets, and he handed me one thousand dollars' worth of "chunked" cocaine in a zip-lock baggy. It was more than enough to send me to prison, but that thought never entered my mind. I used my handy mini kitchen strainer (a tool with which regular cocaine users are intimately familiar) to grind up the cocaine on my desk into a large pile of fine powder. I leaned back in my chair and stared at the volcano-shaped mound for a few moments feeling like Al Pacino's character Tony Montana in the movie *Scarface*.

As I contemplated the cocaine kingdom in front of me, I heard cars pulling up outside, men shouting, and spotted the flashing blue and red lights of a Dallas Police Department cruiser. Maybe the DEA? A SWAT raid? I pulled out my phone, frantically searching for the name of the criminal lawyer who handled my DWI fifteen years earlier. I wondered how I'd explain my arrest to my family. I saw my legal career over. My name splashed over the *Dallas Morning News*: *"Mark Cuban's Attorney Brother Nabbed in Drug Raid!"*

Then I thought of the disbarment proceedings I'd face, and the humiliation of the State Bar of Texas taking my law license and publishing my name for all to see in the *Texas Bar Journal*. At the time, I was working as of-counsel for a personal injury plaintiff's law-firm. My career was hardly distinguished, and the threat of public humiliation made me more anxious than the threat of loss of livelihood. How would I tell my father that his son was a failure and the antithesis of every value he had tried to instill in his children?

I ran to the window, heart rate doubled in panic, and cautiously pulled the slits of the blinds apart as only a paranoid, beady-eyed alcohol and cocaine-addled person can. Then I scoured every inch of the front yard for black-clad agents crawling through the grass. I ran to another window and surveyed the backyard. Nothing was visible. Still, I braced myself for the SWAT team that any moment might swing down from ropes dangling from copters and smash my windows, just like the ending scene from the Chevy Chase movie *Christmas Vacation*. But there were no cars. No police. No helicopters. Just the quiet of the night, and the soft breathing of my dog sleeping in the corner. Outside the flashbulb bursts of fireflies pierced the darkness, and inside I was alone with the ringing paranoia of addiction.

I'm safe, but only for the moment. I was drenched in sweat. Measures had to be taken—I couldn't expose myself to danger like that again. My heart couldn't take it. So I hid my cocaine. Then I got in my car and headed to The Home Depot, where I picked up several electrical outlet faceplates, screws, a saw, and a drill. Back home, I went around to three different closets around my house and cut through the drywall. I put equal amounts of cocaine in separate Ziploc baggies, placed each behind the drywall, and covered the hole with an outlet faceplate. This would not only hide it from prying eyes, but portion it out so I wouldn't "blow" through it all in one night out on the town or alone by myself in my bedroom, as was often the case when I used cocaine.

In my mind, I was logical and brilliant. My law degree had finally paid off. As if the police, DEA, and drug dogs had never encountered that method of concealment before.

Before I packed away my windfall, I (of course) had to sample the wares. *Snort snort*. Heartbeat quickened. Blood pressure rose. I experienced a terrible feeling for a moment, as if I might have a heart attack or just pass out and never wake up. The panic drove my heart even faster. This feeling of dread, morphing quickly into deep depression, was a reaction I was having more and more often when I used coke. It wasn't anything like the high I started chasing twenty years before. Instead, I was overcome by instant shame, instant regret. I knew that I'd continue to snort through the baggies of cocaine non-stop until I finally found the high needed to walk out the door and face the world. I panicked at that thought.

After a few paralyzed moments, I made a decision. I first took a couple of swigs from a bottle of Jack Daniel's to calm my heart down, as I'd done so many times before with a bad high. I then went back to each of the fake electrical outlets and gathered up all the cocaine I'd just hidden and put it back into one baggie. Then I ran to the bathroom and, without hesitation, flushed my nearly one thousand dollars of cocaine down the toilet. There was a sudden sense of relief. *Maybe I can control this*, I thought.

The next night, the Mavs took game one. I was agitated and angry with myself as I sat in the suite with family watching the action. My mind was not on the great game being played on the basketball court, but on the cocaine I had flushed down the toilet. I could be in the arena bathroom doing multiple bumps, but had to settle for Diet Coke instead.

By the next day, the guilt and paranoia of the massive cocaine flush was completely behind me. *The next high will be different*, I thought. *Why did I flush all that blow down the toilet? I'm an idiot! It would've lasted me a week!* I called my drug dealer. Two more tickets traded for more cocaine. Baggies behind the electrical outlets, a bad high, paranoia, panic all over again. Another flush. Déjà vu. The insanity of addiction. The Mavs won those first two games, but would ultimately lose the championship series to the Heat. I was in the process of losing much more.

The Addicted Lawyer. That would be me. It would also be way too many other people I've encountered who are sailing through life play a role in the stress we feel. There is no place or time in the paper chase to deal with or even acknowledge mental health issues.[6]

Whether the pressures of law careers, the culture of lawyers, or genetic predispositions are greater or lesser factors in addiction among those in law careers is not a question this book can answer conclusively. I'm not a psychologist, not an expert on addiction beyond my own personal experiences, and I'm not an academic. I am, of course, also not Albert Einstein. But Albert Einstein said, "I have no special talent, I am only passionately curious." One of the best tools I have to work with is my passionate curiosity. That curiosity—about myself, my choices, about the relationships I've built and lost during my journey—has guided my path toward well-being for close to a decade, taking life one day at a time. My recovery started with painful days of detox and transitioned to many years of difficult self-reflection. That's a normal, ongoing process. I've spent long hours with a therapist talking about my childhood. I've stared at the stained linoleum floor while sharing some of my story and baring my pain in many other ways as "Brian C" in the rooms of Alcoholics Anonymous[7]; and as Brian Cuban, recovering out loud as an advocate, I've written about my experiences with alcohol and drug use, depression, and eating disorders for anyone to read.[8]

As with my first book, I hope that by sharing my own journey here, I'll empower others to seek help and maybe inspire at least one person to better understand his or her journey and take that first step toward long-term recovery. This book contains stories of redemption from law students, other attorneys, as well as interviews with thought leaders in the field. I hope that all of these testimonials together help readers see that no matter how low and desperate we become, as long as we're above ground, recovery is possible.

Today, I consider myself a person in long-term recovery. I've been on this path since April 8, 2007. No matter how many days, months, or years of sobriety I have, it's always just one day at a time. How have I made it this far? It's taken many approaches. I've been in therapy for more than a decade. Frankly, I think everyone should get some professional counseling. The world would be better for it. I went through multiple psychiatrists and psychologists before I found one with whom I was willing to expose my vulnerabilities. There is no stigma to finding the right therapist because finding the right therapeutic fit is a process. I also attend twelve-step meetings, not all the time, but I often enjoy the camaraderie of the fellowship. I will talk about this later in the book, but I will not be preaching AA or any other method of recovery.

Whether active in a long and distinguished career or still imagining one from the halls of law school, whether experiencing addiction or depression first-hand, or touched by the life of some-one who seems to be struggling. I've found identifying with others' stories and learning to share your own can be a critical first step in recovery. That's what the process is about, right? If you're a law student, maybe it means telling your parents, a friend, a professor, or Dean of Students that you need help without fear of being judged. Maybe it means finally reaching out to see what resources are avail-able on and off campus to get help. Maybe that means taking some time off with the knowledge that the hiatus is just a brief pause and not an end of all aspirations to practice law. Pauses are OK.

If you're a practicing attorney, maybe seeking help means finally telling someone in your firm that you're struggling. Maybe it means accessing your in-house employee assistance program or a lawyer assistance program. If fear of professional or academic conse-quences overpowers all, maybe it means taking that first step into the anonymous rooms of Alcoholics Anonymous, Narcotics Anony-mous, or the non-twelve-step-based SMART Recovery.[9] If not those, there are many other types of mutual-aid groups and count-less professionals who treat substance use disorders.

Even for those who have already tried—and failed—to overcome addiction, there's hope. For me, it took numerous relapses, failures, and restarts in my legal and non-legal professional career partly because of alcohol and drug use before I finally found recovery and had the epiphany that I was not put on this earth to be a lawyer. Perhaps you are. As you will see in the stories of redemption later in this book, there is the ability to rewrite the narrative even when we face license suspension, disbarment, family loss, and incarceration.

My wish is that as you read this book, you find hope, information, and inspiration in the law student and lawyer stories of redemption (including my own), as well as from the wisdom offered by other contributors. I hope that's true regardless of your occupation, age, and dreams for the future. Whether it's being able to stay in the profession or having to do something else by either choice or force, you can step into it. You can take the leap of faith into recovery. It's scary, and it's worth it.

1

The Life of Brian

IT'S 1984. I'M at the University of Pittsburgh School of Law in front of the placement office. First year finals are done, and grades are posted. I can feel my blood pressure rise. No doubt in my mind that I've failed. As the grading system is anonymous (students are identified by numbers assigned by professors), computer printouts with only numbers line the walls, and no names appear. I make myself walk up those stairs, step by step, but I'm not getting any closer. Other, faceless students crowd in front of the board, searching for a glimpse of their future opportunities, or lack of them.

I already know I have no future to seek out. No one will let me get closer to the board. They are crowding tightly. They're laughing. *Are they laughing at me?* I remind myself the system is anonymous, but maybe the other students already know what I know. Finally, the crowd drifts apart, and I'm at the board, totally alone. I scour the computer printouts for the number I've been assigned. I don't see it anywhere. There's a twist in my gut, as if finding out someone has died. I head to the Dean's office, try to find my voice, and manage to stammer, "Excuse me, I can't find my grades. Did I do something wrong?"

Nobody in the office seems to recognize me. They stare through me as if I'm not even there. Then I catch my reflection in a window, and I see a chubby, nervous thirteen-year old boy. I blink and look again, and now I'm fifty years old. I feel nauseated. I'm suddenly in my favorite seat at the campus bar that law students frequent. The pretty bartender I want to ask out recognizes me.

"Great to see you, Brian," she says. "Looking good!"

I keep asking for a drink, but she keeps giving me an empty glass instead.

"Give me a damn drink!" I throw the glass against the wall, shattering it, but nobody seems to notice.

Then I see myself in the mirror behind the bar, and I'm a middle-aged man. I'm confused. *What year is it, anyway?* It suddenly occurs to me—I don't exist. None of this is real.

✳   ✳   ✳

It's a dream I've had a hundred times or more. My dreams often play out like full-length movies, films that I must watch again and again and again (kind of like my weekly Sunday ritual of watching *The Godfather*). These films I see each night might be from different genres—some coming-of-age stories, some romances, some about crashed lives. Sometimes the dreams seem nonsensical; sometimes the meaning is obvious.

One thing that they all have in common is that every story seems to use my real past as source material, and many of them appear written and directed by my deepest anxieties. Failed relationships, flunked tests, flying, falling, smashing dreams, dreams of falling back into addiction, and hitting rock bottom again, all cycle through the months and years. Like many others, my anxiety dreams are often rooted in work, and when I look back at my career as an attorney, my memories of the profession often seem like one long anxiety dream. No wonder I eventually came to realize I did not want to remain in the legal profession.

I came to Dallas on Labor Day, 1986, a new graduate of Pitt Law. I grew up in Pittsburgh, so as much as a part of me wanted to get the hell out of the city, another part of me was also afraid to leave my comfort zone. I would've preferred to go to Southern Methodist University Law School to live near my older brother Mark, who had already moved to Dallas. My younger brother Jeff would move there the year I graduated from Penn State, so I would be with both of them. It was a dream scenario for me, but I had neither the grades nor the money to go to SMU. Being a public university, Pitt Law was much cheaper and more lenient to in-state students whose grades were in question. Frankly, I was shocked when Pitt accepted me. I had just over a 3.1 grade point average at Penn State and a slightly above-average score on the LSAT. I suspect that I was on the lower end of the scale of students they accepted, even in-state.

I graduated from Pitt Law in May of 1986 and took the Pennsylvania bar exam at the end of July. After that, I left Pittsburgh as quickly as I could to start a new life. That new life started on Labor Day 1986 with a Trailways bus ticket to Dallas, Texas, and five hundred dollars to my name. Hey, empires have been built on less!

As I didn't have a Texas law license, my legal employment options upon arriving in Dallas were severely limited. Besides the license problem, I'd been a mediocre student at a good, but not Top Ten, out-of-state law school. I didn't get any love from the law school placement office, nor did I have headhunters and recruiters beating down my door. There were no summer associate clerkships with law firms. I would sit in the common of the law school listening to students talk excitedly about their summer jobs with "Big Law" law firms, judges, and public service agencies. As soon as I heard these conversations, I would move away from the animated students so they would not ask me what I was doing over the summer. I wasn't sure practicing law was even something I wanted to do. In fact, I had no idea what I wanted to do. I was simply surviving day to day, and survival was hard enough. But I did know I had to justify the student loans I'd taken out and the hard-earned money my middle-class parents had given me to help achieve my degree.

My first job upon moving to Dallas, non-legal and hourly, was working for my brother Mark at his first company, Micro Solutions, which was a computer consulting/technology business. My job was grunt work in shipping and receiving that allowed me to pay rent until I found something else. Mark, bailing me out as he would many times in my life, offered me the job in late August 1986 after about a month of unemployment. I didn't want to do it because I found packing computers in boxes beneath my high stature as a lawyer, granted, a lawyer without a license to practice law in Texas and a lawyer without much previous legal experience. However, as is the motivation for many decisions in life, I desperately needed money.

Before too long, toward the end of 1986, I landed a gig with the City of Dallas Office of Property Management. My function was as a right-of-way agent, not exactly a prestigious or lucrative position compared to my inflated sense of what a lawyer should be. I made about $18,000 a year to secure easements for various right-of-way drainage projects in South Dallas. So I spent my days thinking about muddy ditches and waiting for happy hour. The job epitomized the word "boring." Many an afternoon was spent sleeping off a hangover in my car alongside one of those ditches. Although the job was an honorable one, I was so ashamed of telling people I was a right-of-way agent that I would often lie (especially to girls) and tell them I worked for the Dallas City Attorney, a much more respectable résumé listing for a recent law grad. It would not be the last time I either exaggerated or outright lied about my résumé. If there was one redeeming feature to that job it was that I had some great coworkers, including some people who are friends to this day. But all things considered, I couldn't wait to get the hell out of that office, one way or another.

During the part of my day when I wasn't thinking about the legal implications of rainwater, I was half-heartedly studying for the Texas Bar exam. I took the test in February 1987 and failed. Already too busy discovering Dallas's booming nightlife, I didn't take a Bar review course. Instead, I came up with the idea of studying while at work so that I wouldn't have to give up on my all-important drinking hours. As a bonus, I'd get to think of something other than how to convince people to give up part of their property without compensation. I'd be done in time most days to hit the inevitable booze, blow, and free-buffet happy hour as soon as 5 p.m. rolled around, all thanks to my creative multitasking.

I eventually stopped doing my job altogether and spent all my time in the lunchroom reading through Bar review study guides I'd obtained from a friend. One day, late in 1987, I was reprimanded after multiple people complained about my lounging around the lunchroom during office hours. My boss went through my files and saw that I hadn't been getting my work done for at least a month. I felt bad, not because I had not been doing my job, but because my boss and I had gotten along well until this encounter. But since I'd been ratted out by coworkers, she had no choice but to come down hard on me. As to the reprimand itself, I didn't care. *Whatever*, I thought. *I'm better than this job anyway.* I'd already decided that type of work was not for me, so I had begun looking around and sending out résumés. The thought of a moral obligation to do my job, even when unhappy, never crossed my mind.

I then took a job as a claims adjuster for Travelers Insurance in their new Serious Injury Unit. "Serious injuries" were defined as direct or indirect bodily injury claims that could potentially be worth in excess of $50,000. This, in reality, could be just about anything ranging from car accidents to fatal shootings in hotel parking lots in which our client was sued for failing to provide adequate security. My employer wanted the unit to be staffed by lawyers, and while I knew nothing about insurance or adjusting, I figured it had to be more exciting than the job at the city I was about to get fired from anyway. It also helped that they paid 40 percent more. It turned out that a lot of the work involved routine auto accidents, but the work was often anything but boring.

On one trip in 1988 to one of the more dangerous parts of Dallas, my job was to take photos of a damaged vehicle. The neighborhood I was in was full of dilapidated and sometimes abandoned homes that had the reputation of being used as "crack dens." I thought I'd be able to get in and get out without much fuss, but as soon as I said my hellos to the woman who owned the damaged car and knelt to inspect the bumper damage, I heard a popping sound and felt something like a bee buzzing past my head. The owner of the vehicle screamed and dropped flat to the pavement. I still wasn't quite sure what was going on, but people who had been standing around nearby were suddenly running or dropping to the ground.

I heard another pop. We were being shot at. Or, who knows? Maybe we were just in the way of someone else being shot at. The vehicle owner scrambled into her car and hit the gas. I ran to my car and followed. *We really should be getting hazard pay,* I thought. I met the car owner back at the office to finish taking a look at her bumper. Although I didn't get a hazard bonus, at least the guys in the office bought my beers that night.

I actually liked adjusting claims. A big portion of it was litigation management, which I really enjoyed. That entailed overseeing the lawyers we would hire to defend lawsuits. I'd approve litigation strategy, settlement amounts, and, of course, legal bills. I could use my law degree without all the stress of actually practicing law. I probably would have stayed at Travelers for a while if I had not been offered a new job with a large raise. I stayed less than a year.

In 1988, after Travelers, I went to work as a claims adjuster with a company called Transport Insurance. I performed well enough to be quickly promoted to the position of "litigation attorney." It had nothing to do with litigating cases in a courtroom. I was a glorified litigation manager focused on accidents where lawsuits were filed, but aside from the raise, I also finally had a title on my business card that I wasn't ashamed of. I could tell people I was working as an "attorney," even though I still hadn't passed the Texas Bar exam.

I finally passed in 1991 while working at Transport, much in the same manner I passed the Pennsylvania Bar—doing the least amount of studying possible, using only Bar exam review books, even though my employer had paid for my Bar review class. The biggest change that got me through it? I no longer had to study during office hours in a lunchroom where people could see me and complain to the boss. My office at Transport had a door.

The company specialized in insuring long-haul trucking companies, construction vehicles, and other commercial vehicles. As you might imagine with semi-tractor trailers, there were often serious accidents that sometimes resulted in deaths. Part of my job also involved traveling to the scene of "serious injury" accident sites within twenty-four hours. This usually meant there was a death involved, so the work could be quite solemn. We worked very closely with the lawyers we hired to try cases, and I traveled to mediations around the country.[10] The parties to the litigation, along with their lawyers would get together and see if we could agree on a settlement before the case went to trial. Such travel often involved hitting the town afterward, drinking with the lawyers involved, with friends in that city, or alone. If I could get my hands on some blow, all the better.

By that time, I'd been using alcohol heavily since college. There is no doubt in my mind that I fit the criteria for alcohol use disorder, in other terms, "an alcoholic," but it was around this time that my use of drugs and alcohol began to accelerate off the rails of addiction.

■ October 1993

I'm at a Dallas Stars hockey game. The Stars, having just moved from the city of Minnesota, are the go-to event to be seen and mingle. (The Mavs were terrible at that time and not a highly sought-after ticket.)

I'm shitfaced. Just did a few lines of blow in the bathroom. I'm also on-call at work if a serious injury accident occurs. That means I might have to travel anywhere in the country at a moment's notice to investigate. I know the risks, but I'm laying the odds that nothing will happen tonight. I'll just enjoy the high and watch the Dallas Stars win. Now it's 8 p.m. My pager goes off. The code "911" appears on the screen indicating that a serious injury has occurred somewhere. I'm supposed to go to the nearest pay phone and call my boss. *Sh#t!* I ignore it. I'll make up some excuse and go tomorrow when I will have a hangover, but at least will have sobered up. I know what I'll say: "Sorry boss, I guess my pager battery died."

I round the corner to get another beer, feeling like I could take off and fly across the rink if I wanted to. Suddenly: "Brian! I'm paging you!" *Where the hell is that coming from? My conscience?* Nope. It's the voice of my boss. He's also at the game. "There's a death just outside of Boston, in Sturbridge. A big accident. I need you to get out there tonight." Suddenly I don't feel so much like flying.

"We have twenty-four hours, John. I'll leave first thing in the morning."

I can see he's getting irritated. "I really need you to go tonight, Brian."

I want to say, "John, I'm fucked up and just finished off a gram of cocaine. Can it wait?" That's what I want to say. Instead, I do what he asks.

I'm on my way, driving home intoxicated and high, one of many times I'd grab the tiger's tail on Dallas roadways before finally getting bitten. Twenty miles under the speed limit. I might as well have an "I'm a drunk, coked-up asshole" sign on my car.

I quickly pack up an overnight bag and a half-gram of blow and drive to the airport, then sleep from wheels-up to touchdown at Logan airport in Boston. After snorting a couple of lines off the back of my hand in the grimy airport bathroom, I rent a car. In an unfamiliar city, in the pouring rain, over an hour's drive to the accident location in Sturbridge, I'm all the more aware I could be stopped by the police and arrested. Somehow I get to my hotel, white-knuckling the steering wheel the entire way there. I immediately pass out. No work done. The next morning, I finish off my cocaine and head to the accident scene. I complete the investigation and report to John that I'd done it the night before. I feel no guilt, only relief that I got away with it.

* * *

Like my time at the City of Dallas, I left Transport just before they were going to fire me for not doing my job. I had a gut feeling it was coming before the conversation with my boss, but I just didn't care.

Déjà vu. "Brian, I'm very disappointed in your performance. When I promoted you, I thought you'd be my go-to guy. It hasn't worked out that way. You're doing half-assed work. I no longer see motivation."

He was right. Addiction had lowered my own expectations for myself. It was the Peter Principle at work. My Peter Principle set-point was certainly lowered by drug and alcohol use. I told myself I was giving maximum effort for my legal clients, but looking back, it was certainly not the same level and same zeal as periods when I was sober or not battling a day-long hangover.

I couldn't look my boss John in the eye after he chewed me out, and this time, I felt intense shame in knowing that I was a failure. I retreated to my office, shut the door, and reflected on my demise, wondering how I'd allowed myself to go from a rising star to a disappointment. Assessing the role of drugs and alcohol in my life was not part of that reflection. I walked back to John's office and without thinking about how I'd support myself, I resigned.

Drugs were more important than job pride and satisfaction, but now I had no more money to buy them. Lucky for me I'd amassed a tidy sum in my retirement fund. I was desperate. Taking the brutal tax hit, I cashed it out. I'd also finally managed to pass the Texas Bar exam. I entered the actual legal profession and went into private practice, not so much by choice but by necessity. Hey, I wasn't going to fire myself, no matter how much I slacked. I had no self-awareness of my problems. The most logical thing was to simply move on and tell myself I was ready to do something else.

I created my own letterhead using software and my home as my office address. My apartment number became my "suite number." I bought a pager, answering service, a computer, a printer, and fax machine. I was ready. Fortunately, it was not long before I had clients. I began getting cases through friendships with chiropractors. The cases were low-level, soft tissue injury type auto accidents. I did have one advantage from my past work: I knew how insurance companies handled cases, including what they looked for, and how they valued injuries. Other than dealing with the expectations of my own clients, it was easy, low stress work. I had no intention of ever stepping into a courtroom.

Because these types of cases can take a while to result in a settlement, I immediately began taking any hourly legal work I could regardless of my competence to handle specific cases. DWIs that I could plead out, wills, you name it. One case that stands out in particular was a DWI. A guy from Ohio was arrested after getting drunk at the Dallas/Fort Worth International Airport. At the initial hearing, the assistant district attorney, sensing my inexperience, told me in no uncertain terms that he would not accept a plea bargain (it was my client's first offense), and that my client would do mandatory jail time since he was from out of state. This was not common practice for first offenders, but I didn't know that. He was taking advantage of my clear inexperience. I almost vomited there in his office as I realized that I was in over my head. Someone's freedom and future were at stake. Fortunately, a sympathetic criminal defense attorney, there to plead out his client, pulled me aside and told me what I was supposed to do. My client went home.

■ 1995

A trip to the chiropractor. I'm not going for an adjustment. I haven't been in an auto accident, but I know many others have. It's how I get my cases—soft tissue injury ambulance chasing. I have relationships with chiropractors around the city incubated during my time as a claims adjuster. Their waiting rooms become mobile offices. I carry blank contingency representation agreements with me in my briefcase, contracts that will grant me a portion of any settlement or trial award. I know the diagnosis by heart: "Soft tissue strain of the lower neck and back. Recommend X-rays of the lumbar or cervical spine, and numerous therapy sessions." In other words, *whiplash*.

"Have you met Mr. Cuban? If you decide you want one, he is an excellent attorney. We highly recommend him. If you decide to retain Mr. Cuban or another lawyer, we will treat you with no money up front."

My personal injury résumé rarely comes up. They don't care. They just want their treatments paid for. I can't sell myself. I have a vague awareness that directly soliciting clients is frowned upon. I walk the line between solicitation and recommendation by sitting mute with a smile and a handshake during the process.

If after the sales pitch by the doctor, the patient is interested, the briefcase opens. Out comes the contingency agreement and the letter of protection which guarantees the chiropractor payment from any eventual settlement. I know it will settle. If the client wants more money, I'll cut my fee, anything to avoid a courtroom. If the client insists on going to trial, I'll refer the case to a lawyer who is not afraid of litigation.

I have trouble looking the potential client in the eye as my legal brilliance is being sold for me. I know the truth. I stare down at the scuffed, ten-year-old black Florsheims on my feet. The client signs, and when the case settles, I'll have a little more money to feed the beast.

During the drive home my mind keeps drifting to Paul Newman. He plays the down-and-out alcoholic lawyer Frank Galvin in the movie *The Verdict*. Frank is also an ambulance chaser. A "drunk." Divorced. Reading the obituaries as if they were want ads. Frank Galvin shows up at funeral parlors. The chiropractor's office is my funeral parlor. I'm Frank Galvin.

I did this type of personal injury work for a few years, but the cases would dry up as cycles of drug use and sobriety repeated themselves. I eventually transitioned to several of-counsel and office-sharing relationships, and then worked for one more insurance company. In 2000, I began working for my brother Mark, again after his purchase of the Mavericks. Finally, in 2007, after a drug- and alcohol-fueled black-out, I would go into recovery. By that time my career as a practicing lawyer had all but disappeared, save for a case here and there.

Reflecting on my career as an attorney, it's clear that addiction issues aside, I never felt the drive to be successful in the legal profession because I never wanted to be in the legal profession. My path to law school and to the practice of law was one of least resistance. That is not to say I regret the path. I have a law degree. I learned a way of thinking that has and will always benefit me in numerous areas, including my long-term recovery. While a license can be taken away by the state Bar, the knowledge of law and the analytical thinking instilled in law school never can be.

But I also learned a lesson during my time practicing and, in fact, as early as law school. I discovered that as much scrutiny as there may have been on the work I produced, I was able to hide my greatest secrets without much trouble. Being a lawyer, after all, often involves masking feelings and motives, a skill I became adept at when hiding my drinking and substance use from loved ones and business acquaintances alike.

Addiction wasn't the only thing at stake. For me, depression and mental health concerns preceded that, and both preceded career neglect. My struggle with mental health was a secret I was able to keep hidden well before—and in some respects well after—I'd hidden my substance use problems. As with many who face problems with drugs and alcohol, it's impossible for me to address these issues in my life without also looking at the hidden interior life that allowed my substance use to flourish and progress.

2

The *Secret* Life of Brian

LATE SUMMER 1987, two A.M. I'm having a night out with my buddy at the new local sports bar, Legends. There's a boxing ring in the middle of the room with the tables surrounding the ring. Televisions ring the room. Yuppies, pool sharks, sports team groupies, and 30K millionaires[11] talking big and spending big regardless of their actual financial situations. I'm one of them. We wear expensive suits we can't afford, fake diamond earrings, and pay way too much for drinks. Anything to convince ourselves and others that we've made it big, even if we're putting it all on the credit card and share an unfurnished apartment with three other guys. That's Dallas in 1987, and I want to be part of it all.

A tall, curly-haired blonde catches my eye, and I walk over to her to start a conversation of lies. *"I work for the City attorney. I played football for Penn State. Of course this Rolex is real."* (Of course, it's fake.) *"I was in the Marines."* (For only two weeks, but I leave that out.) To tell the truth is to face the truth about myself: I'm depressed, shy, scared, and broke. Cocaine (which I always find money for), however, has the power to quickly change that mindset, if only for a few moments. At this particular moment, talking to this pretty blonde, the only thing that matters to me in the world is validation through her acceptance.

My string of lies is interrupted by a moist feeling on my chin. The cocaine I've just done in the restroom has frozen my throat muscles causing a little drool to creep down my face. Soon I'm spitting saliva projectiles with every word, and some of it finds its way to her arm. I can barely control the muscles of my face, which is frozen in an awkward smile. "So, you like Billy Joel?" I ask. "He's my favorite artist." It seems a safe question to find common ground. Eventually, I get her card with her number on the back. I know she won't go out with me after this and is just being nice, and I'll be relieved in a way when she turns me down. But for now, I don't care. I got the number of a beautiful woman. I think back to all the high school girls who in my mind would not give me the time of day. If they could only see me now.

Then, out into the night. It's early morning and nearly autumn, but it still feels like 100 degrees. The lack of breeze is stifling. I'm sweating, as damp as if I'd just stepped out of the shower. Not sure if it's the humidity or the three huge lines I just did. Cocaine is my lunch and breakfast, with tequila on the side. I haven't eaten all day. I hop in my buddy's car and we head to Mickey D's, where I grab five Egg McMuffins. Binging and purging is much easier when I'm drunk. We pull up in front of my apartment in the Village Apartment Complex—at the time, one of the biggest singles apartment complexes in the world. Door opens. I step out of the passenger side and into the street.

As my friend drives away, BOOM! Suddenly I'm airborne. Feet taken out from under me. I'm propelled into a full somersault, a death grip on my McDonald's bag. I slam down into the windshield of the car that's just struck me with bone-jarring force. *What the hell happened? Where did this car come from?* The windshield shatters. It releases from its frame and drops into the vehicle. I'm on the hood of the car and I have a McMuffin in my mouth. My buddy is driving on down the road, oblivious to my street acrobatics. I roll off the hood and onto the street. A man is standing over me. He's shouting at me. I'm laughing. I can't stop.

I notice that my white button down polo shirt is soaked in blood. The trademark insignia no longer visible beneath a growing red stain. A woman starts screaming at me. "You walked in front of us! Call the police!"

I'm still laughing at my airborne somersault. Maybe it's the cocaine.

"Get back in the car, bitch!" the man yells at the woman. Then they're gone.

I'm still lying in the street amid the broken windshield glass. A lot of blood is coming from somewhere. I peel myself off the hot asphalt and hobble into the apartment. Check the mirror. Lots of cuts and bruises. Some cocaine left in my pocket. No biggie. Still have my Egg McMuffins. Just another night in Dallas. Add in three broken ribs. If I do another line, it'll make those ribs feel better. Of course, I'll definitely be calling the blonde. Hopefully it's not the number for Domino's Pizza.

How did I become the person flying high over the hood of that car? I certainly didn't pick up a drink one day or do that first line of blow thinking to myself, *You know what? I really want alcohol and cocaine to take over my life and ruin it for the foreseeable future. I want to go to jail and be divorced three times. I want to lose my friends and family.* Simply put, the act of taking that first drink and doing those first lines were choices, even though those choices may have been strongly influenced by underlying psychological issues and a strong need for acceptance dating back to childhood.

The disease and psychological process of addiction that took hold afterward were not choices. Some will understand that. Many still put forth the stigmatizing notion that it's simply a matter of continuing to make the wrong choices, that there are the strong and the weak, and we can all choose to stop just as easily as we chose to start. *Addiction is a moral failing.* I hear it firsthand and see it all the time in traditional and social media. *It's a choice. Just stop.* If only it were that easy.

Sometimes those who have never experienced addiction (and even many who have experienced it) have a difficult time getting their heads around the nature of the beast. It certainly robbed me of the ability to choose not to drink or to not ingest illicit drugs for any significant period of time.

Did I know right from wrong? Of course. Did I care? No. Did I know I was destroying my life? Yes. Did I care? Yes. Could I stop? No. Addiction overpowered my rational thought process to that extent. Clinical research and limitless anecdotal evidence tells us that my experience is not unique in that regard.

Different environmental factors may or may not trigger that predisposition. Genetically, there is no history of addiction in my family or extended family that I am aware of. I'm the middle of three children. The oldest, Mark, was always the outgoing, entre-preneurial type. He was selling one thing or another as far back as I can remember. He became what the first born might be expected to become and much more, going on to become a billionaire, among other accomplishments. My younger brother Jeff, like many last born, had a little more freedom to just be who he wanted. He was a jock—a nationally ranked wrestler—and also popular with the ladies. I was the middle child, and like many middle children, I was shy and withdrawn, a little less certain. I had an overblown need for acceptance.

I was also someone who internalized every negative thing said to and about me. Fortunately, I had a good relationship with my father, but, unfortunately, I had a volatile relationship with my mom. There was a lot of "fat shaming" between my mom and me. I remember coming home from school for lunch some days starving, so hungry I'd crank open a can of Chef Boyardee Ravioli and eat it right out of the can. My mom would pop in between appointments as a real estate agent, and if she caught me, she'd say, "If you keep eating like that you're going to be a fat pig." It wasn't just the fat shaming. If I did something absent-minded at home or received bad to mediocre grades (which was a regular occurrence), she would call me a "dumb bunny."

What I didn't know then but do know now, is that this was the sort of thing her own mother would tell her when she was young. They were also things my great grandmother said to my grandmother. In her treatment of me, my mother was repeating a cycle of verbal abuse. I'm not starting with this ancient history to blame her or my great-great-great-grandmother for my alcohol and drug use issues. Fat shaming in families is often generational. Parental dynamics can play a role as a trigger for addiction or in the progress of addiction (or, one would hope, the progress of recovery), but those relationships do not *cause* addiction. When I speak to groups, I always make sure they understand that correlation (which is complex environmental factors in this case) is not the same as causation, and I want to start by making sure you understand it too.

3

Who's to Blame?

THERE WAS A time I did blame my mother for my addiction issues. In fact, for a long time, I blamed her for everything wrong with me. When I finally realized that she was not the cause of my problems, and that she was repeating what was done to her, I understood. Then I was able to let go of my anger and forgive.

I forgave my mother, and I forgave the little boy I'd been for the choices he made. I forgave the junior high and high school bullies who made fun of me and physically assaulted me because of my weight. None of those people caused my addiction. They all had problems of their own. Blaming them was one of the ways I avoided confronting my addiction problems, and forgiving them—and forgiving myself— was one of the first steps in my recovery. Today, my mom and I have a good relationship free of the anger of those early days.

I often get asked if I want to confront the junior high and high school bullies who taunted me over my weight and physically assaulted me. It's true that memories of some of those episodes often lingered into adulthood. My dreams often take me back to a pair of pants given to me by my brother Mark and how those pants would, in part, define a lifetime of self-doubt.

Spring 1975: I'm alone in my bedroom watching *Star Trek,* thinking about the upcoming school dance, and idolizing Captain Kirk, the handsome, swashbuckling captain of the *Starship Enterprise.* The looks. The confidence. The women. If I can only be him. I'll bet he was the prom king in high school. I hate school dances. They remind me of what I will never be, and the things I will never see. I will never be invited to the prom. I will never be brave enough to ask a girl to the prom. I will never see a Brian in the mirror who, despite numerous crushes, is attractive and confident enough to even go on a date. I will never command the Starship Enterprise.

I play out fantasies in my head of life with each crush, envisioning an alternate reality of love and acceptance. I see it every day and want it badly. The soft hand touch of the first love. The excitement of the prom planning and talk of booze, hotels, and losing my virginity. I am lost in the fantasy of acceptance and being someone I am not

I am jarred out of my fantasy world by a knock at the door. My brother Mark is standing there holding pair of pants. Shiny. Gold. Bell-bottom. A creation of the new disco craze sweeping the country. Mark is all about the disco. I would hear him playing the hit song "The Hustle" on the record player in our living room. He is handsome. He is confident, with jet black hair from our mother's lineage. I have the red hair and freckles from our father's. Mark has the genes of confidence, the charisma, and charm from my father. I am my mother's child.

"Hey Bri! Check out these babies! What do you think?"

"You're actually going to wear those?"

"I *have* been wearing them. Everyone at the disco loves them. I just bought a new pair. Do you want these?"

Suddenly, I do not care what they look like. They are an offering from my brother, an offering of love, a piece of him that might rub off on me and transform me into a disco-dancing Captain Kirk. I am off my bed in seconds, reaching for the pants. He smiles and says, "Have fun, disco boy!"

I immediately shut my door, strip to my underwear, and slide each leg carefully into the pants so as not to wrinkle them. I stand up. My heart sinks. I can barely get the pants over my ass and up to my waist. I am fat. Mark is not fat. I start to cry, but I keep pulling. Inhale! Stretch! I get them fastened. Exhale. The waistline stretches. I'm in. I can take only half-breaths. I don't give a shit. I am wearing these pants. They are a symbol of Mark's love. They are my ticket to the prom. I will learn The Hustle.

I wore those pants to school. I wore them a lot. The kids made fun of their tight fit on my relatively large body. I was used to being fat shamed and bullied over my weight and never stood up for myself when it happened. As a self-defense mechanism, I laughed it off, playing the self-deprecated clown. One afternoon, while walking home with a group of kids, the taunts started again. Fat teasing then degenerated into violence as several of the kids began surrounding me and ripping at the pants. I felt like prey that had been caught by wild animals.

They tore the pants to shreds, jeering, and then they left me to make a "walk of shame" home in my Fruit of the Loom tighty-whities. As they walked away, one guy suggested that if I was going to go get new pants, I should pick up a bra (for my "man boobs") as well. Did I think about that humiliating afternoon for years to come? Yes I did. The incident was so traumatic that I can go to that spot to this day and point out where it happened. Did wishing vengeance upon my tormentors make me feel better in any way? No it did not. Confronting them years later would have done nothing to heal the insecurities I was facing at the time.

Today, I'm actually connected via social media with a couple of my teenage tormentors. Forgiveness aside, it makes no sense to me personally to confront bullies from a lifetime ago. Life is not a reality show. I'd be confronting middle-aged men, not teens. I have no idea if they remember what happened, and frankly, I hope they don't. I want them to have happy lives and raise wonderful children.

I can hope they've taught them about bullying so those cycles aren't repeated.[12]

However, when we're young, this sort of perspective on past wrongs can be elusive. Episodes with bullies and episodes with my mother would run through my mind often. Blaming others for my issues was a convenient way of justifying long-boiling anger over my childhood and the choices I made. That anger was often a trigger for depression, which was often a trigger for the use of alcohol and cocaine. I was already experiencing fragile mental health and shaky self-esteem long before I ever thought about becoming a law student and attorney. Struggles with mental health started with overwhelming desire for acceptance combined with a very negative self-image dating back to childhood. I wanted to change the reflection of the horrendous monster I saw every time I glimpsed my reflection. A monster born of body dysmorphic disorder.[13]

My mental state as a teenager, in part, would probably be diagnosed today as clinical depression, although I was not diagnosed with it then. It was a different era, and my parents would never have thought to seek help for me. Depression and mental illness in general were not as widely discussed as they are today and not concepts your average baby boomer teen in suburban Pennsylvania would've been comfortable raising with parents, friends, or teachers. Depression was something that was supposed to be handled in private. In silence. In loneliness, so you didn't spread your "sadness" to others. That is how I experienced it for many decades. As something shameful. The shame was intensified as I watched my mother battle her own mental health issues alone. They were something to "just get over."

Depression was still there when I walked through the doors of Pitt Law. It was with me when I studied. When I sat for bar exams. When I sought my first jobs, made my first friends in the city I'd come to call home, and fell in love for the first time. It was there every time I walked into a courtroom or mediation or wrote a brief. The feeling of depression was as familiar as my own distorted reflection, and yet, for most of my life, not something for which I acknowledged needing help. Depression was my "normal" long before alcohol and drug addiction. Even at a young age, my feelings and behaviors became familiar. A deep, gut-wrenching loneliness. Feeling isolated, and crying in my bedroom. Apathy in my studies. Binge eating. Cutting school to drink and smoke weed. Convinced I would never be accepted by my peers.

For some, depression can be triggered by addiction, but for me, it came first. And while I was ultimately able to stop using alcohol and stop doing cocaine and other drugs, the underlying pain of a shy, lonely, little boy remained into recovery and is something I still work on.

Perhaps if the awareness of mental health that exists today had existed when I was a teen, someone might have reached out earlier. For instance, when I began to self-isolate for long stretches of time—my solace was my bedroom where I would spend many hours alone, playing my favorite board game, Strat-O-Matic Baseball with the family dog at my side. Or when seemingly pleasurable things—a trip to the amusement park with my grandmother, a nice word from a friend—would often leave me unmoved. The inability to articulate what I was feeling. But perhaps awareness alone wouldn't have been enough. Even though there's seemingly greater awareness of depression today, it can still be difficult for friends and family (not to mention teachers or counselors) to discern the signs of depression or other mental health struggles in teenagers. After I wrote *Shattered Image* a few years back, some people who knew me in grade school and high school reached out to tell me they simply thought I was shy. Teens are natural experts at hiding feelings from others, often because they don't yet understand their feelings themselves.

For me, the desire to pull away from others and hide my feelings was paired with a desperate desire to be accepted by them. To those

close to me, it might have seemed that I was always eager to socialize, as I always wanted to fit in. That desire to fit in probably led to
my first experimentation with drugs and alcohol.

4

I May Not Have Been Asked to the Prom, but I Could Drink with My Friends

THE OPPORTUNITY TO explore alcohol and "illicit substances" was already there as early as elementary school. At the playground, some kids would whisper about who got into their parents' liquor cabinets, who in class had a connection to a weed dealer. They would talk about smoking their pot and drinking at house parties while parents were away, or in the woods behind the school. I wanted to be included, but I was never asked, and I was afraid to inquire. I was a big, chubby tween already being picked on by kids and adults over my weight. To actually hear that I was unwanted would be devastating. The path of least resistance was to project what I believed others were thinking about me and use those distorted thoughts as an excuse to isolate rather than engage.

I did engage others to experiment with illicit drugs for the first time. I was in elementary school and remember asking about who had the weed near the cluster of cool kids huddled near the basketball hoop on the Herbert Hoover Elementary black top. Eventually, I was directed to the kid who was basically the schoolyard dealer.

It happened to be one of my friends who lived just down the street. He sold me a small cube of hash wrapped in tinfoil for ten bucks. I had asked for marijuana and had no idea what hash was when he told me. He said it was a good deal for ten bucks, and much stronger than marijuana. We had a quick hand-to-hand exchange right there on the court, much like the exchanges I would execute decades later to purchase cocaine. I also had no clue what he actually sold me—it could have been rubber cement and pencil shavings.

I tried to make my own hash cigarette as I'd seen other kids do with marijuana. As I hid behind the school trying to roll the joint, all the hash fell out of the tinfoil into the grass. It was par for the course in how I felt about myself. I couldn't even roll a joint as I saw the cool kids at school do.

I was less shy about experimenting with alcohol. In my early teen years, I raided my own parents' liquor cabinet when they weren't around. I'd pour just a thimbleful of liquid from every bottle, all into the same glass, to make a vile sort of jungle juice. I figured if I could teach myself to drink that concoction and keep a straight face, everyone at parties would think I was an incredibly cool and mature guy. (That is, once I got invited to parties. OK...*if* I got invited to parties.) A year or two more, and some of my happiest moments as a freshman in high school were mixing up a practiced and perfected version of my jungle juice and heading out with a few friends to the woods to drink it.

By sixteen, I was a veteran at drinking. It was a calling card. "Grain Your Brain" parties were regular occurrences, and they involved multiple bottles of grain alcohol mixed with grape soda in a twenty-gallon trash can. I was a big dude, and I could laugh at the kids my own age getting plastered off their first few sips of beer. Soon my friends and I picked up some fake IDs, and we'd road-trip to Ohio or West Virginia, states where the legal drinking age was still only eighteen at the time. We could all pass, easily. We'd return with beer and various types of cheap rock-gut booze that we would hide in the woods.

■ New Year's Day, 1977

I'm sixteen, sitting in a living room in Morgantown, West Virginia. On the other end of the couch is the older sister of my friend "Bender." This is her apartment. There's a few feet between Bender's sister and me, and I'm trying my hardest to make it a few more by clinging to the edge of the couch as if it's a life raft. I'm convinced I'm taking up too much room, that nobody will want to sit next to me because they'll be sucked into the gravity of my huge body.

On the other side of the coffee table, Bender and a couple of other buddies sit. They're cracking each other up by saying nasty things about kids in school, commenting on weight, looks, and girls' butts. I laugh along. None of us are the cool kids. We're all on the margins. Bender, though, is a year older, and to my eyes, seems perfectly content with who he is. Bender's picked on me more times than I can remember. I stood up to him once, when we were younger. We were playing hide and seek when he physically attacked my younger brother Jeff, grinding his face into the mud and dirt of the school yard we were playing in. I wouldn't ever stand up for myself, but I did for my brother. My love for him was greater than fear of the bully. A few hard punches to the gut from Bender, however, reminded me of his superiority. I'm always a little nervous around him for that reason, but he's willing to let me hang around, especially if I have the jungle juice or the beer. He always has weed. Sometimes we get drunk and high and fire off his double barrel shotgun into sacks filled with newspaper in his garage.

With his looks, outsider status, and cutting sarcasm, he's basically Judd Nelson's character from the movie *The Breakfast Club*. I'm the Anthony Michael Hall character (ironically named Brian) without the smarts. The nerd who will do anything just to be accepted. And my willingness to do anything is about to be put to the test.

Friends of Bender's older sister arrive, and before long, she carefully lays out lines of cocaine for everyone sitting around the table. I've never seen blow before. I watch others, then take a rolled up bill from Bender's sister and prepare to alter the course of my life for the worse. But Bender grabs my arm. In a rare moment of sincerity, he says, "Brian, you don't wanna do that. You're too young." At first, I insist on participating. I want to believe there's nothing he can do that I can't. My overwhelming need for acceptance at work. Finally, I grudgingly relent. I'm embarrassed, but agree. Instead, I get drunk.

✳   ✳   ✳

As bad as my problems with coke eventually got, I shudder to think how bad they would have been if I'd snorted those first lines offered to me. I'm not sure I'd be alive today.

I squeaked by high school with mediocre or poor grades. I hardly ever studied. I did have a good short-term memory, so I could usually pass classes by reading the book the night before the test and pull off a C. I would regularly write my own "sick notes" and forge my mother's signature to skip and head to Monroeville Mall where we would smoke weed in the parking lot, get a calzone at the food court, and then head back home in time to pretend I was getting home from school. During those times cutting class, I was my most peaceful and contented self.

All this led to limited options for college. My brother Mark was a graduate of Indiana University, so I applied there as well as to Penn State. Indiana agreed to provisionally accept me if I maintained a certain grade point average my senior year. I didn't. I wanted to follow in Mark's footsteps. I couldn't, so I ended up enrolling in a branch campus of Penn State just outside of Erie, Pennsylvania for my freshman year. I thought it would relieve the pain and shame, but being on my own, away from the antagonists of my childhood, didn't lead to better mental health. It was at this age that I began developing eating disorders as a way to cope with body dysmorphia.

First, I severely restricted my food intake for months, developing the habits of anorexia. I then transitioned to bulimia, gorging on pizza or pancakes at the IHOP whenever I was hungry or depressed, and then purging it afterward in the dorm bathroom with the faucets blasting water to hide the sounds. Oh, yes. College wasn't going to save me. It was only going to offer me more ways to hide.

5

College Daze

THE BOOZE WAS social. The binging and purging were shameful. There wasn't much awareness of eating disorders back then, especially where males were concerned. Of course, drinking was still a big part of my life, and it went hand-in-hand with my eating disorder. I thought that binging and purging to release shame and feel like I was "normal" if only for a few moments, was something I could never admit to anyone. But throwing up because I had too much to drink seemed legit, and nobody in the dorms would think twice about hearing a grown man wretch in the bathrooms night after night.

By my sophomore year, I'd moved onto the main campus of Penn State in State College, Pennsylvania. I also added more unhealthy behaviors to my repertoire. I began misusing laxatives. I'd binge on Big Macs at McDonald's and if I didn't purge, I'd eat an entire box of Ex-Lax. I also started exercising beyond moderation. I gradually worked my way up to being able to easily complete ten- to fifteen-mile runs on a daily basis. This was part of a new eating disorder I was developing. I became "exercise bulimic," which for me was compulsive exercising with the primary goal of offsetting calories. I'd run ten miles in the morning, often missing class. I'd then run the same distance in the evening. I did this six to seven days a week in addition to traditional binging and purging—and of course the drinking. All of these behaviors together put quite a strain on my body. But I kept thinking, *Hey, look good, feel good, and after a few more pounds, I'll have the confidence to be who I want to be. I'll be accepted.* But in truth, no matter how many pounds I shed or what shape my body took, the only way I'd be able to work up the nerve to hang out at parties with other college kids was to get absolutely hammered.

Was I an alcoholic at this point? I'd say so. Not only was drinking affecting my ability to study and maintain relationships, but it had become essential to my sense of confidence around others. I had no intention of stopping, and with as much drinking as there was going on around me, my own behavior didn't seem outside the norm.

The closest I'd come to the concept of recovery was walking into a hamburger joint my junior year and seeing a rack of what I remember to be Alcoholics Anonymous pamphlets. I instinctively pulled one long, rectangular pamphlet out of the rack and nervously peeked inside. The headline asked something like, "Are You an Alcoholic?" There were twenty questions. I answered many of the ones I read positively. "Have you missed days of work or school because of drinking?" *Er, I'm skipping class with a hangover right now, so I guess so.* After a few too many positives, I threw the pamphlet in the trash instead of putting it back in the rack. *Shut up*, I thought. *I'm not going to let some stupid pamphlet tell me I have a problem and take away something so important. I'm in college. Everyone drinks. Everyone gets drunk.* I'm "normal."

I graduated from Penn State with a degree in Administration of Justice (with minors in eating disorders and drinking to excess). I didn't have much of a plan for my future when I finished college. I'd taken a lot of classes related to law enforcement. There was a part of me that really wanted to be a cop. I applied to a few police departments but never did well enough to make the shortlist for hiring. My future as the new Pete Malloy (from the baby-boomer television series about police work, *Adam-12*) was looking bleak. Unfortunately, I really had no "Plan B." One day, I was in the Penn State placement office sifting through potential law enforcement jobs to apply for. I eavesdropped on a couple of guys discussing taking the Law School Admission Test (LSAT) and the law schools they were applying to. *Law school?* One guy mentioned the University of Pittsburgh School of Law.

Although the thought of law school had never crossed my mind before that moment, it instantly became an appealing option. Not because I wanted to be a lawyer, but because I saw the opportunity to spend three more years hiding from myself. I could run. I could drink. I could be alone with my eating disorder. I could exist day to day in the exact same way I'd existed my four years at Penn State. I could repeat the cycle of behaviors that had become part of my self-identity. That, and the thought of attending law school being proof that I was worthy of acceptance from those who in my mind thought I was never going to amount to anything. My mother. The bullies. My high school teachers.[14] That is ultimately why I enrolled at Pitt Law. I didn't want to change the world. I didn't want to be the next Clarence Darrow or Atticus Finch. I wasn't motivated by money or social justice. My motivation was simple and logical in my mind. I didn't want to change my habits, and continuing from Penn State into graduate school seemed like my best chance to keep them concealed. It was simply the path of least resistance.

I spent my early time at Pitt Law just as I had at Penn State: often drinking to excess, exercising to excess, going out to the law school bars, and occasionally dressing up in my only suit and playing lawyer at the more upscale Pittsburgh nightclubs. Trying to figure out where I fit in with my fellow students whom I perceived as having more drive, better grades, better looks, more friends, and higher IQs than I.

I thought I was the only one who had secrets—my unhealthy relationship with food, with drink, and with that old, familiar feeling of shame and loneliness. Of course some of my fellow law students were struggling as well. I'd come to find out years later from other alumni that some students were using marijuana, cocaine, stimulants, and prescription pills to keep their own problems at bay. Many of us were drinking, and that was clearly visible at favorite off-campus bars. But at that age, drinking—sometimes to excess—seemed normal, even for young professionals. Of course, by this time, my alcohol consumption was anything but normal, and was already deeply affecting my future prospects. I was lost.

One of my favorite movie lines is from a 1994 dark comedy entitled *Swimming with Sharks*. With "sharks" in the title, you might think it's about lawyers, but it's actually about the cutthroat world of Hollywood producers. In one particular scene, the character Buddy Ackerman, a top movie executive played by Kevin Spacey, is on the phone berating a subordinate over differences in opinion concerning a movie production. He closes with, "Say this one time with me: 'Would you like that in a pump or a loafer?'...Good. Now memorize it, because starting tomorrow, the only job that you're going to be able to get is selling SHOES!"

When I saw the movie as an adult, I instantly flashed back to the feeling I had as I walked out of my first (and last) moot court competition at Pitt Law. What is moot court? For the non-legal types reading this book, it is a competition between burgeoning litigators, appellate gurus, and other law students who want to hone their debate and critical thinking skills in various legal subjects. It's typically an extracurricular activity—students in law schools across the country *volunteer* to have our legal arguments verbally hacked to death by law student judges, professors, and sometimes, actual judges.

For me, volunteering to participate in a process that would further degrade my sense of self-worth was akin to agreeing to be water-boarded. So how did I end up sitting before a moot court panel of law student "judges" trying to argue the ins and outs of the Fourth Amendment implications of *Illinois vs. Gates*? I decided that if I could survive the process and argue my case well, it would be more proof to other students that I deserved to be there, and so it was a chance to boost my self-esteem. Unfortunately, the closer it came to oral argument day, the worse the anxiety and self-doubt got. The morning of the event, the only way I could get myself out of my apartment was to "loosen up" beforehand. Moot court, meet Jose Cuervo.

I often wonder if I'm the only law student ever to show up for such a competition not sober, if not quite legally intoxicated. I feel safe in saying I'm probably in an "elite" group in that regard. My decision to drink before the session was akin to decisions I'd make throughout my life before leaning on drugs or alcohol: I wanted to face my fears, but I too often decided the only way to do so was to change how I felt through drugs or drinking.

Safe to say, alcohol did nothing to enhance my performance in moot court. The student judges "eye-rolled" and sighed all the way through my barely competent arguments. My biggest concern was not getting close enough to them so they could smell the booze on my breath. It wasn't just the drinking. I'd also prepared in much the same way I had approached all facets of my education. Last-minute cramming was my normal preparation. A legal brief written in a few days using other students' notes. A week later, I walked out of my evaluation and ran into my moot-court partner, Eric. "I think I did OK," he said. "They told me I had the potential to be a star. How did you do?" I told him I did about as well as I expected, then walked away thinking about my future career as a shoe salesman.

6

Big Haired Barbies, Booze, and Blow

AFTER PITT LAW, on to Dallas. While my career as an attorney grew slowly, I advanced rapidly in my experiments with substance use. Dallas was a swinging town in the mid-80s, and I wanted to be part of it. Opportunity abounded. At the same time, I was still battling severe body dysmorphia and the feelings of loneliness and low self-worth that had followed me since childhood. The combination of psychological vulnerability and abundant opportunity led to my first experiments with harder drugs.

The first time I used cocaine was in 1987. I was in the downstairs bathroom of one of the nicest hotels in Dallas, befitting my outward status and appearance as a licensed attorney (at least in Pennsylvania, as I had not taken the Texas Bar yet). Shiny marble, mouthwash, breath-mints, and the ultimate bonus, a toilet door that closed completely so no one could see in. With the bathroom attendant standing just outside my door handing out towels and mints, I carefully laid out three lines of cocaine given to me by the drug dealer I had been introduced to for the first time twenty minutes earlier. I rolled up a twenty-dollar bill and bent over the white Kohler

34

commode. The three white lines looked harmless, and my only hesitation was the grime, germs, and undoubtedly the past drug residue from previous guys like me.

Then I went for it. As the cocaine began its journey up the rolled bill to change the course of my life, I had a thought. I thought about a man I'd never met. I thought about Lenny Bias. Lenny was a first round draft pick of the NBA Boston Celtics in 1986. Lenny was a "can't miss" future NBA prospect. He died of a cocaine overdose two days after being the second overall pick in the draft—it caused a deadly arrhythmia. No warning. No second chance. Just dead. I was thinking about him just three months after he died as I stood there with a rolled-up bill in my nose. It occurred to me in that moment that I had no idea what I was putting in my nose any more than Lenny did. But I was determined. I was going to do what it took to be part of the fun. That could never happen to me.

After I snorted the lines, I opened the stall door, walked over to the faucet, washed the residue off my hands, swigged a mini-cup of generic mouthwash, flipped the attendant a 5-spot, took a mint, and pushed open the restroom doors to exit into my new kingdom, at least for as long as the high lasted.

I was on the apex of a feeling I had never experienced before. A feeling I loved and knew immediately I had to have again, and again, and again. *This is what I've been looking for all my life*, I thought. I finally felt in control, and I walked confidently through the dim light of the already addicted, the non-addicted, the weekend coke kings, big-haired beauties, doctors, lawyers, students, and fellow 30k millionaires. I was now up for the battle. The King of Dallas. Nothing could stop me as long as I felt that way. In that moment, in that bathroom, I was instantly addicted. Not necessarily in the sense of physical dependence, but in immediate psychological dependence—I instantly felt I couldn't survive if I didn't try to maintain such a wonderful feeling.

Cocaine had the power to make all my anxieties seem trivial and the formerly impossible, possible. I was able to party, socialize, and feel good about myself all at the same time. It was as if the drug made my problems go away, if only for the brief period of the high. But of course, my self-medication was only papering over deeper issues, not resolving them. Cocaine did not make me better at building and maintaining relationships: it just helped me overcome my often paralyzing fear of being rejected by women and worrying less when the relationships fell apart. Coke didn't help me focus in my career: it just helped me recover from the hangover from the night before and not lose self-confidence despite poor performance. Coke didn't cure my depression: it only masked it for the short term. It did not help me take control of my life: it just offered the illusion of control and self-acceptance as things slowly but surely spiraled downward. Decades after my first experience with coke, I'd watch the Ziploc baggies of cocaine I'd traded for Mavs Championship tickets spiraling down the toilet bowl, but the vision of those baggies wasn't enough to help me see just how out of control my life was.

Through my early years in Dallas, I moved beyond cocaine as well. I was a huge fan of ecstasy, for instance. "X" offered a longer-lasting and more predictable high than cocaine. As good as it made me feel, cocaine could sometimes have terrible side effects, including a racing heart, all-night jitters, insomnia, and its own flavor of anxiety. I soon learned to come down with Xanax, Ambien, more booze, or some other depressant when I had a bad high. Ecstasy was a little easier on the body, and I didn't have to worry as much about the deep slide into regret and depression that often accompanied coming down from a cocaine high. But it wasn't as easy to get as cocaine, which was available on a daily basis with a phone call and available funds. It was also simpler to deal with from a going-to-jail perspective. Much easier to pull a tiny pill out of my pocket and quickly pop in my mouth than finding a bathroom to snort in.

But I always had a little fear with ecstasy because there was no way to tell what was in it. While I can't speak to the mid-to-late 1980s, when I was popping ecstasy, a 2016 study found that in addition to the primary ingredient MDMA, ecstasy (or "molly") pills may contain dangerous ingredients such as "bath salts," which can be, well, many things.[15] The point being, caveat emptor, and the caveat is that you can die or sustain permanent physical disability. Studies aside, there is plenty of tragedy-ridden anecdotal evidence online and in print on a regular basis to prove this. Of course, without a chemical analysis, there was no real way to tell what was in the cocaine either, but after a while, I became kind of a self-described "cocaine connoisseur." In my mind, I could judge the "safety" and quality by smell, feel, and consistency. I could tell what it was cut with. No way to do that with a pill.

As much as cocaine became a psychological obsession, though, I was still just as dedicated to my "first love," alcohol. I found the two worked together to give me the feeling I wanted. It developed into an art form, and I came to know just how many Jack and Diet Cokes I needed on a given night before heading to the nearest bar or night-club bathroom to do my first line of the night. Drinking numbed the pain and helped me forget. Of course alcohol is a depressant and counteracted the effect of my antidepressants. That created an even deeper low that I'd use cocaine to pull out of. The more experience I had balancing the two, the more I figured I could be in charge of how I felt every day. What could possibly go wrong? It turns out, a lot.

There is a popular internet meme that is often attributed to the actor Robert Downey Jr., although I can't figure out when and if he actually said it, and many twelve-steppers claim it originated in the rooms. "I don't drink these days. I'm allergic to alcohol and narcotics. I break out in handcuffs." Not long into the start of my Dallas party days, I broke out in handcuffs.

✳   ✳   ✳

■ **August 8, 1992**

I'm getting hammered on giant beers and peach sweet cider ale at the Gingerman Bar in Dallas. I know I'm hammered, because I keep telling my buddy that I'm hammered.

I take a trip to the bathroom with my newly purchased cocaine "one hitter" from a local head shop, but it doesn't make me feel any less sloppy. Finally, around 1 a.m., the cocaine is gone, and I've had enough to drink that my mood darkens, I start to feel sorry for myself, and I head home.

Soon I'm flying up the Dallas North Tollway at about 75 mph. The cocaine has me on edge, but I'm not edgy enough to notice the state trooper parked on the side of the highway waiting for someone just like me. Too late. I know immediately that he's on me, and sure enough the lights come on. He pulls me over within walking distance of my house. He asks, "How many have you had tonight?" I give the answer given by thousands of intoxicated individuals across the country right before they are arrested. "Just a couple, officer." After the roadside tests, which in my drunken state, I believe I execute perfectly, he tells me I'm being arrested on suspicion of DWI. As he slaps the cuffs on me, I blurt out, "I passed those tests. Why are you arresting me?" He smiles, shakes his head, and guides me into the back of his cruiser. Fortunately, he doesn't ask about any other drugs I might be on.

The trooper is a nice older guy who even pulls over to loosen my cuffs when I tell him they're cutting into my wrists. We carry on a pleasant conversation the entire trip to the Lew Sterrett jail, which is the main jail and holding facility for the city of Dallas. I ask him if he'd take me back to my car when I blow under .10 (the legal limit in 1992). He laughs and says that he doesn't think that's going to be the case, but promises if I'm not booked, they will get me back.

He's right. I blow a .11 on the breathalyzer. I fail to follow the legal advice I gave time and time again. *Don't blow*. But like any drunk, I've convinced myself I'm not intoxicated.

Being handcuffed on the side of a public highway was humiliating. It was nothing, however, compared to the assembly line booking process staffed by Dallas County deputy sheriffs. Rightfully so. I've earned the verbal abuse. It's open season. One of the deputy sheriffs leans across the table, sees my fake diamond stud earring, places his face inches from my nose, and starts yelling for all to hear: "YOU'RE A STINKING LAWYER? ONE THING IS FOR SURE. YOU DO STINK! YOU'RE A DISGRACE TO THE LEGAL PROFESSION! I HOPE THEY KICK YOU OUT!"

I agree with him. I don't say a word. It's at this point that I realize my job and legal future might be at risk. Then I'm put in a large holding cell (otherwise known as "the drunk tank") that smells of puke, urine, and the stench of the non-showered. Men, some much younger than me, dressed in their hip nightclub shirts and alligator shoes are crying uncontrollably in shame and uncertainty for their futures. *They're beneath me*, I think at first. *I'm a lawyer!* But then, after a few minutes sitting on a concrete floor, I realize they *are* me. I am them.

I stand close to the phone in the drunk tank waiting for the shirtless tattooed dude to finish using the phone. He's screaming into the phone in Spanish and gesticulating wildly. Then he slams the phone down so hard, it draws the attention of the guard, who silently stares the tattooed guy back into his spot on the concrete floor. Only outbound collect calls are permitted. *Who will I call?* Family is out. I'm too ashamed to let either of my brothers know. Will anyone even pick up the phone for a collect call at 2 am? After several failed calls, my best friend John finally answers. A wave of calm momentarily washes over me when he promises to immediately head to the jail to post bond and take me home.

Arraignment time. I'm sitting with a bunch of drunks in a room looking at a television monitor. A guard suddenly calls my name. My heart begins racing. *What did I do wrong?* (beyond the obvious). I slouch back in my seat in relief when he simply tells me that my bail has been posted. Not everyone in the room is calm. Especially a guy in the back. "This place sucks! The cops suck! Fuck all of you!"

The deputy sheriff responds. "Sir, if you don't shut up and calm down, we're going to put you back in the tank, and you'll have to wait for the next arraignment. Keep quiet!"

Uncomfortable pause. He's contemplating. Heads turn in anticipation. "Fuck You! You All Suck!" Two burly deputy sheriffs are on him. He's in a bear hug, and then in handcuffs. Then he's gone. He won't be going home today. I chuckle to myself. *Hey, someone has less sense than I do.*

About ten hours after my arrest, I'm released. John drives me home. My first call is to my father. I cry uncontrollably in shame and fear of the unknown consequences to come. My life is over. I vow to him and myself that "I'll never drink again." My next call is to my brother Jeff. He's circumspect. "Yeah, you f#cked up. Deal with it. Learn from it. Get a good lawyer." My last call is to another friend to take me to the tow yard to get my car. Standing in the "line of shame," I notice another guy who had been in the drunk tank with me there to get his car. I don't feel so bad. Misery loves company.

■ Monday, August 10

Back to work at Transport Insurance, fresh off my first night in the slammer. I can still hear the crying in the cell, and my own sobbing with my father on the other end of the line. Despite numerous hot showers to wash away the memories of the drunk tank, I can still smell stench. My brief moment of clarity brings memories like a looped cassette tape playing over and over.

Now I'm crying in my office, wondering about my future at work and as a licensed attorney. *Do they let convicted felons keep their law licenses? It's sure to come out. Will I get fired?* My boss knocks, and I wipe the tears away. He wants to talk about a case going to trial. I need to get the shame off my chest. If I'm going to get fired, so be it.

"I was arrested for DWI over the weekend."

"Did you hurt anyone?"

"No, spent the night in jail. I'm sorry."

"It happens, Brian." He repeats the advice I had received from my brother Jeff. "Get a good lawyer and learn from it." Sigh of relief. I'm not getting fired.

I managed two weeks of sobriety after getting out of jail. Just as long as it took to feel secure again in my established routine. My DWI should have been a learning experience. It was not. Or rather, it wasn't the learning experience it should have been. Like many addicts who are humiliated, repentant, and swear off drinking, drugs, or whatever else in the immediate aftermath, the farther the event was removed in time, the easier it was to tell myself it would never happen again. I only learned it'd be better to take cabs to and from the clubs. That way I could drink and do as many drugs as I wanted without getting busted.

Perhaps it didn't help that I ended up beating the rap. I pled not guilty. I approached my friend who was with me at the bar that night and asked him to lie for me at trial. Having more integrity than I did, he refused. I still chose to try the case and challenge the breathalyzer results. I was lucky. The state trooper did not show up for trial, so the charges were dismissed. I remember my attorney handing me the dismissal. When I thanked him, he said to thank the assistant district attorney for dismissing the case. I had no idea he was being tongue-in-cheek. I stuck my head in the ADA work room next to the courtroom and with a big, ear to ear, teeth-baring grin, said, "Thank you!" They were not amused. The look in their eyes told me I should have humbly stayed quiet. I high-tailed it out of the courthouse before they changed their minds. No thought about how I'd gotten to that point. No thought of being in desperate need of treatment. Just relief that I had dodged a bullet. No hard conse-quences other than the few grand I gave my lawyer and getting my car out of impoundment. My attorney told me not to get too giddy over it because they could refile the charges. I got drunk and snorted cocaine to celebrate. They never refiled.

I may have beaten the DWI, but cocaine and alcohol had taken over my life and were robbing me of my ambition, my ability to focus, and the stability of all my relationships—professional and personal. Before long I'd lose my job for not meeting expectations. And just as drugs and alcohol were interfering with my career, they were wreaking havoc on my personal life.

7

Liars Dance

DURING MY YEARS in Dallas, I learned both the two-step and the liar's dance—a dance with which all addicts are familiar. I perfected each of my liar's steps in each of my failed marriages, and that is a major reason they failed.

■ **Summer 1997**

I'm married—and not for the first time. My first marriage started with a bar pickup and ended as my others would—with me putting exponentially more effort into concealing my addiction and other mental health issues than into working toward a healthy marriage. My new wife is someone I met in a bar as well, and is also someone from whom I hide my secrets. The cycle repeats.

My spouse is a newly hired nurse in a neonatal hospital intensive care unit (NICU). She has long night weekend shifts. Like my first wife, she is at first unaware of my dark side. Drugs. Alcohol. An eating disorder. Anabolic steroid use. Untreated clinical depression. The depression however, will become clear to her during our marriage. Day-to-day demeanor is front and center in a relationship. Her concern and questions about what was wrong will be met with deflection and silence. These days I'm working as a personal injury plaintiff's attorney. My income is settlement-based, and the new wife doesn't know about every settlement. My deceit goes beyond just hiding my dysfunction. All I have to do is quickly turn settlements to cash, and suddenly I have money to party. It's not unusual for me to head over to a friend's house when my wife is working the night shift. A friend with cocaine. My wife is working hard, saving the lives of newborn children, and I'm working hard at destroying my life and eventually our life together. But I think the arrangement is great: I can party with my friend and be in bed when she gets home. This particular night at my friend's house is a rager. Two eight-balls of cocaine for three people.[16] Morning comes with the nauseating sounds of birds letting me know to get my ass home before her shift is over.

After the bleary-eyed drive home, I toss my clothes in the washing machine and hop into the shower. I'm an expert at destroying all evidence of my other life. The hot water washes away some of my guilt.

Suddenly the shower goes dark. I can't see! My heart rate triples. It won't go down. I'm having a reaction to the cocaine. I drop to one knee in the shower. Am I having a heart attack? Sheer panic and fear. Deep breathing. No help. I call my brother Jeff. He tells me to bite the bullet and call 911. If I do that, I'm discovered. My marriage is over. There has to be another way. I run to the liquor cabinet and chug a leftover bottle of Cristal champagne from our wedding and pray that the depressing effect calms my heart. I drink the entire bottle. No change. My life is over, either by death or divorce. I pick up the phone to call 911. A feeling of faintness washes over me. It's the lightheadedness of a sudden change in my heartbeat. It's back to normal. Falling back on the bed, I start crying. Not tears of guilt or self-awareness—tears of relief that I won't be caught today. Back in the shower. Toss the champagne bottle. I'll tell the wife it broke. Throw back some mouthwash, and rehearse my story of what I did the night before.

Within a year, my second marriage officially breaks. Along with my career, my personal relationships followed the same cycles. Every crisis, whether divorce, job-loss, or some other humiliation inspired a short period of sobriety, only until I felt I had my life back again—I'd meet someone new, I'd find new work, my family and friends would show they still care.

Then—sometimes slowly, sometimes all at once—drugs and alcohol would creep back into my life. Even if I could hide my substance use from my immediate loved ones, drug and alcohol use were as ingrained in my life, part of my history, part of the landscape wherever I traveled, part of dozens of relationships I'd formed with fellow users through the years.

■ Winter 2004

Las Vegas; Miami; Los Angeles. All places that hide my secrets. Drugs delivered to my hotel room in Vegas. Coke deals done with quick hand-to-hand exchanges under the cover of darkness just feet from the calming waves of the ocean in South Beach. I often require a high-end backdrop for the high-end product I was purchasing—it makes me feel like the false image I tried too hard to project. Of course, the dealers I meet don't care about the ambience. They just want to make a sale and not be seen.

Today, however, it's a bitter cold day in Chicago, hundreds of miles from any sun or ocean. Not a nice hotel. No drug deals along the scenic shores of Lake Michigan. This evening I'm cruising the crack dens and dilapidated drug houses of the Chicago slums. I'm terrified, but I'm not alone. My friend Mike, also a cocaine addict, knows where the best stuff is. My trips to Chicago to visit him always involve tense visits to seedy parts of town to score from his dealer. Hotel rooms and all-night cocaine binges are a regular staple. The cocaine money eventually runs out. The weekend ends. I always head back to Dallas and my addict life. He stays in Chicago in his. Those with addiction never really think about the lifestyles of others with the same problems. The impulse isn't to think about the ways their families might be torn apart, or the grief, anger, and despair that might be a prison in the same way coke addiction might be. The quest for white powder to drive the masking of pain, guilt, childhood, and loss.

I have my secrets. Mike has his. My drive is for the acceptance of a thirteen-year-old bullied little boy. To change a horrifying reflection that I saw in the mirror. The drive for the elusive feeling of being loved. Mike's struggles are touched by loss, profound loss. The loss of a son, his only son at the time. A tragic July 4th weekend years before. The pain. The guilt. The blame. He would never recover. His marriage would never recover. Addiction does not distinguish between the trivial and the tragic. Neither do secrets.

I wait in fear while Mike goes into a housing project apartment to score for our upcoming binge. My fear is not that he'll be harmed, but that if something goes wrong, I won't be getting high. But he emerges, prize tucked away, and a smile on his face. *Now there's a true friend.* Thoughts of the grief he carries are out of my mind. Thoughts of my own depression, my own wrecked relationships also seem miles away. *Who needs family, when you've got friends like this?*

Another tragedy was around the corner for Mike, and it hadn't been revealed to either of us. He was dying. Colon Cancer. I'd see him only one more time before his death. I never had the chance to speak to him outside the prison of addiction and despair. He died before he was able to find recovery.

I was luckier. I saw plenty of wreckage in my life as a consequence of addiction. Another failed marriage. A career that sputtered to a near stop. But eventually, I found a way out, and was lucky to find that path before I too died.

Looking back, it's hard to say there was an exact date when the seeds of positive change were planted. And those positive changes for me were often a razor's edge away from the kind of tragedy Mike experienced.

Maybe it began on July 22, 2005, when I first sat in a room with an attending psychiatrist, a psychiatric nurse, and my two brothers at the psychiatric facility at Green Oaks Hospital. On that day, my younger brother had awakened me from a stupor and confronted me about the loaded .45 on my nightstand. He had been alerted by a friend who was worried about me. My brother Mark would also intervene. The intervention may have helped save my life, but it wasn't enough to break the cycle.

Or maybe a better date is April 7, 2007. On that date, I was on my way back to Green Oaks again. This time I was driven there by my girlfriend of just over one year, the one person close to me who hadn't known about my battles with addiction. The worse my problems got, the more effort I put into concealing them, but only to those who hadn't known me for years. Hiding my addictions was a mentally and physically exhausting process of deceit. My girlfriend discovered my secret that morning of April 7 after coming home to a terrible scene when she was supposed to be away on a business trip, and I told her the truth and told her where I needed to go next.

That second trip to Green Oaks was the last time I touched cocaine or alcohol. But I can't say that was when I left drugs and alcohol behind. Substance use disorder isn't like an on/off switch, and despite the narratives that come from movies and novels, recovery isn't like bouncing back to sobriety after hitting some mythical "rock bottom." As with battling the addictions themselves, repairing personal and professional relationships and earning trust again is an ongoing journey. But I've found it is possible. For me it requires remaining alert to my past, not shutting it out.

■ 2015

A dream one night. I'm thirteen years old again, in the house I grew up in. Searching for the cold blue lockbox my father often kept money and coins from his trips abroad. As a child, I loved to explore it and steal mementos of his trips to foreign lands that, to me, were full of mystery. I would look up the countries in the bound volumes of Encyclopedia Britannica that was a staple in so many baby-boomer homes. I think he purposely left it unlocked to allow me to begin my exploration of other cultures. Now, in my dream, I find photos of my old friend Mike and me, and I begin to cry uncontrollable heart-wrenching sobs of a little boy mourning. I awaken from my dream, a grown man, sobbing in the middle of the night.

8

My Reel Life in Addiction

LET'S PLAY A GAME. Let's play, "What addiction movie are you?" Not necessarily your favorite movie, or the one that should have won an Academy Award, but the one that most accurately reflects your journey—whether it be the struggle, the recovery, or both. The one with that one scene or line of dialogue or character that really hits home.

I've previously mentioned the excellent movie *The Verdict*, but there are some others I would call "Brian movies" as they so closely mirror my experience in some way that I actually become the characters when I watch them. The image of Jamie Conway, the cocaine-addicted aspiring writer, standing alone on a dance floor in New York City as the club closes in the movie *Bright Lights, Big City* hits hard for me. I see in Jamie the loneliness of addiction, the all-night cocaine and booze binge, waiting for something to happen, the friends who are also addicts, and the career slipping away due to addiction and the Peter Principle in action. And then that scene, being the last man standing at the nightclub. That was me so many nights on the club scene in Dallas.

The final scene of the Dick Van Dyke movie *The Morning After* always puts a knot in my stomach. It was the first film I ever saw on the subject, and Van Dyke's character is a successful executive destroying his life with alcohol. I still cry at the end with the final image of Charlie alone, drunk, and hopeless on a deserted beachfront with a rendition of the Beatles' "Yesterday" playing. A beaten alcoholic. It happened to me. It happens every day of the year around the world. We *must* challenge prevailing attitudes and behaviors that simultaneously encourage unhealthy lifestyles while discouraging help-seeking. We must disrupt the sick and dysfunctional status quo. From law schools, to Bar admission agencies, Bar associations, legal regulators, lawyer assistance programs, private firms and beyond, it is time for *all* stakeholders to step up and get actively involved. It is the duty of each entity to evaluate what it can do within its respective role, and then do it. The list of possible solutions is long, but it might include an emphasis on early referral to behavioral health services at the first signs of a problem, encouraging and de-stigmatizing help-seeking behavior, establishing and supporting policies and procedures that de-emphasize the use of alcohol within work settings and at work events, and promoting overall wellness and balance. The common denominator in all of these ideas? Change. The old ways of thinking and acting just won't cut it anymore.

But when I think of moments of hopelessness followed by the slow march to recovery, I also see the character Daryl Poynter, played by Michael Keaton in the movie *Clean and Sober*. Keaton plays a successful commercial real estate executive deep in cocaine addiction. He's destroying his professional life thanks to the alcohol and cocaine. His personal life is full of superficial relationships, as would be the case with anyone who won't let others see who they truly are. One morning, Daryl wakes up in bed with a girl he barely knows who has overdosed. She ultimately dies. The scene is hard for me to watch. That look of bewilderment on his face, not knowing for a moment where he is, who he is with, what is happening, and why. I never had someone OD next to me, but I did have those mornings, waking up next to someone I barely knew, not sure how I got there or how she did, a love of drugs being the only tie that brought us together. Also like Daryl's character, my life became an exhausting struggle to maintain a world of lies and deceit, anything to avoid facing the possibility that I was addicted to drugs and alcohol and engaging in a host of other destructive behaviors. After the woman he's with ODs, Daryl begins his journey through rehab, skeptically at first, and then starts into twelve-step. The final scene of him at the twelve-step podium sharing his story brings back vivid memories of my own recovery. When he holds that thirty-day chip in his hand with no promise of making it through day thirty-one, I can practically feel one of my desire chips pressed against my palm. Daryl's progression from denial and lies to acceptance that he could not do it on his own resonates with me.

The last of my favorite "addiction" movies is, believe it or not, *American Psycho. Is Brian Cuban like Patrick Bateman? What could a movie about a mentally disturbed mass killer have to do with addiction?* Sure, Patrick Bateman is a high-powered stockbroker during the day and mass murderer by night. And I'm in no way trying to equate the mental health issues I or other addicts might face with being a monstrous serial killer. But there are ways that movie reaches me. For one, it does an amazing job skewering the late-1980s coke and club culture, with Bateman spending long nights chatting with his co-workers about who has the best business cards and whether or not the club has a good bathroom to do coke in, and then griping when they get scammed on a cocaine buy and end up snorting Sweet 'N Low. I've been there.

But more than the depiction of materialistic culture, the movie resonates with me in the way its anti-hero's polished façade is just a mask. Early in the movie, in describing himself, Bateman says, "There is an idea of Patrick Bateman, some kind of abstraction. But there is no real me, only an entity, something illusory. And though I can hide my cold gaze, and you can shake my hand and feel flesh gripping yours, and maybe you can even sense our lifestyles are probably comparable...I simply am not there." For me the experience of having addiction to drugs and alcohol and hiding it away from my respectable world felt a lot like this. I might look as if I'm here, shaking your hand, but I'm not. In my mind, I'm already at the bar with a drink and an eighth ounce of coke. You are seeing what I want you to see. A respectable lawyer. A happy lawyer. From that standpoint, in the practiced disguises of addiction, I was Patrick Bateman. (And I'm still trying to get that reservation at Dorsia.)

For me, these are just a few fictional stories that come to mind that I identify with so strongly in some ways that to watch them makes my heart beat a little faster. It's difficult but also cathartic. Other addiction stories might not reach me as easily or powerfully, but might touch others more closely instead. In a movie like *Requiem for a Dream,* I can recognize that abyss, the deep hole that the characters fall into as they succumb to heroin and amphetamine addictions. But their stories don't brush up against mine in quite the same way as Daryl's or Jamie's, for instance.

Anyone who has had to confront addiction either as the person dealing with addiction or as the loved one of someone facing addiction has those moments of recognition. You might identify with another movie, song, painting, dream, or even a smell that takes you to a different time and place and brings a long recessed memory into the present. How many recovering from cocaine addiction will, out of the blue, take in that ether-like smell that reminds them of the white powder? How many have drug dreams? It happens to me quite often. When I experience them, I often have a moment of sadness, and then hope when the technique of mindfulness reminds me the smell is an illusion of the past. But that illusion is also a reminder to stay in the present in my recovery.

For some, these brushes with familiarity aren't welcome regardless of whether they come from triggers in the real world or from fictional accounts. Maybe they trigger feelings of need that come with addiction, or memories too painful to bear. I've had those moments. But I've learned from recovery that sharing and hearing stories is the best way to understand my own life experience, and understanding my own experience has been instrumental in my recovery.

For that reason, I've opened this book up as a testimony not only of my own experience, but of the experiences of other attorneys who have stories to share.

I suspect that while our "addiction movies" might all be different, we all share some key experiences, and they are the ones I hope to identify. If there's one common bond all addicts share, it's that the consequences can be pretty consistent for those of us who can't find the way to recovery.

The differences in our stories are important, too. There are different environmental stressors attorneys face, for instance: the area of practice, private practice versus law firm, hours worked, family stress, genetics, childhood trauma. The list goes on. Because I wanted to know the whole story and not just the moments of self-destruction or moments of hope and recovery, I asked attorneys I knew how substance use played a part in their careers, including application to law school, student life, substance use, and their careers, as well as any grievance process they may have faced. I wanted to know what their addiction movies were like.

Many were willing to open up about how substance or alcohol use affected their personal lives. As you might imagine, it was not an easy task finding current and former lawyers willing to go on record. The stigma. Employment fears. Family privacy. I get it. I did find some extraordinary people willing to talk about their journeys. Some of the attorneys I spoke with are still practicing law. Some are not. Whether we stay in practice or not, we all have the choice to move forward with our lives.

I want to start with Marsha. Her story offers plenty that I can identify with, those moments that seem as if we are in the same addiction movie. Other aspects of her story are different from my own experience, and reading about those moments can be just as illuminating as reading about the familiar.

I connected with Marsha, as I did all of these contributors, by networking in addiction recovery and legal circles looking for attorneys and law students willing to share their journeys with me. I am grateful to each of them for being willing to recover out loud and share their journey here.

Marsha began drinking in high school and continued through college. When she was twenty-two and married to her college sweetheart, whom she describes as, "my best drinking and using buddy," she did cocaine for the first time. Two years later, they were living on the Outer Banks of North Carolina, had three children, and were going through separation, something they would repeat many times during the eight years prior to their divorce in 2002.

"Looking back, I can see that my dependence on alcohol and cocaine was progressing," she told me. "At the time, however, I had zero awareness or concern about my relationship with substances."

One day, Marsha had what she describes as "a sort of epiphany," remembering that she was a good student and once won a debate competition in high school. The idea of becoming a lawyer entered her mind, and she took the LSAT and applied to a few law schools. She was accepted and earned a partial scholarship to North Carolina Central University School of Law in Durham, North Carolina, which she started in August of 1996.

As she progressed in school, so did her drinking and using, she says: "I remember coming to class very hungover and reeking of booze to the point that my classmates would comment and tease me. I went on a spring break trip and was MIA for most of the trip because I met up with some old drug buddies, and we did cocaine around the clock."

After the first and second year, Marsha got an internship for the summer at a law firm and was unable to fulfill her duties due to being hungover during the day, so much so that she sometimes missed work.

"I specifically remember saving cocaine from the night before and taking it into the law firm the next morning and doing lines on my desk to try to stay awake and functional," she says. "Not surprisingly, this firm did not offer me a position upon graduation."

In her third year in law school, Marsha was standing in her kitchen, high on cocaine, and about to pour herself a drink. Her seven-year-old son walked through the door, and she noticed that the pants he was wearing did not reach the floor, and the shirt he was wearing was too thin for the season; it didn't even reach his waistband.

"I suddenly realized that I was expending my meager resources on alcohol and drugs rather than properly caring for my children," Marsha says. "However, that clarity was quickly supplanted with the thought (delusion) that any single mother in my situation, under the stress of law school and raising three children alone, would be drinking and using to cope with the stress as I was. I honestly believed that as soon as I was done with school and had a good job, I would stop drinking and using for good. I believed that financial security would solve my problem."

She did graduate. She passed the Georgia Bar and moved back to her hometown in Georgia, where she accepted the position of assistant district attorney of the Southern Judicial District. Marsha didn't share the truth about her substance use on her application for character and fitness, nor during the interview process for the job with the DA's office. She justified her dishonesty by rationalizing that any behaviors she had denied or omitted were a part of her past, and that she had made up her mind to not drink excessively, not do any drugs, and to be an upstanding citizen and attorney. "And I meant it with all my heart. I had no idea I actually suffered from a disease."

Marsha was the first female assistant DA in her hometown, where her stepfather was a prominent attorney, and her aunt was the probate judge. Marsha was assigned all of the felony crimes against women and children, as well as a scattering of other felony crimes in the district, and of course, she was under a good deal of pressure and scrutiny. Her plan and commitment to herself to straighten up was short lived. During the three years of 1999–2002, her disease really took off.

"I was drinking every day by this point and becoming intoxicated most evenings," she told me. "I used cocaine whenever I could. Gradually I began to wake up during the night and had to drink to stave off withdrawal symptoms. I also began to drink in the mornings. I was living a double life, prosecuting people during the day for the very behaviors in which I was engaged during the evenings. My friends and family began to notice I had a problem (which I always denied). My children suffered from my erratic behavior and neglect."

In 2002, while under the influence, Marsha had a bad car accident. She was asked to resign from the DA's office, and shortly thereafter, her family did an intervention on her. Marsha went to treatment for the first time at Talbott Recovery Campus in Atlanta, Georgia.

"While at Talbott, I looked at my drinking and using with some honesty for the first time. I learned something of the genetic component of addiction, and I learned that other people were getting and staying sober. Still, I mostly blamed my drinking, using, and associated behaviors on my life circumstances."

While she was at Talbott, Marsha got into a romantic relationship with Jim, another patient, and they left the program together before completing it. Jim would later become (and remain) her husband.

Marsha and Jim moved to Asheville, North Carolina, stayed mostly sober, married, and blended their families into a life that she describes as looking "pretty good on the outside."

According to her, "I had a few slips with alcohol and also on occasion took pain pills from a doctor. I marginally participated in recovery; however, looking back, it was the epitome of half measures."

She took the North Carolina Bar and got her license to practice in 2003 or 2004. She had to sit in front of an ethics committee prior to being fully licensed due to having been to treatment but was ultimately licensed to practice in Georgia and in North Carolina.

North Carolina has what is called the PALS (Positive Action for Lawyers) Committee, which is a peer assistance program designed to help attorneys with chemical dependency. Through PALS, Marsha was assigned a mentor with whom she also worked as an associate for a couple of years. Marsha later opened a private practice in Asheville but was still a member of PALS.

In February 2007, she was "stark raving sober." As she puts it, "I was abstinent from alcohol and drugs but not involved in a program of recovery. I wasn't going to meetings or taking care of myself spiritually at all."

Instead, she distracted herself with work and acquisition of material things in an attempt to soothe the feeling of being "restless, irritable, and discontent" as they say in the twelve-step fellowships. And in her experience, that only lasted so long until she picked up a drink or a drug.

One day, she bartered legal services for cocaine from a long-standing client. "I told myself that I'd only do the cocaine and not drink any alcohol, blaming alcohol on all my prior problems. This was a failure of course, and in short order, I was doing massive amounts of cocaine and drinking. My husband relapsed with me, and together, we were off to the races."

At this point, Marsha was barely getting her work done, missing deadlines with clients, not showing up to court. In the fall of 2007, she entered a six-week program. Very quickly thereafter, she relapsed again and was drinking and using on a daily basis.

In February 2008, she was introduced to crack cocaine. "I remember sneaking cocaine into the courthouse and smoking it in the bathroom there. I was powerless. I could NOT stop. If alcohol and powder cocaine is a sumo wrestler, crack is a ninja, and my life went up in smoke in a period of one hundred days. From February 2008 to May 6, 2008, I lost my car, my house, my job (I was locked out of my office by my partners), and Child Protective Services came and took custody of my five children and placed them in the care of my mother. Every penny I'd ever earned I used for drugs."

To make matters worse, when Marsha's own money ran out, she wrote checks to herself out of her client trust account, promising herself she would replace it "tomorrow."

One night in that moment of "incomprehensible demoralization," she reached out to her old employer a PALS mentor, and he contacted the North Carolina Bar. A representative from the Bar Association contacted a long-term treatment center and made arrangements for Marsha to go with the NC Bar, somehow negotiating a discounted rate and paying her tuition.

She entered treatment on May 6, 2008, finally willing to surrender and take direction, and she has been clean and sober ever since. Marsha signed agreements to pay back (and did) the NC Bar for her treatment. She also paid back all the clients who sought reimbursement from the Bar for fees she accepted for work that wasn't performed. She was required to sign a "Consent Order for Disbarment" for five years in both North Carolina and Georgia, and to this day, she is technically disbarred in both states.

Today, Marsha is not only a Juris Doctorate, but also a Licensed Chemical Dependency Counselor and the CEO of a well-known and respected treatment center outside Austin, Texas. Although she no longer desires to practice law, she would like to have both state licensures back one day, simply as a testament to the power of recovery.

"I am crystal clear that I suffer from a disease called addiction and not of a moral failure of some kind," she says. "I'm also crystal clear that there exists at this very moment of this very day, a young parent and budding professional just as I was, who is engaged in a process of behaviors that will ultimately bring them to their knees. At this moment, I would like to be a beacon of light and hope to that person and their family. There is hope. Recovery is possible."

Like me, Marsha started using alcohol early, and it disrupted her work and her personal life early. Like me, Marsha screwed up some of her earliest career opportunities because drinking and drugs were more important to her. And it hits close to home for me when Marsha describes her younger self feeling as if her destructive behaviors were only temporary, and once she made her life what she wanted it to be, she'd be able to stop. If only young Brian had been able to talk to young Marsha about our problems, maybe we both would have realized we shared a common self-deception fed by addiction.

Of course, there are many ways Marsha's story is completely different from my own. While I was by myself when starting out my career, Marsha was already divorced and raising three young children. She mentions the stress of law school as a factor in her developing addiction. I didn't feel stressed about law school performance much. My environmental stressors were more about my past and achieving some kind of social acceptance. Our paths to recovery were different as well—Marsha was able to use the support system offered by her state Bar to help move into recovery, a path I never followed, but a path that I hope readers of this book will see is not one that should be feared, even in the face of professional consequences. Careers can be paused, changed, and redirected. Lives cannot be brought back.

As someone once said to me, as long as we are above ground, recovery and redemption are possible. As legal professionals, we need to move past looking at Bar-directed help as a battlefield and see it as a tool of moving forward into long-term recovery.

Another important similarity to my story is that Marsha is no longer practicing law, and has instead made helping others with recovery the focus of her work. Not every attorney with whom I spoke has left the law. In fact, I know many incredible attorneys who are in long-term recovery and continue to love the law. If you or a loved one is struggling with addiction and worried about the professional implications of exposing your problem, know that doing so is far more likely to help than hurt. And no matter what you want to do professionally, think of it this way: *How is addiction keeping you from maximizing your passion and effort?*

Regardless of your career decisions, most important, it's better to put yourself in a position to recover from addiction so that recovery is *your* choice and the career "choice" is not made for you by your school, the criminal justice system, or your state bar in suspension or disbarment proceedings. There is no shame in being an "addicted lawyer" or a law student struggling with these issues. Addiction is not a choice. It is not a moral failing. Recovery is a choice. You have to do more than just want it. You have to take steps. They don't have to be big ones. Baby steps are fine.

Regardless of what people tell you, how people judge you, how people stigmatize you, how low you've sunk, and how much damage you've done to yourself, family, and others, you still have choices to make. It's never too late. Maybe you're being called before your respective state bar for misconduct. Maybe you've already lost your law license through temporary suspension or permanent disbarment. Maybe you've dropped out of school. Whatever your situation, it still boils down to this: How you choose to take that first step in the face of fear is what will define you. If you slip, stay the course. Get up and step again.

When you're deep into the consequences of addiction and depression, it's easy to feel as if nobody else could possibly understand what you're going through. Maybe it feels like so many things are happening in your life that you can't even make sense of it all. It's important to know that you always have the opportunity to look and to listen. You'll find stories like yours sooner than you think.

They may be hard stories to watch or hear for you, but there's a good chance that making connections with experiences outside your own will help.

That was my pep talk. You might have heard something similar before from friends, family, or professional colleagues. For those who have heard it all and still haven't been able to change their lives, believe me, I get it. I've been there. It's a common feeling among those battling addiction. A stranger writing a book isn't likely to tell you something your family cannot. But I believe continuing to reach out and to share stories is one of the critical tools of recovery.

Now let's take a look at the start of nearly every lawyer's path, the first year of law school. This is a time often fraught with decisions and actions that have long-term implications for future lawyers' career paths and mental health. We have some available data that many law students struggle with addiction and mental well-being. We'll also find out what some addiction thought leaders have to say on these issues—things I wish I had known and concepts that may help you navigate your recovery and professional choices. I'll continue to share my stories and the stories of other attorneys who have battled addiction, and I hope you will see that no matter what addiction movie you might feel trapped in, you are not alone. Furthermore, you can still believe and even witness happy endings.

9

Chasing Paper, Booze, and Belonging

BY THE TIME I had entered through the wide glass doors of the University of Pittsburgh School of Law, I was lost and overwhelmed before I had finished my first step into the expansive lobby. At the time, I thought I was the only one who felt that way. Now I know better. Back then, a brisk and sunny fall day in September 1983, I was sweating as if it were the worst, humid, hot July day Pittsburgh had to offer. I was now a "1L"—a first-year law student.

Walking through those doors brought about a sick feeling in my stomach I knew all too well from excessive alcohol use and bulimia. I felt sick because I was no longer in the comfort of my small apartment at Penn State with my routine of survival.

I was alone when I was in college, but I felt safe there. I'd run up to twenty miles a day to ease the pain of loneliness and the overwhelming obsessions I had with the fat, ugly, monster I saw in my reflection every minute of every day. Drinking to excess had become my new normal, but I never dreamed I was an alcoholic—college students were never alcoholics, I reasoned. Too young. And bulimia? I'd never heard of it, even though I was living it.

The short time I had between college and law school hadn't exactly been a time of personal growth either. I spent the summer living with my parents in the Pittsburgh suburb of Mt. Lebanon while I saved up some money. I worked as a store detective at the now defunct Joseph Horne's department store in downtown Pittsburgh: long, mind-numbing hours of endlessly circling the men's clothing section with handcuffs and a walkie-talkie, broken by shifts hiding inside a two-way mirror waiting for the moment when I'd spot someone slipping a pair of dress socks into a pocket, and I'd suddenly spring from behind the mirror, startling the thief and slapping on the cuffs. Those shifts hiding behind the mirror trying to remember not to hum along with the Muzak and the spike in adrenaline before I sprang into arrest mode were as close as I'd ever get to my original dream of being a police officer. But they didn't do much to help me prepare mentally for the rigors of law school, or the intensive socialization that's often part of law school life from day one.

That first day, as I watched other first year students milling around in the lobby, talking, and getting to know one another like the first day of camp, I felt alone and isolated. *That's OK*, I thought. *It's what I'm used to.*

Then, within those first few days at Pitt, I was quickly swept up in meeting students, socializing, taking classes, and studying on top of my personal challenges. It was a lot to add to the problems I already had, but I badly wanted to fit in, even if my desire to succeed in school wasn't much of a motivator.

I felt I was never going to truly belong, however, until I found a way to move out of my parents' home and closer to campus. But as a broke law student, roommates were essential to being able to cut loose from parental support.

Dave and I met early as L1s, and ours was an arrangement of convenience. We both needed a roommate, and we were both fairly quiet, reserved people. But it turned out that we were like oil and water. Him: preppy; conservative; socks and shirts neatly organized by color. By that first day together, he made sure I knew the top shelf in the fridge was his food. Bottom shelf, my food. For an alcoholic and active bulimic such as myself, such food boundaries were meaningless. I ate his food regularly, often after coming home drunk.

For Dave, law school was *real*. It was competitive. It was one step toward something: life as a successful prosecutor, maybe, or a judge, or even a life in politics. Maybe Big Law. For me, it was a step away from figuring things out for myself.

Soon Dave proved he was not only an incredibly tidy and organized roommate, he was also a good student. He got in with the top study group. He got good grades. He seemed to want to spend evenings in quiet study, and I never saw him drink. I was beginning to suspect there was something seriously "wrong" with Dave. The problem was that he was not like me.

What I wanted to do was sit around watching television and drink whenever possible. Isn't that what people our age were supposed to be doing? In the evenings, a time Dave seemed to think was appropriate for his quiet book reading, I chose to do high impact aerobics (popular at that time) to music in the living room. *Hey, you live your life, I'll live mine*, I thought. Soon he was spending more and more time at the law school library while I did endless knee kicks and jumping jacks in the living room to the song "Footloose" by Kenny Loggins. Our new arrangement was fine with me. I ruled the roost.

More than that, to see him was to be reminded of what I was not. I was a slob (OK, I'm still kind of a slob), but it was easier to pretend I was living that way on purpose when he wasn't around. Dressers and closets were mere ornaments—the floor was a more efficient clothes storage system. Sweaty running gear sat piled up near my door, ready for wear at a moment's notice. Empty six packs of passion fruit wine coolers added a festive, tropical note to most rooms in the apartment. I would drink the entire case after going on a long run. And it seemed like fun little pranks to leave dishes piled up in the sink for him (I knew he'd wash them eventually) or gobble down his healthy, expensive grocery purchases when I came home intoxicated. *Aren't we an odd couple! Can't wait to see the look on his face when he has to take off his cufflinks and scrub the day-old mac n cheese out of the saucepan!*

In short, I was a constant source of irritation to Dave. And that was even before I started having to dig around under the couch cushions to find rent money. Even though Dave demonstrated incredible patience, I started to become paranoid about what he thought of me. After all, the evidence of my dysfunctional life didn't require much investigation. When I'd see him at school, my mind would run wild with his imagined plot to ruin my life for being such an awful roommate. I had it in my mind that he was telling everyone else what a slob, a drunk, and a loser I was. But of course, he was just a law student trying to survive and excel in the hardest year in law school.

As we both grew to hate the arrangement, I spent more and more time away, sometimes staying with my parents. When I wasn't at the apartment, I'd go to the local bars alone or at night or pull my pre-exam study binges at a local twenty-four-hour Roy Rogers restaurant (with their unlimited salad bar to keep me fueled) so I didn't have to interact with Dave. In fact, I didn't want to interact with any of the students who were even a little like him—motivated, organized, and looking forward to promising careers. I didn't want to hang out with any of them and be reminded of what I'd never be: A real lawyer. So while Dave and my other fellow first year classmates studied, hung out, and even dated, I stayed to myself and nursed my own obsessions—exercise, alcohol, and avoiding looking myself in the mirror.

The amazing thing was, even after I'd reestablished my unhealthy habits and alienated peers like Dave, I was still surviving as a student. And that may be true of many who go to law school with substance use problems. While some who struggle might drop out, it's possible for others to do well despite underlying issues. Some of us give less than full effort and squeak by. Fate is certainly not predetermined by addiction and other mental health challenges, but probabilities of success (however you define that) are certainly affected.

Starting that first year of law school, I went the "squeak by" route, and getting through that tough first year without the consequence of outright failure was enough justification to me that I was doing well enough, and that my problems weren't really problems at all. *Can an alcoholic be able to make it through the gauntlet of L1?* I wondered. The answer, of course, is yes, and just being able to get by isn't confirmation that the problem isn't real, it just means the consequences are being put off until later, when the consequences of failure may be much greater and affect clients, family, and career.

There's good evidence that, as in my case, many law students come to school with problematic substance use, alcohol use, and mental health challenges already developing or fully developed.

A study called the "Survey of Law Student Well-Being" published in the December 2015 edition of *The Bar Examiner* magazine (one of the studies I referred to in the introduction) contains some revealing statistics in terms of law students who are dealing with mental health issues while simultaneously trying to stay afloat and excel in the hyper-competitive law school environment.

According to the report, it is the first survey to assess drug and alcohol use in law students since 1991. (I took particular interest in the 1991 date as that is a mere five years after I graduated.) As one might expect with such a stigmatized topic, even when anonymity is a condition of the survey, the response rate was just under 30 percent. But some of the numbers are eye opening. Some of the major findings include:

1. As mentioned in the introduction, nearly 25 percent of law students responding to the study fit standardized criteria to

be considered for further screening for problematic use of alcohol.

2. Eighteen percent of law students reported that they had been diagnosed with depression.

3. Nearly 40 percent screened positive for anxiety, with 14 percent meeting the criteria for severe anxiety.

The "Survey of Law Student Well-Being" also addresses some substance use, and compares numbers to results from the 1991 survey. For instance, in 2014, 25 percent of respondents had used marijuana in the last twelve months and 14 percent had used it in the last thirty days. That compares to 21 percent and 8 percent, respectively, in 1991. Numbers for cocaine use were also slightly increased: 6 percent in the last twelve months and 2.5 percent in the last thirty days, compared to 5 percent and 1 percent in 1991. In terms of other substances, between 9 percent and 15 percent reported using prescription drugs with a prescription (including sedative/anxiety meds, stimulants, pain meds, or antidepressants). Between 3 and 9 percent used those same categories of drugs without a prescription. These numbers are concerning, but not especially high. Again, though, are students possibly shy about reporting substance use problems even in anonymous surveys? It's a question that's difficult to answer. But there's good evidence in the study that the stigmatization of substance use issues is holding some students back from seeking help, if not also keeping them from self-reporting issues.

Aside from exploring the numbers of law students who might struggle with alcohol, substance, and mental health issues, the well-being study also asked students what the top barriers were to seeking help for those issues. According to the study, those top obstacles are:

1. Potential threat to job or academic status
2. Social stigma

3. Financial reasons
4. Potential threat to Bar admission
5. The belief that they could handle the problem themselves
6. Not having the time
7. Concerns about privacy

I see this list, and the item that jumps out to me most is number two, the stigma. Let's talk stigma and stereotypes.

This isn't a story about addiction specifically, but it illustrates how mental health is constantly subject to stereotypes. In 2013, I gave a lunch talk to a group of family lawyers. When I spoke of my battles with drugs, alcohol, and use of twelve-step in my recovery, there were nods of acknowledgement and understanding. When I got to the part about being in recovery from eating disorders, some of them looked at me as if I were someone from Mars. Shock and disbelief. *A guy can get an eating disorder?* Many had never heard a man talk about having one or even read about it. Of course most knew that singer Karen Carpenter's death was related to an eating disorder. It was something that happened to women, not men. In sharing my story and recovery, I had educated a group who now know that eating disorders also affect all of us. I helped break through the stigma and stereotypes.

But it took decades to get to the point where I could even admit to myself that I had a problem with eating disorders, let alone share that part of my story with others. Stigma can be a powerful disincentive to seeking help. But more than that, it can be a powerful enough force to keep us from admitting the truth about our mental health or addiction problems even to ourselves. That's why, I believe, many might avoid registering problems with alcohol or substance use even on an anonymous survey.

But all this is just *my* story. One problem in relating my story as a law student is that it occurred decades ago. I'm a baby boomer. Was the law school experience in the early to mid-eighties the same as it is today? Are the results of the well-being study speaking more for a newer generation of students? To better understand the experiences of contemporary law students, I reached out to many, and I share some of their stories here. These young law students are remarkable for their bravery in sharing their stories as well as their self-aware-ness at a young age. Unfortunately, many other law students might still be unaware or unwilling to acknowledge they have a problem, as I was at that age.

As I write this book, Melissa is a second-year law student at New England Law/Boston. She is also in long-term recovery. Melissa grew up in New Jersey in a small town with a mom and dad and siblings. To her, they seemed like the perfect family, complete with a nice house and pool in the backyard. Both of her parents owned businesses and were always there for her.

She relates that her dad was the typical guy who everyone in the world thought was great—everyone but his immediate family, that is. Her father was an alcoholic.

"He was Dr. Jekyll and Mr. Hyde," she says. "Fun-loving one moment and enraged and drunk the next."

As she was growing up, her mother always said, "Don't drink, Melissa. We have alcoholism in our family. Not just your dad, but your grandfathers." And it wasn't just drinking. Her father's brother, George, was addicted to heroin and took methadone on a daily basis pretty much until the day he died.

Melissa's mom tried really hard to be there for her and keep her out of harm's way. But in school, Melissa always felt like the outsider, the one who didn't belong anywhere. In middle school, she experi-enced bullying and often came home crying.

Melissa started out as many kids do, experimenting, drinking on weekends. There was always alcohol in her house. To her, drinking was just a big game, and her abuse of it was fun and easy to hide.

By her freshman year, Melissa, was drinking regularly but with-out consequences. She was freshman class president. She played basketball and softball. Then, not even six months after she started high school, she started getting into hard drugs. The first time she tried drugs was at a high school party.

"When I got there, and people were doing ecstasy, coke, and drinking, I just wanted to fit in," she says. "There was no second thought. There was no pause."

She had been searching for a group of friends she didn't have to constantly try to keep up with or who just accepted her as she was. That night she found them. And not only had she found a group of "friends"—but she had found something that made her feel invincible. She had found drugs.

At sixteen years old, Melissa was hanging out with the same group of people at someone's apartment and she was asked, "You want to do a line of dope?" She accepted the offer. She told me that her heroin use quickly turned into a daily habit. She, however, did not limit herself to heroin.

"I was a 'garbage head,'" she says. "I would take any drug that was given to me."

At that time, people from school knew she was a "junkie" and she was going to live up to that title.

"I thought I was a badass," she says.

When she was about seventeen years old, she started injecting heroin. After using heroin for a while, she quickly noticed that she wasn't getting as high as she had previously. Her tolerance had grown. That's when Melissa went even farther in her addiction.

She told me, "I remember hanging out with my boyfriend and just begging him, crying, because I wanted him to shoot me up."

She had the same boyfriend since she had started doing drugs. Upon learning of his arrest, she had a "meltdown," withdrawing and desperate for heroin.

"I got my fifteen-year-old brother cornered in the kitchen," she says. "He was sobbing, saying, 'Melissa, I don't want you to die.' I couldn't understand why he was crying."

Her mom walked into the kitchen just then, and for the first time Melissa admitted to her that she was doing heroin. Her mom called the cops.

The police showed up, and they took Melissa to the hospital. "I was on a psych watch," she says. "After my psych hold was over, I was strapped to a stretcher in the back of an ambulance and sent to a long-term adolescent therapeutic community. I cried for four days straight. I honestly did not believe that I was an alcoholic or addicted to drugs. I looked around at all these other people, and I thought: *You guys are scumbags, and I don't have a problem.* In my mind, I really believed that I was having a good time. I thought I could stop if I wanted to, but I just didn't want to."

Melissa told me that a lot of people always ask her, "Why didn't you get clean the first time you went to rehab?" Her answer is that she was still in denial. She realized that maybe she had a problem with heroin, but she definitely didn't think she had a problem with alcohol or weed. Her mindset was: How could I have a problem with alcohol when I am only seventeen years old?

Melissa left the treatment facility after about six months, and keeping with that mindset, she tried to just drink and smoke weed— no heroin. She did not understand that, for her, replacing one drug with another wouldn't solve the problem.

Melissa graduated from high school and applied to college. She relates that she wrote one application essay about how she was a seventeen-year-old recovering heroin addict. She ended up getting a big scholarship.

But she didn't stay sober. She tells me that she was high the entire first year of college. She was also homeless.

"Today, people who knew me at college and hear of my addiction issues, say, 'But you were really active as a freshman. You went to the church groups, and you did all this stuff.' And I say, 'Do you know why I did all those things? It's because I was homeless. I wasn't going there because I wanted to. It's because I had nowhere else to go.'"

During her freshmen year in college, there was a point where there was no more couch surfing, and there was no more staying at her boyfriend's house. There was no more living in her car and sleeping on the side of the road in Newark. She had burned every bridge. Melissa ended up going to a shelter in Easton, Pennsylvania.

"Of course, like any good drug addict, I was seeking out the drug users," she says. "I got there and found out that I couldn't get dope, but I could smoke crack."

By that point, she bounced between long-term programs and detoxes, going in and out of nine different programs, including Suboxone programs. She was told by one doctor that she'd have to be on methadone for the rest of her life because she was "too far gone." She was only nineteen years old.

"I lay in bed at the Hotel Lafayette, covered in bed-bug bites, roaches running across the floor every time I opened the blinds to let the light into the room," she says. "Needles on the dresser, the floor, empty bags everywhere. I prayed to die. One last shot of heroin. I hoped it would take me. I didn't want to live anymore. The anger I had the next day when I woke up in that shelter was like no anger I've ever felt since."

The next day she went to a social services office and told them she had a problem and was going to die if they did not get her into safe and sober living environment. They put her in a "beautiful new facility," she says. "One morning I just said in the middle of the group, 'I want to get high.' My counselor said to me, 'Of course you do, because you're a drug addict,' and it all made sense in that moment. It was so nonchalant and just like, *All right, so let's move on.*"

This was the first time Melissa successfully completed a program. She went to a halfway house, which was her first time in a sober-living environment. She was there for about a month and a half before she got kicked out, and not for getting high.

"I thought it was impossible to get kicked out of a halfway house for any reason besides getting high," she told me. "I was wrong. Even though I'd gotten a sponsor, was going into meetings, was working the steps, and hanging out with sober people, I was an asshole. My character defects were running rampant. I did what I wanted. I said what I wanted."

Horrified of spending the rest of her life in church basements, and not drinking, and not drugging, she went to sober dances, drove to meetings all over the state, and even went to sobriety-themed conventions. She began to see how good things were getting.

Melissa then went back to college, and "outed" herself to let people know what was going on with her recovery. The support, she says, was "amazing." She graduated from college on time despite taking a semester off when she got sober.

"After working my butt off in 2014, I got into law school."

Melissa then moved to Boston to begin her legal education. She got a new sponsor, made new friends, and continued to live a life of recovery. She was even lucky enough to mentor a first-year law student also in recovery.

"It's been a huge blessing in a world of law school where drink tickets are the main attraction at all school events," she says. "It's good to see another sober face in the halls at school."

Every few months she receives a phone call about the death of one of the friends with whom she used to get high.

"Every time I go to one of those funerals," she says, "I kneel down next to the coffin and ask myself why I was so lucky to have found recovery."

Melissa tells me that she knows today that in an instant she could be back to where she used to be if she doesn't continue to work on herself.

"Addiction is cunning, baffling, and powerful, and I need to work on my recovery every day for the rest of my life."

Melissa is still active at her undergrad college. She started a recovery effort because it was frightening for her to go back into school and think that no one was going to understand her. Today, she says, "I am so blessed to have my family and my friends back in my life. I see the future and I continue to work on myself, and it's not easy."

In October of 2015, Melissa worked on a national campaign called Unite to Face Addiction and was able to help organize a rally on the national mall in Washington, DC. She organized in Massachusetts and Rhode Island and helped a portion of the 30,000 people from around the country come out to destigmatize addiction and fight for better treatment. The day after the rally, her team was invited to the White House for a reception. "My mind was blown standing in front of those 30,000 people, but it was exploding as I went through security at the White House," she says. "I mean, I used to shoot heroin, and now I'm invited to the White House! That's a good story, one that I will continue to tell because it is important for people to know that we do recover."

Though Melissa's recovery has been difficult (as they all are), she at least has found self-awareness at a young age. Not only that, she's not afraid to live her recovery out loud, and has sidestepped the worry of stigmatization by being open and honest about her history with addiction. Unlike me, for instance, Melissa was in a position where she had to confront addiction's role in her life at a young age.

However, for many prospective law students, addiction is something more easily swept under the rug. There may be not only a lack of criminal history, but also no gaps on the résumé, no awareness of the problem on the part of family or friends, and no time spent in rehab or other recovery institutions. In such cases, it might seem preferable to ignore that a problem might exist at all. But that is often a mistake. Whether students who have had difficult histories with drugs or alcohol admit those difficulties to law schools or not, it's critical that they at least admit those problems to themselves.

As I write this book, Hannah is starting her first year at law school in DC. And although she could very well have started law school as

I did with no self-awareness of her problematic use of alcohol, she took the first critical step of admitting that she had a problem.

Hannah grew up in suburban Maryland raised by a single mother.

"My mom is my hero," she says.

When Hannah was eleven, her mom got married to a man Hannah describes as "a great guy." When she looks back on her childhood, she remembers "a time of simplicity and happiness."

So what went wrong?

In middle school, Hannah began to experience symptoms of obsessive-compulsive disorder and depression.

"The obsessions that began to crowd my thoughts were horrifying," she says. "Shame and mortification prevented me from telling anyone what I was going through."

Around the same time, she had her first inkling that she was attracted to girls. Throughout middle school and high school, she slipped in and out of denial about her sexuality for fear of rejection and loss.

"I grappled with a lot of shame, confusion, and fear," she says. "It was in this context that I discovered marijuana and alcohol."

Hannah always had a talent for compartmentalizing. Externally, she was a straight-A student, playing year-round varsity sports with lots of friends and a perfect family. However, internally she felt like a pariah, "apart from," and "feeling like a fraud."

She started believing that the "good Hannah" everyone saw was a mask for the horrible person underneath. "It was a chasm that I always felt," she says. Alcohol was the first thing that bridged this gap.

As soon as she took her first drink, Hannah knew that she was meant to *be* there. That sense of detachment from the self that she saw and the self that others saw disappeared. The first time she drank, she kept going until she passed out. The next day, she demanded that her friend bring a water bottle of vodka to her cross-country practice. For the next few years, Hannah drank and smoked weed relatively infrequently but always heavily. She drank "alcoholically" from the start and says that her primary motivation at the time was just to have fun and feel present. But her substance use took on a different dimension after her first serious breakup in college.

Hannah drank for two reasons—to numb herself and to punish herself. She quickly spiraled. She started to drink or use most days of the week, and the substance use coupled with self-harm with increasing frequency.

"For the next two years, I felt like I was in the middle of a centrifuge, spinning, with my components always on the verge of tearing out of me," she says. "To keep myself together, I had to drink. I started to lie, to cheat, and to deceive. I lost the honest and present Hannah that I knew. Any moment alone with my sober thoughts felt like torture."

It took Hannah a few years of living this way to grasp that she had a problem. By her second year of drinking, she was experiencing fleeting moments of clarity that she might be going down a dangerous road with her alcohol use. She knew that her mom and biological father were addicts, and she recognized that her behavior was abnormal, but this knowledge only drove her desire to continue.

"I loathed myself and felt that I deserved punishment," she says. "Why not make that punishment addiction and kill two birds with one stone by numbing myself in the process? However, most of the time, I couldn't see that I had a problem. It is easy for young addicts to believe that their behavior is normal while living on a college campus. As far as I knew, most students were drinking like I was. Of course, they weren't. College students are socialized to think that substance use is a natural, normal, and expected part of being a student. Furthermore, there is a very prevalent myth that young people, particularly college students, can't be addicts."

As Hannah's substance use progressed during her undergraduate years, she learned to hide her reality, especially from herself. She received her B.A. with honors. She was involved in student organizations, and she kept a smile pasted to her face in most contexts.

"I can count on one hand the number of times anyone has expressed concern to me about my substance use," she says. "Even my mom—an incredibly intuitive woman in recovery to whom I am very close— never fully saw what I was going through. But as my alcoholism progressed, this compartmentalization became increasingly difficult."

By the end of her junior year at George Washington University, she learned for the first time that she was not alone. She stumbled across a student organization called Students for Recovery (SFR) and attended an event called "Raise High for Recovery Day." She had tried to curb her substance use a few times before learning about SFR and about the wider recovery community, but she lacked the support of people her age who were grappling with the specific doubts and challenges of college students facing addiction.

"Students who are suffering from addictions face a wall of myths, stigma, and rationalizations that they must break through in order to acknowledge that they have a problem and reach out for help," she says. "They often feel incredibly alone and isolated, as I did. Never in my wildest dreams could I have imagined how different my life is now, in less than a year, since I discovered Alcoholics Anonymous."

Hannah initially chose twelve-step recovery because this was the only option with which she was familiar. Her mother is in recovery, but they never talked in-depth about her experiences before Hannah entered the program.

"I knew that she got sober through AA and NA," Hannah says. "She is a living example of twelve-step recovery working. She encouraged me to try AA, and I immediately felt like I was in the right place."

For Hannah, a twelve-step program provided the perfect balance of structure, through sponsorship and stepwork, and individual flexibility. She says that she was provided with the essential tools and guidance necessary to stay sober as well as the space to make the program her own. She immediately felt welcome and included. It was the first place in years that she felt as if she belonged without self-medicating herself.

"Recovery is hard. I didn't get sober immediately. Slowly, each day gets better," she says. "Not all days are good days, but even on the bad days, I have a community of people who understand, who love me unconditionally, and who will welcome me with open arms. I'm beginning to develop a new tolerance for discomfort and uncertainty, and am discovering new tools that provide me with sustainable relief."

Her relationships are blossoming again. Above all, she is slowly learning how to love herself. She also recognizes that she is early in sobriety. She admits that she has much to learn and a lot of space to grow.

"Relapse is always a possibility," she says, "so I must live life one day at a time."

In discussing her transition to law school, Hannah says that she didn't address her recovery in her law school application. Instead, she had had few in-person conversations with current students and alumni who either have experience with recovery resources for law students or who are familiar with the university's mental health resources. As a person in early sobriety, she is still learning to navigate when it is or isn't appropriate to mention her recovery status and has stayed fairly quiet about it throughout the law school process so far.

"Truthfully, I have no idea what I'm in for," she says. "I've heard mixed reviews on the degree of difficulty and competitiveness of law school, but regardless, I know I am in for an education much more challenging than undergrad. God willing, I will have achieved six months of full sobriety and over a year without alcohol by the time my 1L year starts this fall."

She feels incredibly lucky to have gotten sober when she did. She managed to maintain her grades while actively drinking during undergrad but understands that such a strategy wouldn't suffice in law school. She knows that alcoholism is a progressive illness, and inevitably, she would derail herself before graduation.

"Now, I have the incredible opportunity to start school without an unmanaged addiction," she says. "What a relief it will be to live without such a crippling and omnipresent obsession preventing me from fully focusing on anything else."

On the flipside, Hannah is also scared. She knows that that the pressure of law school will prove challenging, and that cravings can sneak up on her unexpectedly. She hopes she will have access to the right support for those times. She feels fortunate to be staying in the same city for school, so she will have access to her established AA network and her sponsor. She does worry that between school, studying, and taking care of her dog, she won't have the time to get to enough meetings. She is also worried about having trouble finding a community of fellow law students in recovery. She is currently on the hunt for a roommate, and she is struggling with how to disclose her recovery status to a stranger in order to find someone who won't keep alcohol in the apartment.

Hannah envisions, one day, a law school campus with an on-site therapist who is well-versed in addictions and local resources. She envisions a student organization on-campus for law students in recovery, and a centralized location where local resources are posted. Although she feels lucky to already be in recovery and aware of many local resources, she is concerned about fellow students who are just coming to terms with active addictions.

"I want these students to understand that they are not alone," she says. "I want them to understand that I am there too, and that they need to know that we can get through this together."

10

Beyond the Study:
Acing Exams and Addiction

IN BOTH HANNAH and Melissa's stories, there is both hope that their schools and profession will offer support in recovery and concern that professional gatekeepers might frown on a history of addiction, or that the pressures of the profession might not be conducive to recovery. Fear of professional failure, judgment, and stigmatization no doubt color students' unwillingness to seek out additional help through their schools. It's understandable. When I was in school, these concerns just weren't addressed by academic institutions, let alone law schools where competition was ruthless.

But has the situation changed since my time? Are there people within law school institutions and on the front lines of academia who work to make students with mental health and substance use concerns feel safe? I asked David Jaffe, who co-authored the law mental health study and deals with these concerns as the associate Dean at the American University Washington College of Law. Here is what he had to say about students seeking help within the support structure of a law school, and concerns they might have about stigma and long-term career prospects.

If a student comes to you and says, "I think I have a substance use issue and I am afraid if I seek help, I will have to drop out and will never make it back," what do you tell her?

Noting that there is a far greater number of law students struggling with a substance use or mental health issue than those who approach their dean of students, the first thing I do is acknowledge the student's bravery for having come forward, let her know that she is in a safe and confidential environment. In most instances I respond initially to the student in an indirect way, but for a specific reason: I ask the student, "Do you want to be a lawyer?" The immediacy (or delay) in the response is almost always a clear table setter for the remainder of the conversation. A student who, but for the substance use or mental health issue facing her has her heart set on becoming a lawyer, will answer almost immediately in the affirmative. Conversely, a student who hesitates with the reply often has something else going on that is not related to the immediate issue (such as having started law school as a least-worst option, or owing to pressure from parents, and so forth). For this latter student, a substantive conversation must be held to glean if proceeding with law school is in her best interest.

Assuming the student's response is in the affirmative, my goal is to do everything in my power to have the student receive help without dropping out of school. In some instances even a twenty-eight-day inpatient stay may be effectuated without the student having to leave school. A dean of students will have a good relationship with the student's faculty and should be able to facilitate a temporary absence. In the event that a course is heavy on interaction, and too much class will be missed, the dean of students should be able to arrange for a withdrawal from the course without a complete withdrawal from the semester. Further, even in the instance that the student chooses to (or needs to) withdraw from one or more semesters, maintaining contact with the student will send a positive signal that there is a place for her. I worked with a student who withdrew partway through one semester and took another semester of leave prior to returning to earn his degree. We met every couple of months off-campus just to talk, during which time I was able to reassure him that we were prepared to receive him back (and provide ongoing assistance, if necessary) when he was ready.

In sum, a student who want to earn a law degree should not be prevented from doing so due to a substance use or mental health issue. If the student is committed to assistance and recovery, so too will be the law school.

What would be the top three-to-five things you tell either an incoming student like Hannah, or a more advanced student who is looking to find a more solid recovery support structure in a high stress environment?

What strikes me about so many of the conversations I have with students near or in crisis is the palpable relief when I share that they are not the first student (sometimes in that same week) to have come to me with an issue. Law students really will go it alone because, among other things, they believe all of their classmates are doing just fine. The stigma and fear associated with getting assistance is real; it will only be overcome by a growing acceptance in the practice and in society that adverse mental health behavior and regular substance misuse are diseases, and should be treated no differently than the care and empathy one would give, say, to a cancer patient.

Hannah is right to seek if not expect a law school campus with at least a part-time onsite counselor who can provide ongoing assistance for her work, as well as one or multiple locations that can provide a ready list of resources. Students who cannot find these sources should ask their student affairs staff why they do not exist, and should support their creation. If budgetary concerns exist, regular access to the university's resources may have to stand as a fill-in. Inviting staff from a local Lawyer Assistance Program to put in some hours might also exist as a possibility.[17]

The establishment of a student organization dedicated to law students in recovery can be a slightly larger challenge—not necessarily owing to any administrative opposition—but for the mere yet profound fact that a student has to be comfortable enough in her recovery and really comfortable taking in one or more classmates to be involved in this level of support. We have explored Friends of Bill meetings (and, with a church nearby our new law school location, will explore that avenue), as well as Thursday night gatherings that are not meant to combat the "Bar reviews" that permeate the law school atmosphere but are intended to provide comfortable space for non-drinkers. In each of these instances, the challenge is developing a circle of classmates, ideally to become friends, who can trust one another over the long haul that is law school.

Finally, a word about the Bar admission process and the character and fitness questionnaire. The notion that a student who shares with a dean of students his or her personal issue is going to get "jammed up" (not admitted or conditionally admitted) is often more perception than reality. What a Bar examiner (properly) wants to know is if the applicant is prepared to represent clients in the particular jurisdiction. A student having mental health or substance use issues is only going to do himself a good turn by a) reaching out to those who can help either directly or by providing resources and b), starting or continuing to address the issue(s) by getting the help he needs while in school. Having a dean of students or a member of a LAP speak in support of the candidate, if the candidate has actively sought assistance, will help in the end. We want our students to be lawyers, but we want them to be healthy ones.

David's advice is comforting, and it does seem as though law schools around the country may be doing more to support law students who seek help. I was also struck by his advice to law students that acknowl-edging problems and documenting help received goes a long way toward easing concerns about addiction and mental health worries that a state Bar might have. What about the concerns of law schools themselves? For students who are aware they have problems with drugs or alcohol, is that something that they should reveal as early in the process as possible, including the law school application itself?

To help shed light on this question, I spoke with Ann Levine, who is considered one of the foremost experts in the country on what needs to be done to maximize the chances of getting into the best possible law schools. She has written two books on the topic, and her website, the Law School Expert (lawschoolexpert.com), is very popular with aspiring law students. I asked Ann several ques-tions regarding what she recommends when advising a prospective law student who may be dealing with alcohol, drug, or other mental health issues.

What are some of the substance use and legal issues connected to that use that prospective law students have come to you with?

I've worked with a number of law school applicants whose substance use issues coincided with their undergraduate studies and, as a result, their grades were inconsistent or low across the board. These issues primarily revolve around alcohol or marijuana. Sometimes these issues are accompanied by DUIs, possession arrests, and/or drug- and alcohol-related college discipline issues that need to be explained on law school applications.

In your experience, what are the three biggest mistakes prospective law students make with regards to dealing with their substance use as they try to get into law school?

Definitely lack of candor is a huge mistake, because applicants can be dismissed from law school and/or be refused membership to the state Bar if they are found to have been dishonest in their application. Another big mistake is to acknowledge issues without taking responsibility for mistakes. Last, neglecting to let some time pass between the date of sobriety and/or criminal issues and the date of applying to law school would be a mistake. It helps to show law schools that you've been sober/clean for a significant period of time, making it less likely that these issues will plague you in school. It also helps to point out accomplishments achieved after seeking help—whether holding a fulltime job, completing school with better grades, or volunteering with organizations. Those accomplishments demonstrate that you are now exercising good judgment and making good decisions.

Based on your experience, in general, what are the three most important things a prospective law student who is struggling can do as soon as possible to put himself/herself in the best position to get into law school and succeed?

To get sober and stay sober, to show that the applicant has taken the issue seriously and attended AA or some other recognized institution of recovery, that the person is now a mentor to others who are going through similar issues, and to have something on his or her résumé or in their academic record to show how they are now prepared to focus and excel.

Ann reminds us that at any stage in the journey of becoming a lawyer or practicing law, the profession expects candor. Still, this points to a problem that none of the stories in this chapter have addressed so far. Honesty is often one of the first casualties of addiction. Self-awareness is often another. I marched through law school without ever believing I had any addiction problems. In that sense, I "got away" with not confronting those problems at that early stage. But, as I'll describe in the next chapter, addiction was already taking a heavy toll.

Law schools and perhaps some law firms may be developing more up-to-date attitudes toward providing support for students or workers with substance use or mental health issues. But when those problems go unacknowledged, law school and law careers can just as easily be environments that exacerbate rather than ameliorate those concerns. Until the individual experiencing the problem admits that there's a problem, very little can be done.

11

Do You Really Want
to Be a Lawyer?

DO YOU REALLY want to be a lawyer? As you just read, it is one question David Jaffe asks students who come to his office seeking help for mental health and substance use issues. And it's a question I wish I'd been asked. Law school is arduous, all the more so when real motive isn't present.

Once upon a time, long after I graduated from law school and long after my career as a practicing attorney had run its course, I hosted a segment on a syndicated morning news show called *Eye Opener TV*. My segment was called "Cuban's Legal Briefs." The premise of the segment was to provide short, provocative commentary on legal issues in the news. For instance, the question might be, "Is burning the American flag protected by the First Amendment?" My trademark opening would be, "Are you an idiot? Of course it is!"

For those baby boomers from the East Coast who remember commercials for the Crazy Eddie electronics chain, I was kind of the Crazy Eddie of *Eye Opener TV*. The actor in the commercial would gesticulate wildly while yelling at the viewers that Crazy Eddie's prices were "insane." Those videos of my ranting are still on the internet for those interested. Let's play the Crazy Eddie "Legal Briefs" game with law school. "Are there good and bad reasons to go to law school?"

"Are you an idiot? Of course there are!"

My reasons were far from good. I wanted to use law school to continue to escape my problems. I went to law school because I had no idea what else to do. And I went to law school because I thought maybe its structure might transform me into a more disciplined person. I did not go to law school because I wanted to be a lawyer.

When I relate this story to students, I always say, whatever your reasons for considering law school are, don't go for the reasons I did. Law school is too great a commitment, the competition for jobs is too intense, and the practice of law too great a responsibility to use as a way to avoid confronting mental health issues.

Getting the degree is just the beginning, and carrying those problems into a career along with the degree isn't going to fix anything or prove that the problems aren't really problems at all. For those who think the rigor of law school will help them simply "grow up" and leave substance use or psychological problems behind, it just doesn't work that way.

Still, I carried on past my first year, denying that I had any problems and not worrying too much about my own lack of interest in the material in which I was supposed to be immersed.

I didn't spend my entire time in law school without a sense of purpose, however. For one brief period after my first year at Pitt Law, I had a clear vision of what I wanted out of life. Unfortunately, it was a vision based in fantasy and escapism, and one that allowed me to pretend I could become someone new without confronting the alcoholism, depression, and other psychological problems that were quickly progressing in my life.

After my first year at Pitt Law, I tried to join the Marines.

I'd never thought of myself as military material growing up. I have vague recollections of watching the news from Vietnam with my parents, and I remember the mandatory selective service registration that began in 1980 in response to the Soviet invasion of Afghanistan. I was nineteen then, and this was an era when we were closer to World War III with the Soviet Union than any time since the Cuban Missile Crisis. It was quite a shock to those of us first required to register. But in general, trouble overseas seemed far away and detached to a middle-class kid from Pittsburgh. For me, the battle to be fought was the one with my mirror and the self-hatred and loneliness I experienced every day.

The military I knew was for the most part the fictional (and generally comedic) shows I watched. *Gomer Pyle*, *Hogan's Heroes*, and *M*A*S*H* were staples of my television military "experience." On the movie front, I watched and re-watched *Kelly's Heroes*, *Patton*, *The Dirty Dozen*, and *Stalag 17*. Of course, the reality of military service is far from the fantasy these shows present, but I knew nothing of that reality.

Growing up, I was oblivious to the effects of war on my community, my recent ancestors, and even my immediate family. Although my father's friends and relatives would show us the numbers tattooed on their arms, I didn't grasp their significance. I knew little of the Holocaust, or the fact that my great aunt, her husband, and two children on my mother's side were murdered by the Romanians as they perpetrated their own mass murder as part of the Holocaust.

Neither my mom nor my father talked much about it, even though my father had served as a Navy Seabee in the Pacific theater during World War II, where he fought in the battle of Okinawa. He also cleared mines in Korea, but he rarely talked about the reality of his military service, and I rarely asked.

When I did ask questions, he'd offer terse responses that often ended in his tears and silence. Not even that was enough to keep me from seeing war as a game. I'd spend whole days playing with my neighbor Pete's GI Joe collection. Pete's father, like mine, was a combat veteran. Pete kept his GI Joes in an old military-style foot locker. We'd take out the war toys and arrange columns of soldiers with hand grenades, flanked by tanks. It would take hours to prepare our troops for the ultimate battle out on his driveway. Then, when we'd watch the carnage in Vietnam on our black-and-white TVs, it looked like the same thing. *It's war, it's just plastic figures toppling over.*

At ten years old I was curious, though, about that old wooden crate nailed shut in the upstairs bedroom in our house in Mt. Lebanon, Pennsylvania. I knew it contained memorabilia of some sort from my father's time serving during the war. I understood there was some deeper reality in that crate, some profound secret about adulthood, duty, and the kind of sadness that would grip my otherwise cheerful father when he spoke of war. It smelled of musty wood and a journey of thousands of miles from a battlefield in the Pacific.

One day, I could stand it no more. While my parents were at work, I got a hammer from the garage and pulled out the nails. I'd planned to hammer them back so my father would never find out that I'd come to know those secrets that I was certain he wanted to keep hidden from me. I slowly pulled out the rusty nails pounded in decades before and grew nervous as they bent, making it impossible to put things back the way they were. But I kept going and finally pried off the creaky lid.

Before me was a dull, grease-stained .45 semi-automatic. I took the weapon out of the box and began aiming it at imaginary targets outside the upstairs window of my bedroom and then dry-firing it at imaginary Japanese soldiers. I imagined myself coming to the rescue to save my father and his comrades. In the wooden box, I also found a long wooden Japanese sniper rifle with a still-glimmering bayonet attached to it. There was also a Japanese battle helmet with a star on it. I put on the helmet, and dust and particles rained down onto my shoulders. I didn't care. I was General Brian. I'd lead the attack.

I had no idea how my father came into possession of the items. One day he'd tell me that that there was the head of a Japanese soldier in the helmet when he found it, and he'd had to boil the helmet to disinfect it. That was the reality of war. The reality of someone's son. Someone's brother, like my brothers. Someone's husband. But to a boy of ten, it was all just a powerful fantasy. Decades later, fantasy would transition to a dangerous reality with a gun I owned and suicidal thoughts. But after my first year of law school, I was still searching for the fantasy. It was clear by then that I'd never love law, but I'd already invested so much, and my family had invested so much, that I didn't see a way to step off the path that I was on. But what if there was something I could do that would make everyone even prouder than if I simply became a lawyer? What if I could do something bigger, better, even more exciting to me?

The problem was, I had no idea what that new path could be. Then I ran into Danny. He had grown up just down the street from me. We went to the same high school, and my family knew his family, but we weren't friends in any sense at that time. I saw him around the law school, and we'd acknowledge each other with waves and small talk. Danny was an avid runner and weightlifter, and this gave us some common interest. I was training for my second marathon. Ironically, it was the Marine Corps Marathon. I'd also run it the year before. As we became workout buddies, Danny related to me that having finished his second year at Pitt Law, he was going to enter something called Officer Candidate School and then go on to be a military attorney.

I was intrigued, not by the thought of being a lawyer in the military, but by the thought of being *in* the military. A part of my mind long dormant was activated. I remembered that sense of mystery and deeper truths I'd felt when opening my father's hidden war memorabilia. But it was more than that. Being in the military seemed both more respectable and more exciting than simply being a lawyer. Visions of Richard Gere in *An Officer and a Gentlemen* came to my mind. I'd recently seen the movie for the first time. Gere's character went from an angry loner to a man, shedding his character defects and getting the girl. This was everything I wanted.

Maybe my Debra Winger was waiting out there for me, and if I wore the uniform, I'd find her. Gere's character in the movie actually reminded me of a roommate at the time. Jack was a tall, blond, muscular, good-looking guy who had visions of doing commercials on television. A good student and very popular with the ladies, he would fill each weekday with stories of his weekend conquests. I wanted to be part of those exploits. I could never look like Richard Gere, but I could be an officer and a gentleman, and that would be the great equalizer.

Through the Marines, I thought I'd have a shot at a complete rebirth. I'd be able to wipe the slate clean. The Marines would make me not only a lean, mean fighting machine but also a self-confident, well-adjusted person. I wouldn't just win on the battlefield; I'd be able to win at life.

I decided I'd follow Danny's path and join the Officer Candidate School. First I'd go through OCS, then the Basic School in Quantico, Virginia, and then onto the JAG corps in Newport, Rhode Island, and I would become a Marine lawyer. For once, I was looking forward to the future: I'd transform myself, mentally and physically, with every stage of the training.

Danny was enthusiastic about joining the Marines, and his enthusiasm was infectious. We were from the same place. If he could do it, I could. Danny gave me a couple of Marine Corps handbooks that he had gotten from someone who had completed OCS, and we trained together to take the required physical fitness entrance test.

The test at that time was a timed run, pull-ups, and push-ups. The run was no problem, but I had no upper body strength and was terrified of doing the pull-ups and push-ups. The test would take place in downtown Pittsburgh along the Monongahela River, where many people ran at lunchtime. Danny and I would go there and practice the three exercises. Even though I had gotten into pretty good shape, I still couldn't do many pull-ups. Danny would be ripping them off, one after another, and I'd think back to high school, and how I'd do everything I could to avoid days where there'd be games in the gym between shirts and skins. When I knew it was coming, I'd stay home sick. Now, training for officer candidate school, I was having nightmares and flashbacks to those high school days that brought out my deepest fears about my own worth.

Slowly, however, one day of training at a time, the workouts on the banks of the Monongahela were doing something important. More than getting in better shape, I was actually planning for a future for the first time in a while, a future that excited me. Sure, it was based on a fantasy, but it was a fantasy that was helping me drink less, put my eating disorders to the side, and even face myself in the mirror from time to time. The fantasy of a real future didn't make my problems vanish, but the fantasy did give me something else to focus on.

Fantasies, though, can be as ephemeral as a high. Like seeking to transform my reality through drinks or drugs, hoping to become an entirely new person by having someone else transform me was not only unrealistic, but it was ultimately self-defeating.

The PT test came, and I basked in the glory of my under-seven minute miles. I did a respectable number of sit-ups. I even managed a pull-up or two. Hey, not great, but I felt my run more than made up for it.

I passed. My dad drove Danny and me down to the Federal building in downtown Pittsburgh for processing. I was proud to have my father see me take this step in my life. The truth is, my father would have been proud of me no matter what path I chose, but I felt as if he were watching me become initiated into the secret rights of adulthood. At the time, I still didn't know some of the horrors he'd seen. I didn't know that he still had dreams of his patrols on Okinawa and stumbling upon burned and mutilated corpses of fellow G.I.s. But even if he was worried for me, he'd never try to scare me away from making my own choices. That's always been important to him.

Next thing I knew, I was on my way to Washington, D.C., where I'd then board a bus to Quantico for Officer Candidate School. This was really happening. Once in D.C., Danny and I went to the assigned spot outside the airport and began congregating with other OCS arrivals from around the country. Then a man showed up in uniform and introduced himself as a gunnery sergeant. He didn't crack a smile as he ordered us all to fall "in line." The gunnery sergeant spoke to us as if we were children. I didn't exactly expect a handshake and a cold beer, but the gunnery sergeant's barked orders were immediately unnerving. My fantasy was about becoming a new man—stronger, healthier, more certain and determined. That fantasy had nothing to do with feeling like a bullied child first.

We made the hour-long bus ride in silence, did our best to obey every order, and were in our bunks around the time I was usually getting warmed up with a few swigs of tequila before hitting the clubs. I remember lying awake in my bunk, staring at the ceiling, feeling like a child stuck on some Boy Scout camping trip from hell. The thought occurred to me that I'd made a huge mistake, and I cried.

The next morning, in what was almost a scene right out of the 1987 movie *Full Metal Jacket,* we were jolted awake by what sounded like a metal garbage can being rolled past our bunks. It turned out that's exactly what it was. *Is this basic training or a frat hazing?* It only got worse from there. After struggling to make up my bed just the right way while having abuse showered down on me from my sergeant instructor, I had the opportunity to meet with the platoon captain for a brief interview.

I did my best not to fidget while he examined some papers and then stared right through me.

"Son, what were your scores on the PT test?"

One of our first lessons was that we were required to speak about ourselves in the third person, so I replied, "This officer candidate thought he did pretty well."

"Son, let me tell you something," he said. "You're pretty arrogant. You did not do well at all. You're not in very good shape. You can barely do pull-ups. If you don't get those scores up, you won't make it here."

The captain went on about how unfit I was to be a U.S. Marine, trashing the one remaining pillar of my self-confidence—my physical fitness. I heard the voice of my mom calling me a fat pig and a dumb bunny. I heard the voices of everyone who had ever picked on me or made fun of my weight. I felt queasy and longed for that security of privacy I'd had in law school, a feeling I realized I'd likely not have again for some time.

The next morning, after chow, we were told that we were all scheduled to go have our hair shorn. *Of course.* Now I remembered the opening credits of *Full Metal Jacket* with all of the new recruits getting their heads shaved. The movie must be the most effective advertisement for steering clear of boot camp ever made. Had it come out a couple of years earlier, I might not have joined. Trivial as it may seem, for someone who was struggling with body dysmorphia, the prospect of losing my hair was nightmarish. I knew right then I was not staying in the Marines.

I did not want to DOR (Discharge On Request), as that would humiliate me even more. It was made clear within the platoon and by the sergeants that DOR was a badge of shame, failure, and unworthiness. As it so happened, I'd been having some knee pain as was normal for someone who was running more than eighty miles a week. Nothing out of the ordinary, and nothing that limited me. I, however, now had a way out—or at least some time to think. I immediately complained of intense right knee pain. They sent me to the military hospital at Fort Belvoir, Virginia, to be examined. I knew I had "runner's knee" if anything at all. It was something I'd lived with and could have lived within OCS. After some conversation, the Navy corpsman who examined me knew what the deal was. He'd seen it before.

He asked me a simple question. "Do you want to go home?"

I gave him a simple answer. "Yes."

My time in the Marine Corps was over. They pulled me out of the officer candidate barracks and stuck me in a White Elephant, an old World War II-style barracks, with all the others who had been discharged for one reason or another. They might as well have painted a big "L" for loser on the side of the building. I couldn't look any of the other rejects in the eye because I knew if I did, I would see myself. I could not look at the officer candidates heading to "PT" who were sticking it out. I could feel what they were thinking about me. I was a quitter. A loser. A relieved loser, but a loser nonetheless.

The fantasy was over. As with law school, I'd joined the Marines for all the wrong reasons. If it hadn't been for the threat of the buzz cut, who knows? Maybe I would have squeaked through military training just as I squeaked through law school. I'd never be at the top of the class in either place, but I proved I could pass. For me, the lesson of my short-lived career as a prospective Marine should have been that I alone was responsible for fixing myself. That even though the support of others is critical, no person or experience was going to transform me. Instead, I learned once again to hide; I couldn't risk that sort of emotional vulnerability again. I went back to Pitt Law with my dreams of traveling the world to exotic bases as the Richard Gere of the JAG corps now ended.

That doesn't mean I was satisfied with picking up where I left off at school. It became clearer to me that my future, whatever that was, was not in Pittsburgh. I began to set my sights on Dallas, Texas, where my brothers had already relocated. How to get there was the question, though. I had no prospects, no plan. I decided for the time being to stick with law school. It allowed me to hide out, anyway, and it gave me time to figure out the next steps. *Hey, at least I'm still in great shape,* I thought. *They can't take that away from me.*

My second year of law school was consumed once again with trying to fill a void I felt in my life rather than focusing on the work at hand. Before the school year started, I moved into a boarding house run by a guy named Rand, who was well known in the Pittsburgh film and public television community. He owned several houses in the neighborhood known as Shadyside and would rent them out at reduced rates to students in exchange for housework and yard work. I'd spent the first year of law school isolating myself through running and doing aerobics in front of my TV and heading out to bars by myself. Thus, I was deeply envious of some of the other law students who all socialized, studied together, and even dated each other. The boarding house was full of people about my age, and I hoped I'd fit in with some of them better than I did my law student peers.

I felt incomplete, and part of my desire to transform myself was to find my place socially, and, quite frankly, to find a girlfriend. I'd all but given up hope that I'd ever meet someone who would be attracted to me since my first day at Penn State, when a pretty brown-haired girl passed by my dorm window, saw me, and shouted for the gods to hear that I was "ugly." Since then, more than ever, I was on a mission to transform myself to become worthy and find the nerve to talk to women. I ran until I lost most of my body fat. I got drunk to take away anxiety. I'd even tried to become Richard Gere in Marine blues, and I was still searching for the right mask to present to the world.

Then, along came...no...not Polly. Nora.

She was another tenant at the boarding house, and we started talking at the end of summer before my second year started. A graduate of Brandeis working on her master's degree at Pitt, she was thin, pretty, artsy, into meditation and self-discovery. I didn't join her in those pursuits, but I was attracted to her sense of calm. Nora was confident in herself and in her body, which again, was a completely novel and wonderful attitude to me. I couldn't even look at myself in a mirror unless I was drunk. In my mind, Nora was exactly the type of girl who wouldn't give me the time of day.

Except she did. She told me she found my shyness attractive. She found my lack of self-confidence endearing. In a way, she took me on as a project. I didn't mind. I'd been my own project for years, and I was happy to let someone else into the laboratory. Of course that type of relationship won't usually last, and ours didn't.

I ended up losing my virginity to Nora on a blanket in the basement of the boarding house. I was drunk, of course. Alcohol took away some of my self-loathing and fear of intimacy in that moment.

I was inexperienced. I had no concept of what sex should be like, and was ashamed of my body. I was afraid to look at her, because that meant she would be looking at me. Our eyes never met the entire time. I did not find the sex itself shameful, but I felt mortified at being exposed as an inexperienced child. She had to know it was my first time. *Twenty-three years old! What guy waits that long?* What I should have remembered with fondness instead became something that made me ill to think about. *Women want men, not children.*

Still, I walked into class at Pitt Law that next day feeling as if the weight of all the bullies, the horrible relationship with my mom, and my lackluster class performance were taken off my shoulders, if only for a short time. I remember the confidence I had in answering when called on in my Insurance Law class that morning. Finally, I was the man!

But somehow, as uncomfortable as I was with Nora, I didn't spoil things entirely. One night after our basement encounter, while we were watching television together, she casually suggested that we have dinner sometime. A real date. She must have known I'd never initiate anything on my own. She was right. I would never have said a word.

■ September 16, 1984

My first romantic date ever. Prior to the basement with Nora I had never kissed a girl. *What do people do on dates?* Dinner meant I could get drunk. Conversation might be easier with alcohol. Still, I could not imagine being comfortable just sitting across from a date all night, being studied. I'd have to come up with something else besides a romantic dinner.

I didn't know much about soul music, but I had recently heard for the first time George Benson's rendition of "On Broadway." I loved it, and it ran through my head constantly. I put myself in the place of George and imagined what it would be like to be driven. To be a star. To be talented at something. Memories of those childhood dreams permeated my thoughts. But just like the song, looking at beautiful women could give me the blues.

I knew exactly what George was singing about—wanting to be part of the beautiful crowd had made me feel down for a long time. But I had more than the blues. I was clinically depressed. I had no idea what that was or meant in terms of my life. I just knew it sucked. If I could only be "on Broadway" it would all change. I had never been to New York City, but my Broadway was the mirror in my bathroom. I wanted to be able to see myself in bright lights—or at least flattering lighting. Now I had a woman interested in me, and maybe it was time to chase my dreams again.

I had to hear George sing the song live. It would inspire me to seek more than simply to get through each day. The song would be my anthem. With George in my corner and Nora by my side, I would make a fresh start, and this time, it would last.

Not long after we agreed to go out on a real date, I saw it in the paper: *George Benson is coming to Pittsburgh's Syria Mosque.* I had my date plans set. Nora and I went to the concert together. It was a powerful, energizing performance that gave me the fresh resolve I'd hoped for. George had brought me partway to Broadway. That night, I was a man.

Nora and I started dating. I was wanted! It was a new feeling, to be desired. But even after we'd been together a while, I never let Nora know about the extent of my problems. I couldn't even admit to myself some of the dysmorphia-inspired thoughts and feelings I was having. There was no way I was about to discuss them with a woman who seemed to be attracted to me. Still, Nora was smart enough to figure out some of them. My drinking was already serious enough that she tried to help me move past it, along with my incredible shyness and introversion. Soon, she encouraged me to try out therapy for the first time.

At Nora's recommendation, I tried EST (often written as "est"), which stands for Erhard Seminars Training. I knew about EST already from my mother's participation. She had pitched it to me years earlier, and I refused. I viewed it as just an extension of her screaming-in-the-closet therapy. Ironic that the first girl I ever dated was, like my mother, involved in EST. I wonder what Freud would say about that.

EST was a popular group-treatment method in the seventies and eighties, supplanting the fads of the previous decade. It found numerous celebrity adherents such as John Denver, Diana Ross, and Yoko Ono. It combined group dialogs with healthy doses of psychoanalytic language and a splash of Zen Buddhism, all whipped together by Werner Erhard, a former encyclopedia salesman. Training seminars were held across the country and would typically take two intense weekends to complete. The goal of the seminars was to talk through self-inhibiting patterns and replace them with a mental state of enlightenment and purpose. Those who broke through to enlightenment over one of the weekends were said to have "got it."

With Nora set to participate with me, and with money given to me by my mother (who was thrilled I was going), I participated in an EST seminar in Cleveland. I remember a bunch of people sitting on the floor of a giant meeting room listening to people tell us how to "get it."

Going in, I had no idea what I was supposed to "get," but I was becoming more self-aware that I had issues. I did not know how to define those issues in terms of specific disorders, but I knew that my behavior was becoming more and more destructive. I knew I was drinking too much. I knew that I felt alone in the most crowded of rooms. While I still did not know what bulimia was, I knew that running fifteen to twenty miles a day and then binging and purging at night was not healthy and was intensifying my state of depression. These had become compulsive behaviors. I could not help myself. That was enough at that time to at least move me in the direction of reaching out for help.

My memories of the weekend sessions in Cleveland are hazy. They did not allow us to use the bathroom during each day-long session. I recall that some people had catheters going into bottles. The only other lessons I took from the seminar were that I should talk to strangers in elevators and give the company behind EST lots of money.

Though EST didn't work for me, one thing was clear: I was searching. Searching for that magic spell that would rid me of my demons. Perhaps for people who are relatively sound psychologically, self-help sessions such as EST can be positive experiences. Primal therapy, group meditation, or even a motivational self-help book might be all they need to feel that they are back on track with their lives. But for those who suffer personality disorders, substance abuse problems, or other grave psychological conditions, quick fixes through such self-help programs can do more harm than good. They can lead to greater discouragement and depression when they don't work. Sometimes they can be traumatic. There are solutions out there, but they take time and commitment and can't be achieved over a couple of weekends—even without bathroom breaks. BDD recovery is a long-term process that differs for everyone.

Nora couldn't build me into a new person, and she wearied of trying. That was that. Back to what I'd become so comfortable with, the path of least resistance. I thank Nora for what she gave me. Without her, I don't think I could have made it through my second year. But after she and I broke up that year, I went back to my old habits, old compulsions, and old goals. I ran, I exercised, I drank alone, and I dreamed of transforming myself into something else.

Some of my strongest memories from my second year are of running and fantasizing about being normal, about ways I could fit in. About making law review. About being in the cool study group. About having Big Law interviews for summer internships lined up daily. In real life, I had neither the drive nor the desire for any of those ambitions, but during those runs, I was a law student my family could be proud of, and I could be proud of. Those fantasies of what I would never achieve brought on terrible bouts of depression that only running long distances seemed to alleviate. Soon I was training for marathons again, which was the only sort of achievement that seemed immediately accessible to me, and the only form of achievement that really seemed to pull me forward day after day.

■ **May 1985**

I'm finishing up my second year of law school and now participating in what really matters to me, another race. This time, it's the Pittsburgh Marathon. I'm flying along at a great clip! Then, at the fifteen-mile point, our eyes meet. My Marines corps recruiter is standing there, cheering on the runners. He sees me, and a puzzled look crosses his face. I look away, face blazing. *My knee is all better. It's a miracle. I can even run marathons again!* As I pass him, my gaze is fixed on the steps in front of me. *Just take it one step at a time.*

That's what I do: one step at a time, without looking too far ahead and without the rigorous honesty needed to begin recovery. I make it through a post-second year internship, and then start my third year. I know if I stay on my current path, I won't finish anywhere near first at school, but I won't finish last either.

■ **Fall 1985**

By just putting one foot in front of the other, I'm now in my last year and close to the finish line of law school. Now it's time for the Race Judacata, a five-kilometer trail-run put on by the law school for the legal fleet of foot. The name of the run is an obvious take off of some

Latin legal phrase, the meaning of which I should probably know as a law student.

The race doesn't draw many runners. Law students have other priorities: studying; graduating; maybe going out drinking the night before the Sunday-morning run. They see time taken from the pursuit of their dreams. Running may simply not be their thing, but it's practically my only thing. The prospect of the race excites me more than figuring out what the Latin term means. It's a chance at redemption. I'm shy. I'm lonely. But I can run.

Other than myself, there are two big-time runners in the law school. They're both the more classical long-distance runner types— shorter, thin, and fast. I'm not the typical distance runner at 6'2" and 200 pounds. Although I know I have no real hope of beating either of them, in my mind, a third-place finish would be tantamount to a statement to everyone else in the law school that, at least in this instance, in what is important to me, I am better than they are.

There is only one thing standing in my way. One person, really. My roommate, Mark (not to be confused with my brother Mark). Mark is not really into running, but he's athletic and decides that it's his duty to prevent me from achieving my coveted and anticipated third-place finish in the race. He's having fun with it, treating me like a brother he couldn't let win. Mark, who knows nothing about my underlying psychological issues, begins announcing to every student who will listen that even though he mostly drank chocolate milk and beer and ate pizza and hot dogs from the Original Hot Dog Shop, he will soundly defeat me in the race. It won't even be close. I begin to doubt myself. If Mark beats me, it's a sign that I truly am unworthy. I've pinned my self-worth around an event that is meaningless to everyone else other than a diversion from the stress of law school. Everyone but me.

Race day. A cool, clear fall morning. There's even wagers being made, not on who will win the race, but on whether Mark will beat me. Gun sounds, and we're off. I quickly fall into fourth place behind the two runner guys and Mark. At about the two-mile point, Mark begins stopping intermittently and throwing up. Apparently he really has been out drinking beer and eating pizza the night before. The irony is that it was one of the few nights that I didn't drink because I so badly wanted to beat him in the race. I pass Mark and finish third. To me it's a complete victory. Not over Mark alone, but over what our competition represents to me. As playful as Mark's taunts had been, beating him was like beating all the middle-school bullies, the hurtful comments growing up, the cool kids who would not invite me to the parties, the law school cliques, who in my mind, were laughing at and pitying me every day. A victory for a shy little child wanting to be loved. A meaningless race that is held by law schools around the country and is nothing more than a diversion from the rigors of law school life, is all that to me. *Now* I can graduate. In terms of how I've come to gauge accomplishment and self-worth, law school is a piece of cake.

■ Summer 1986
Soon enough, I make it to the end of the law school race, and although I don't finish first, I don't finish last, either. Now I'm a law school graduate. I don't even bother to show up for graduation, convinced I don't belong with the other students, who worked hard and strived for their dreams. I can't bear to see my own sense of failure and uncertainty reflected back in their hopeful faces.

Still, I have recurring dreams about being at graduation. In the dreams, the Dean of the law school pulls back my diploma as I reach for it, telling me I didn't really graduate, that I had failed every course. Maybe I subconsciously regret blowing off the ceremony. But whatever the reason for the dream, after graduation, it's time for the Pennsylvania Bar exam. I approach it with the same zeal I approached my three years at Pitt Law, with indifference. I don't care about the law. I don't care about a job. I don't care about my future as a lawyer. My plan is to get out of Dodge (Pittsburgh) as quickly as possible. However, I feel that I must take that Bar exam because that is what we're supposed to do as law school graduates. That's what everyone else is doing. If I don't take it, I will confirm to other students and myself that I'm a loser.

I have no intention of practicing in Pennsylvania or any desire to practice law at all. But I have to justify the student loans, the money from my parents, and the years of fooling myself that this is my destiny. After taking the Bar without much concern about my score, I get on the bus to Dallas. During that two-day bus-ride, the thought of a career in the law, or any career at all, are the furthest things from my mind. Thoughts of the fun bars my older brother took me to during my visits and all the beautiful girls he knew are more important. I don't want to be a lawyer. I want to be him.

* * *

By some standards, I'd "succeeded" in law school. Although I'd made it through all three years and taken the Bar exam, my success was in many ways a huge failure. I'd sailed through three years without coming to terms with my addiction or underlying mental health issues. On top of that, I'd set myself up on a career path I had no real interest in pursuing.

Conversely, many law students experiencing substance use or mental health issues might feel they've "failed" when mental health or substance use issues come to a head, and they must suspend or quit law school. Nothing could be further from the truth. Any action that leads us to better self-awareness and sets us on a path toward what we truly need and want is a success. Nothing illustrates this better than the story of another law student who responded to my call for stories. Like me, Parker had hoped that law school (or in my case, the Marines or my first girlfriend) might transform him into a new person and leave addiction behind. It didn't. But unlike me, Parker knew he truly wanted to be a lawyer, and so setbacks ultimately proved positive in some ways.

By the time Parker turned twenty-six, he had graduated Phi Beta Kappa from the University of Texas, been accepted to Teach for America, been elected Teacher of the Year on his campus, won the annual Outstanding Young Educator award for Houston ISD, and received the full-tuition Root-Tilden-Kern scholarship from NYU Law.

"But I couldn't juggle," he says. And that's when everything began to fall apart."

On the first afternoon of a group-building retreat in late August, Deb Ellis, the Root-Tilden-Kern faculty director, brought him and his fellow scholarship recipients outside and passed out beginner's juggling kits.

"It was a low-hanging metaphor," he says. "The ability to *juggle* several obligations at once was critical to success in law school and beyond."

She assured everyone that they would all, that afternoon, learn how to juggle and said that, in her years of facilitating the activity, no student had ever failed to do so.

"As the minutes passed, it seemed as though she was right," Parker says. "One by one, the students went from fumbling to figuring it out to bona fide proficiency. No matter how hard I tried, though, I kept dropping the balls. Eventually, I gave up."

Parker says that his failure was inevitable. An hour before going outside that afternoon, he had folded half of a crushed OxyContin tablet and a couple of anti-anxiety pills into a piece of toilet paper and swallowed it whole. He had maintained a steady, if ever-increasing, dose of both medications in his system for years prior to that afternoon, and although they had long since ceased to provide more than a fleeting degree of pleasure, they continued to impair his coordination.

"No matter how hard I tried, I couldn't juggle," he says.

It wasn't always that way. Although he'd struggled with substance use disorder since he was fourteen, he worked incredibly hard to keep the discordant realities of his life separate. The progression of his substance use, however, eventually required morning-to-night abuse of opiate painkillers and anxiety medications to stave off debilitating withdrawal symptoms. His friends and family were concerned about the symptoms they could spot, but Parker assured them (and himself) that he didn't have a problem.

"I desperately hoped that going to law school would fix me," he says "I had wanted to be a lawyer since I was a child and had worked for nearly a decade to get into a top school. Something had to change, and surely the new environment and challenge of law school would provide that opportunity. Either way, there was no Plan B."

But nothing changed, in spite of the new environment and challenge of law school. Parker's addictions exploded, his hope faded, and he was isolated in his dorm room whenever he wasn't in class. Suicidal, longing for the safety and security of his family, he withdrew from NYU Law in late November and moved back home. Five months later, he entered a residential treatment program for substance abuse and began his winding road to recovery.

"Ten months after checking into treatment, six of which were spent in the grip of a brutal heroin addiction, I, along with the help of a therapist, my family, a loving church community, and a twelve-step support group, was finally able to begin building the foundation of a sustainable, long-term recovery from substance use disorder."

Slowly, Parker's life began to improve. His relationships healed, and some long-lost self-respect returned. Years of shame began to fade, and he learned how to laugh again. He reveled in the simple joy of early recovery. One day, out of the blue, an old counselor of his offered him a newly created job position—director of Three Oaks Academy, a high school program designed specifically for students in recovery from substance abuse.

"I was surprised and more than a bit intimidated," he says. "At the time, I had been sober for only six months. But I stepped through my fear and accepted his offer, a decision for which I remain indescribably grateful."

Parker says that his experience at Three Oaks was transformative, both professionally and personally.

"During my time (there), I saw many young people restored to health and wellness, and their families healed, thanks to the full continuum of care provided by the recovery school and alternative peer-group models, from initial treatment to ongoing recovery and academic support," Parker says. "I've had the privilege of serving on the boards of the Association of Recovery Schools and the Association of Alternative Peer Groups, and, about a year ago, the advocacy work I've been able to do with both organizations, in addition to my participation in *Generation Found,* a documentary that focuses on Houston's unique support network for young people in recovery, inspired me to return to law school."

Parker plans to study education law and policy with the long-term goals of using legal, policy, and advocacy mechanisms to expand the national network of recovery schools and increase the amount of recovery support services within public schools. He says that he had to work through a tremendous amount of fear to even consider returning to law school, but, with the help of the same support network that carried him through his early days of sobriety, he realized that it was a risk worth taking. He studied hard to retake the LSAT, applied to several excellent schools, and was accepted to Stanford Law in early April 2016.

Parker says that the contrast between his life today and the mere existence he was "eking out' when he arrived at NYU Law seven years earlier couldn't be greater.

"Instead of investing all of my hope in a 'geographic cure,' I'll arrive at Stanford with a solid recovery foundation and a plan, devised by me and my therapist, of the specific ways I will maintain my physical, mental, and spiritual health while I'm in school, along with how I'll have fun and relax. There are twelve-step meetings on campus. I look forward to attending those and to learning more about the Stanford recovery community. I'll continue to be an advocate for school-based recovery support systems, and I hope that, moving forward, my story can help persuade more schools to provide their students with ongoing recovery support, not only in the name of saving lives but also to create stronger and healthier student bodies, ones with a diversity of life experiences, comprised of students who are well along the road to happy destiny."

Parker's relationships today—with his family, his friends, and his partner—are stronger than ever, He is comfortable in his own skin, and his life has newfound direction and purpose.

He did what was best for his situation. He withdrew, sought treatment, and, at this writing, is entering one of the top law schools in the country. However, it is possible to navigate law school while also getting help. Once again, the larger lesson here is that real self-awareness and positive action toward acknowledging and addressing mental health and addiction problems can save our careers, our ambitions, and our lives. But as I'll explore next, it's possible to let mental health and addiction problems progress without acknowledging them. Even with the added scrutiny of employers and clients, young professional adulthood can offer plenty of opportunity to hide our issues from our colleagues, our families, and even ourselves.

12

From the Bar to the Bar

YOU'VE MADE IT through law school and now you've passed the bar exam—one would hope the first time around, but hey, it took me three tries in Texas. (It took me three tries to get my driver's license as well.) Assuming you have not gone into some other professional field or are unable to find employment, which can be a stress trigger in itself, you're finally a practicing attorney. Time to get up off that barstool and deal with life as a grownup.

Now that you've made it, how likely are you to seek help for those mental-health issues that tend to be become progressive without treatment? The studies, the anecdotal data, and our understanding of stigma tells us it's not very likely. Once you're set in your career, how long before those issues develop to the point that they affect your work? Maybe it's already happened. Maybe you've now "borrowed" some money from that client trust account to fund your substance use disorder, for instance. You're missing client meetings or court hearings. Those billable hours are becoming lower quality or simply just...fewer. Or maybe it's not that bad (yet). *I would never do that!* The famous last words of many former and once "high-functioning" lawyers who struggle with addiction.

The period of time after law school graduation is one where, as aspiring attorneys, we receive a lot of attention and scrutiny—through the Bar exam, through early job interviews, through the watchful eyes of our supervisors in our first jobs. But none of this scrutiny will necessarily lead us to confront mental health or substance use issues if we haven't already begun to acknowledge them. For many of us, it isn't a time that allows for much self-reflection. We want to reap the benefits of three long years of study. We want to succeed. And we've already figured out that success in the professional world is not measured by how well we're able to face our demons.

Still, to be admitted to the Bar requires a series of trials that compel us to put more than just our book learning on display. First, there's the application to a given state's Bar, which requires filling out "character and fitness" information about personal and professional history. Although the character and fitness application and interview seek to uncover obvious red flags that might interfere with an attorney's professional responsibilities and might trigger a telephone call—or even worse, an in-person interview with a Bar representative—it's not an attempt to get at applicants' deepest, darkest secrets. For plenty of young law grads such as myself at the time, there's simply no paper trail of mental-health or substance use issues. No documentation, no problem.

My own character and fitness applications for Pennsylvania and Texas were so long ago that I can't remember the specifics of my answers relating to addiction or other mental-health issues, or what specific questions were asked. I can state that in 1986 I had absolutely no concept that I had a drinking issue and two eating disorders (traditional and exercise bulimia). I was not in treatment or counseling at that point in my life. I'd never been diagnosed with a problem, never been in trouble with the law, never experienced any academic sanctions or probation. Assuming they asked me anything that would require me to answer in the affirmative to mental-health issues, I would have answered no. I must have also submitted details related to my internships and other employment during law school, but only the most superficial facts were required. If they'd required detailed, honest accounts of my previous three years, I doubt I would have finished the application at all. "Rigorous honesty" was not yet in my vocabulary.

I can close my eyes now and imagine a different sort of interview that might have taken place right after I graduated from law school, one where the interviewer had perfect access to the truth. One where the interviewer could get me to reveal my deepest hopes, fears, and anxieties that in most cases I hadn't even admitted to myself. How? Who knows? Maybe this interviewer is a cross between Perry Mason and Sigmund Freud. Maybe he or she has given me an injection of sodium pentothal. Maybe this person can read my mind, and there's no sense in trying to hide the bullied, depressed thirteen-year-old at my core. Or maybe speaking with this individual is like looking into a flawless mirror, one that shows me who I really am instead of the distorted image I see most days.

This interviewer might ask, *"Mr. Cuban, what are your biggest weaknesses?"* And I might answer, "Well, I'm an alcoholic, clinically depressed bulimic with little to no interest in practicing law. I'm really not fit for this sort of work at the moment, and I'm not sure it'll ever be right for me." And that would only be the beginning.

"Brian, just make yourself comfortable. The truth serum should really be kicking in about now, so let's continue. It says here that in your second year of law school you spent three months interning with the Allegheny County District Attorney's office?"

"Yes. I took the internship in the DA's office mostly because I could usually get a better grade through an internship than classwork. I didn't really have any special interest in becoming a prosecutor. And as soon as I started, I had even less interest. I mostly worked on low-level drug offense cases. I'd sit next to a real assistant DA, who would correct me when I asked the wrong question. I'd try not to think too hard about how, in many cases, we were prosecuting kids who'd been caught with nothing more than a joint, something I'd been 'guilty' of plenty of times myself as a teen. Of course it was a different culture in 1986 than 1976. We were in the midst of Reagan's ramped up war on drugs, including weed, and there was a lot of pressure to land convictions.

"I remember one day in court, questioning a young girl who was charged with marijuana possession while an assistant district attorney (ADA) watched over me. I'd ask the wrong question, the defense would object, and the judge would sustain the objection. I was getting nowhere, frustrated and embarrassed, and the ADA had to whisper in my ear the right way to ask the question to avoid drawing objections. I asked the question again, the right way, ashamed at my own incompetence.

"Then I looked into the eyes of the young girl and saw fear and shame on her face as well. She was starting to tear up. She knew she'd done something wrong in the eyes of the law but had no idea that the young man interrogating her about it had done the same thing many times over. I was stunned that I was part of a system that was doing this to her, but more than anything, I just wanted to be done for the day so I could go for a run.

"Then while watching this girl start to cry, I remembered a time when at age thirteen or fourteen, I was out with my friends with a BB gun. Egged on by them, I'd shot a robin out of a tree. I didn't want to hurt the animal, I just didn't want to disappoint my friends. I wanted to be accepted. I'd shot the bird out of the tree and left it on the ground, slowly dying. I wanted to put it out of its misery, I wanted to cry, but I couldn't show my feelings in front of the other guys. By the time they'd left and I returned to the bird, it was already dead. I'd bawled in my room for hours. I'd always felt great empathy for animals. I'd see a stray dog, and it felt personal for me. Killing that bird has haunted me all my life. But I didn't feel more than mild pity for this girl. I could block out those feelings with people. *But how alone does this girl feel? Why don't I feel the same empathy for her?* Suddenly, I did. The girl was like the robin I'd shot as a kid. I couldn't block out the feelings anymore. *I can't do this,* I thought. *I can't stand to carry other people's pain like this. I can't help ruin people's lives.* I knew then I'd never be a prosecutor. It wasn't just that I cared too little about being a lawyer; I also felt too much to handle these sort of responsibilities. I could not bear the thought of feeling the pain of both the accused and the victims. I had no ability to see my work as an objective exercise of the law. And it wasn't just kids I might be prosecuting. I knew the only way I'd be able to hold the burden of my clients' traumas was to push the feelings away, preferably with a bottle of tequila. I hope that answers your question."

"Yes, very instructive Mr. Cuban. And then I see going back a little farther, before your second year, you did something quite different. You entered the United States Marine Corps Officer Candidate School. Please tell us how that came about."

"Well, aside from problems with alcohol, I also have unacknowledged mental health concerns, including depression. I often long to escape my reality by changing my life completely. In the case of Officer Candidate School, I basically thought I go could reinvent myself as Richard Gere. Turned out it was a terrible idea. Having a drill sergeant try to break me down and make me feel worthless wasn't the best medicine for my already tenuous mental health."

"And just one more item here related to internships. After your second year, you clerked for a private practice?"

"Right. It was for a solo practitioner in downtown Pittsburgh. My only project was a legal memo on 'stock churning.' It was eight hours of dull every day. Drinking and marathon training were more important to me at the time. I stopped showing up for work before the internship officially ended. A sign of things to come."

"Well Mr. Cuban, it seems you don't have much interest in practicing law, joining the military, or really any clear career ambitions at all. What is it you'd say you truly care about?"

"What do I care about? Well since I suffer from untreated clinical depression, I care about things that allow me to isolate myself and still appear to be a highly functioning part of 'normal society.' I care about running long distances. In three years, I have four marathons under my belt. Running is the one area I knew that I was better at than more than 90 percent of the other students. I knew I'd never make law review, and I knew that I'll never get a job in Big Law. I'd rather drink than study. What I could do was run. What I could do was get drunk. Not necessarily in that order.

"I also care about doing high-impact aerobics daily at the local gym. Doing these things allows me to offset enough calories for the inevitable binge and purge in the evening. I also care about finding a steady girlfriend. And I want to get the hell out of Pittsburgh. I want to swig Jose Cuervo out of the bottle to numb my shame. Most important, even though I do not yet really understand my destructive behaviors, I care about hiding them from the outside world because, deep down, I'm ashamed. All of these things matter more to me than the Pennsylvania Bar exam. In fact, I've already decided that as soon as I take the exam, I'm packing up my clothes, borrowing five hundred dollars from my father, and taking a Greyhound bus to Dallas, where I hope to have a little fun and hang out with my brothers."

So what would you say are your long-term career goals?

"Oh, probably not much different than my academic goals have been. Find someplace—anyplace, really—where I can do enough to get along and not have to reveal my real struggles to anyone."

"OK, Mr. Cuban. Thanks for coming in, and good luck with your future career. We happen to know of an athletic shoe store around the corner looking for a new part-time sales clerk. Maybe something to consider. Seems like you might have the relevant experience needed."

I hadn't blown off thinking about my future career completely while I was in law school. I'd made some minimal effort during my three years to go through the job-hunt motions. Once again, it seemed that it was what I was supposed to do, as I was still dealing with the obsession of "fitting in." However, graduating in the bottom half of my class didn't exactly put me in a prime position for the Big Law firms that put out sign-up sheets outside the law-school placement office. My one trip through their doors for advice constituted a look at my grades, what I thought was a snicker, and a "Have you considered private practice?" I had not considered it. (And I wouldn't consider it until eight years later when I set up a private practice simply because I needed to eat, pay rent, and buy drugs and alcohol.)

So in the end, I took the Bar, packed my bags, and headed for Dallas, just as I'd planned all along. I couldn't wait.

13

Working Hard and Playing Hard; Playing Hard and Hardly Working

MY OLDER BROTHER Mark had lived in Dallas since 1980. My younger brother Jeff was there now too. We'd all be together. I found comfort in that and instinctually felt being with them could help mold me into someone the Marines could not. Staying close as brothers was also something my father had consistently stressed since we were children. As the middle of three boys himself, he would jokingly say to us, "Mark, Brian, Jeff, wives may come and go, girlfriends may come and go, friends may come and go, but as you go through life, the one thing that needs to stay constant is your love for each other. Wherever your lives take you, wherever you live, always pick up that phone and call each other. Ask how things are going. Tell each other you love them." (As I write this book, it is no accident that 1,200 miles from where we grew up, decades later, Mark, Jeff, my father, and I all live within walking distance of one another.)

Prior to my graduating from law school I would sometimes go down to Dallas for visits and always had fun. Those trips were about girls and booze. I have vivid memories of one such trip with Mark to a club called Fast And Cool. I wore a blue-and-white striped beach-style short-sleeve shirt he loaned me. A pretty girl walked up to me and told me she loved my shirt. I never would have dreamed such a pretty girl would say anything positive about me. It was like being asked to the prom. I stole the shirt from my brother.

Mark was very popular, outgoing, and charismatic. Jeff was good looking and also not afraid to strike up conversations. Maybe some of that would rub off on me in Dallas, Texas.

It wasn't until I was in Dallas that I got the letter informing me I'd passed the Pennsylvania Bar exam. *That's great*, I thought, *but there's no way I'm going back.*

Dallas was all I wanted it to be, at first, young, free, and having fun. I arrived by Trailways bus in Dallas on Labor Day, 1986, and had a blast for two months. I was living with my brother Mark. I'd poke around looking for a job in the daytime, and then party all night. But after a few weeks, Mark started getting frustrated at my lounging around his place, drinking, and eating all the food. I was the roommate from hell.

"You need to work harder looking for a job, Brian."

"Mark, I'm sending out résumés but don't have a Texas law license. I'm even applying for paralegal jobs."

"Well you may have to consider finding something else until you pass the Bar. Lots of law firms are looking for part-time help. Are you calling them? Pull out the yellow pages and start cold calling."

Cold calling. The phrase sent tingles down my spine. Cold calling in my mind translated to *intense fear of rejection.* Everyone experiences that to some degree or another (and I suspect fear of cold calling is not unusual), but it was a mindset that dominated my existence and played right into the antithesis of what was important to me: my need for acceptance. I would view any rejection, even over the phone, as a personal attack on me. The faceless lawyer or secretary on the other end would know my fears. They would know I had no sense of self. They would know it the minute they said hello. Mark could cold call and get a job any day he wanted, but as much as

I wanted to, I would never be Mark. I would never be a salesman. But I didn't want to disappoint Mark, and I recognized I needed a job. Desperation overcame the fear. I pulled out the Yellow Pages. (For the millennials reading this, we didn't have the internet in 1986.)

I started with the "As" in the law-firm section and started dialing. After about two hundred phone calls, a bunch of "We only hire law school interns," quite a few "Have you passed the Texas bar?" and one "We'll think about it and get back to you later," I gave up. I hadn't even been able to get past the receptionist to someone who actually had some say in the hiring process. I'd only confirmed I was a failure.

Broke and desperate, I begged Mark for a job at his company, Micro Solutions, while I tried to find legal work. He agreed. I boxed and shipped computers. I hated it. *I can't do this grunt work, I'm a lawyer*, I thought. *Well, I have a law degree anyway. I've got to find a way out of this situation.*

Then for the first time in my brand new career, I crossed the line. I changed my résumé to read "Micro Solutions, Corporate Counsel." I started to include "securities work" on my résumé, among other areas I didn't have a clue about. Soon an attorney friend of mine suggested I send my résumé to his law firm. I got a call. "We have reviewed your résumé and are interested in your securities background. Can you come in for a chat next week?"

The next day I headed to the Southern Methodist University Law School bookstore and bought a textbook on securities law. I'd be ready! You can insert your "eye-roll" and snicker here. I remembered some law from my corporations class. I knew phrases like "closely held," "public offering," and "Securities and Exchange Commission" and convinced myself that my knowledge of these words and boning up from the books I purchased would give me just enough familiarity to sound competent for a half hour or hour. I could fill in the rest of the details after the first interview.

Interview day! I was feeling good enough, despite having had a few too many the night before at Dallas Alley, a popular downtown nightclub. I got home in time to review my key phrases and steal a couple hours of sleep. Then I put on my Sears three-piece suit that my dad had purchased for me as a graduation present from Penn State and hopped the bus downtown.

"So Mr. Cuban, tell me about your securities work at Micro Solutions. Are they going public?"

I stared at the distinguished-looking man interviewing me. His nostrils seemed to flare, and I imagined he could smell the hangover on me. Booze wafted from every pore in my body. Awkward silence. I cleared my throat as a stall mechanism. *Which phrase that I memorized will help me here?*

"Well I just started working there, so I'm not up to speed on that yet."

The attorney said nothing for a moment and just looked at me. Then he glanced down again at my résumé.

"Thank you, Mr. Cuban. We'll get back to you."

Of course they never did. He knew immediately that I was full of shit. I knew that I was not going to be able to bluff my way into a job in a profession I did not even want. Time for plan B.

■ Late Fall 1986

Filling out an application to be a police officer for the City of Dallas (DPD). My fallback is consistent with my major at Penn State. Law enforcement. During my time at Penn State, I had interned with one police department in Upper Saint Clair, Pennsylvania. I'd taken a few police officer exams. One in Mt. Lebanon, where I grew up. One in State College, Pennsylvania, where Penn State is located, and one with the Pennsylvania State Police. I'd not scored well enough to make the short list for hire on any of them. Not that it would have mattered. I would not have been hired. Police departments generally required minimum uncorrected vision and being free from color blindness. I was blue-green color blind and legally blind without my glasses decades before Lasik would become a reality. I was ineligible for hire from almost every police department, but as was the case when I believed myself eligible for hire at that Big Law firm, I went ahead hoping to somehow slip through.

Of course, there was something else that would make me ineligible for the Dallas Police Department. I had smoked both hash and marijuana, which was a no-no. I applied anyway.

Initial interview day with DPD! Unlike the morning before my Big Law interview, I am alert, sober, and rested. I've strung together some days of sobriety in preparation for the drug test I knew would come. The officer is looking over my application. He notes my law degree.

"You'll be a short termer here. Gone in five years. The lawyers always are. They either go to the District Attorney's office or switch to the dark side—criminal defense. We'll be glad to have you until then. We just need to get you set up for the entrance exam, the physical agility test, drug test, and...polygraph."

As I leave the building I think to myself: *It took ten minutes for a law firm partner to see through me, I'm certainly not going to B.S. a polygraph about my drug use.* I never finish the application process.

On to Plan C. I have no Plan C. Just as I'm leaving the municipal building after the interview, I see the job board for all the City of Dallas civil service postings. One post is for their "Office of Property Management." *Law degree preferred.* The job is doing something called "Right of Way Acquisition." *What the hell is that?* It doesn't matter. I need a job. I head back into the building, fill out an application, and hop the bus home.

Waiting to hear back on my job application with the city of Dallas, I read the jobs section in the now defunct *Dallas Times Herald*. My eyes lock on a half-page ad announcing, "The CIA is hiring." I read the qualifications. So far so good. Then I see *Proficiency in Russian preferred*. The wheels start turning. *Russian? I can speak Russian!* Well, I know some Russian. My high school was one of the few in the country that offered a four-year Russian program. I did all four years, albeit not very well. I also took a course at Penn State. Why? Because Mark had also taken Russian at Mt. Lebanon High School. He had traveled to the Soviet Union with his class. I wanted to be like Mark. Maybe that would be enough.

Why were they interested in a Russian language background? This was 1987. Just months earlier, Ronald Reagan had given his famous "Tear Down The Wall" speech, calling on General Secretary Gorbachev to tear down the wall separating East from West Germany. A few years earlier on television and at the movies, military conflict and nuclear holocaust based on U.S. and Soviet tensions were the themes with such titles as 1984's *Red Dawn* depicting a joint Soviet and Cuban (the country, not my family) invasion of the United States, and the 1983 film about a Soviet Nuclear strike on the United States, *The Day After*. As I read the ad, I have visions of CIA analyst Joe Turner (played by Robert Redford) in *Three Days of the Condor*. I'd failed to be Richard Gere in the Marines. Robert Redford wasn't a bad alternative. I think, *I could be on the run from assassins with the beautiful Faye Dunaway. The CIA is for me.*

As one might suspect with the CIA, even the directions to their office were secretive. My interview would be held in a room marked only with a number at the old Federal Building in Dallas. I received a letter with instructions on how to find it. Not being a detail person, I forgot to bring the letter or write down the room number. I spent twenty minutes walking around the building asking where the "CIA Room" was. I finally got there.

One of the employment recruiters—a woman with longish brown hair, greeted me.

"Thank you for coming Mr. Cuban," she said. "Did you have any trouble finding us?"

"Yes," I replied, "a little bit."

"Please tell me that you weren't asking around about where we are. We like to keep a low profile."

"Uh...no..."

"What do you know about us, Mr. Cuban?"

"Only what I read in the ad and what I see on television."

"Well, let me tell you what we envision for you," she said. "You'll officially work for the State Department based out of Washington, D.C. You will, however, be overseas with rotations back to the states. You'll take immersive Russian language classes, among other training."

"Sounds good," I said. *Rotations?* I thought.

"This job is about meeting people and getting them to trust you," she said. "You'll attend parties and other events as well as travel extensively. You'll love it. As you're probably aware, we don't have a domestic charter. We have no domestic positions for what you will be doing. You'll live overseas."

I stopped listening after "no domestic positions" and "meet people." I didn't even want to get my hair cut in the Marines, and now I have to go overseas *alone*? I have to actually interact in social settings? I have to get drunk first just to go out at night. *I don't get it. In* Three Days of The Condor, *Joe Turner was stationed in New York City!* In this tiny office however, there's no Redford, just the reality of my life.

Every flicker of a career ambition I have has been quickly snuffed. I wasn't nearly prepared enough for Big Law. I couldn't admit the truth about my drug use to the Dallas PD. And I'd never hack it in the CIA with my unaddressed mental-health issues. What was left for me after strikes A, B, and C?

On to Plan D. Being a right-of-way agent for the city of Dallas is not sounding so bad now. *If they offer. I'll take it.*

They do. I do.

Not quite parties and international intrigue, but I'm safe. Fixed hours. The job sounds simple. It sounds boring. But that's great—it means I can continue to hide. I'm safe. I'm home.

It had been a bumpy ride, but I'd made it to the land of the gainfully employed, although it was soon clear to me that I wasn't going to gain much through my gainful employment without the law license to boost my prospects. I still had no interest in pursuing any avenue of law, but I needed a better salary if I wanted to take advantage of all the fun that Dallas had to offer. And if I wanted to be a licensed attorney, I still needed to pass the Bar. There was also my old friend, shame, an emotion that had historically driven so many of my decisions. This was one of the few times it would drive a productive action. I was ashamed to tell people in Dallas that I wasn't licensed in Texas. I'd been lying about it when it would come up. Something had to be done.

■ 1987

Bar Exam number two. This time it's the Texas Bar exam. I'm still working for the City of Dallas, and I have to deal with that damn character and fitness investigation again! Nothing has really changed. I've never been arrested or officially sanctioned in any way that needs to go on the application. I'm in good financial standing (for now) and have never defaulted on any loans, which would have to go on the application. Of course by this time, one small detail has changed. I now regularly use cocaine. I have no idea I'm already addicted. I just think cocaine is still fun. Alcohol is still fun. Ecstasy is fun. Just one long six-day-a-week Dallas party.

I see no reason to change the study habits that got me through the Pennsylvania Bar exam. Get someone's Barbri Books and notes and pull a couple of all-nighters at a no-tell motel in Fort Worth. I head out to the Will Rogers Memorial Center in Fort Worth and pass! Right? Wrong.

The Texas Bar exam was different than the Pennsylvania exam. It was over three days as compared to two in PA. In addition to the multistate and essay portions of the exam, there was a one-half day exam on Texas criminal procedure and evidence. Shit! I didn't even know Pennsylvania procedure and evidence, and I went to a Pennsylvania law school. I fail the Texas bar exam.

Finally, in 1991, almost five years after my move, and two more tries, I passed. I'd absorbed enough through osmosis and occasional study that I was able to crawl over the finish line. I was officially a lawyer in both name and practice.

I was also addicted to cocaine and alcohol.

By this time, my substance-use problems were fully developed, and they were affecting my work. But I'd still never been arrested and never sanctioned in any way that would throw up red flags for the state Bar. That changed soon enough. In 1992, I was arrested for my DWI. A year after that, I lost my job. My problems were finally surfacing in a public way, but it was still possible for me to keep my reputation somewhat intact. After all, my arrest never led to a conviction, and when I went into private practice in 1993, I never had to tell any of my clients about the employers I'd let down along the way. In my mind, I was still functional. My "new normal" was fully integrated in my life.

Despite all the scrutiny and testing lawyers face as they leave law school and seek credentials and employment, there's no part of the process that is certain to force those young attorneys to confront substance use or mental health problems. Once we are settled into a career, there can be even less incentive, at least, that is, until the consequences finally start piling up. For many of us, that pile of consequences can become a virtual mountain before we admit to ourselves that we have a problem.

Lawyers have a reputation for working hard and playing hard. I knew many lawyers who struggled with alcohol and substance use issues, though it could be that I was attracted to a social circle where substance and heavy alcohol use was the norm. Of course, I also knew many who had no issues with drugs or alcohol and could have a good time within healthy limits. One way to reduce or mask shame is to put yourself among people engaging in the same behaviors. I immersed myself in that culture—the underground drug culture of Dallas. I wasn't the only lawyer hanging out in those circles, although there were people from all sorts of backgrounds. It didn't matter to me. Here's what did: Who had the blow, the private tables, the bottle service, and where I could "bust the line" at nightclubs because of my last name were all that mattered. They were the most important things in my life.

According to the "2016 Hazelden Betty Ford Foundation Study," not only do attorneys have nearly triple the rate of self-reported problematic alcohol use as the general population, but they have double the rate of doctors, another high-stress profession. According to the study, problematic alcohol use among young attorneys is through the roof, according to the study, with lawyers under thirty at 31.9 percent and junior associates at law firms at 31.1 percent. That's almost one-third of all young attorneys admitting anonymously to problematic alcohol use. Astonishing.

Perhaps there is something to attorney culture being a contributing factor to these numbers. In an interview with the *Washington Post*, Patrick Krill speculated that this might be the case. According to Krill, the lead author of the Hazelden study, attorneys might "prioritize success and accomplishment over things like balance, personal well-being, health, and so forth. You put them through a training (law school) where they are taught to work harder, play harder, and assume the role of a tough, capable and aggressive professional without personal weaknesses or deficiencies...Heavy drinking, lack of balance, and poor self-care are entirely normalized... That's the behavior that young lawyers see being modeled all around them, and throughout the profession."

Culture is one factor. Personality might be another. As I mentioned previously, there's certainly a lawyer personality stereotype in pop culture. And lawyers often seem to be driven, Type-A personalities who might in some ways be at higher risk for addictive behaviors. Perhaps the ways we fit the lawyer "type" has something to do with propensity for mental health issues and addiction. Or maybe sometimes it's the way we *don't* fit in that matters. I certainly felt more stress through the years from the ways I *wasn't* a typical lawyer than the ways that I was. I've already made it pretty clear that I never felt particularly stressed from the desire to excel either in law school or as a lawyer. I was stressed because I was miserable for other reasons. I'd chosen an occupation for all the wrong reasons that had no relation to who I was as a person.

I believe part of the issue was that being a lawyer often required putting aside personal feelings to meet client objectives. That was never something at which I excelled. I'm a person who cries at movie trailers and at every Facebook mention of a dog that passes away. I'm the guy who has harbored the guilt of shooting a bird out of a tree as an adolescent all my life. As an intern with a district attorney's office, I almost lost it when I helped prosecute a young girl who was being tried for a minor drug violation. I wear my emotions on my sleeve. My decision-making process is often a direct construct of my emotional sense surrounding the issues. In short, I'm a "feeler."

As part of my exploration of my journey through the legal profession, I decided to take the well-known Myers-Briggs personality test, which is based on the writing of Carl Jung in the early twentieth century. It's not a perfect tool but can provide some insight into how we process information, complete tasks, and interact with others. Had I taken it at the start of my career, it may not have persuaded me to go into a different profession, but it could have helped me anticipate some of the ways my personality fits (or doesn't easily fit) a law career.

According to the test, I'm considered an "ISFJ" personality: *Introversion, Sensing, Feeling, Judging.* How does that compare to other lawyers? Luckily I'm not the first to ask that question. In 1993 a study was done by attorney and management consultant Larry Richard in which 3,014 lawyers were surveyed on Myers-Briggs personality type. My personality type of ISFJ was relatively rare in the legal profession, accounting for only 4.25 percent of those responding to the survey compared to roughly 14 percent of the general population. Comparing my results to lawyers as a group is interesting.

As a "feeler" already with underlying mental health issues, choosing law was one of the worst decisions I could have made to fit my personality. Mental-health issues combined with an aversion to conflict and criticism for me certainly seemed a volatile combination that often led to dissatisfaction, depression, and triggering behaviors.

While I have no doubt there are "feelers" doing well in the law and happy with their career choices, with that personality type and all the baggage I was already carrying, the odds were not good that, without being in recovery, I would succeed. And what happened when I went into recovery? I veered to a profession of feelers: mental-health advocacy. Now I'm happy. To my fellow lawyer "feelers"—the law is full of opportunities to catalyze on empathy and emotion. Not everyone is meant to be a hard-ass. Pivot. Juke. Set your new path. Get healthy doing it. Be happy doing it. Exploring the ways you are a unique individual can certainly help with recovery.

This test could also apply to students who are in recovery or deciding whether to reach out to someone for the first time while dealing with the stress of the law school environment. Who better to quote than Socrates, the Greek philosopher, whose method of stimulating critical thinking, The Socratic Method, forms the fundamental core of legal education? In order to succeed both in law school and in recovery, "Know thyself." Of course, the legal profession is full of all sorts of personalities. Individuals are unique, and personality indexes tell only part of the story.

It may have been the personality-type mismatch with my profession that fed my depression, which fed into addiction. For other lawyers, work might have fueled addiction in other ways. To get a better sense of the friction that lawyer culture can provide, I reached out to other attorneys to get a sense of their experiences. One such attorney that responded was Susan, who, unlike me, worked in a high-pressure environment where drinking to "blow off steam" might have been part of the professional culture.

As a child, she always dreamed of becoming a lawyer and living in Washington, D.C. Not that it was expected of her. Susan's mom stayed home, and her live revolved around her family; her dad was an ironworker who had never graduated from high school. So where did this dream come from?

"It was a direct result of my grandmother's influence on my life," Susan told me. "Adele T. Broderick was a woman way ahead of her time and had devoted herself to a life in public service and was involved in politics. Throughout my childhood and teen years, she would bring me to DC for visits, and from a very early age, I developed a passion for the law and for justice."

In 1989, Susan began her professional career as a prosecutor in the Manhattan DA's office, "the most incredible job I've ever had." The hours were long, the pay was low, but there was an amazing feeling, she says, that came from standing up for the victims and putting the bad guys behind bars.

Eventually she was working on homicide and child abuse cases, dealing with horrific crimes and countless tragedies. "Some of the cases I worked on were so awful, so vicious that it was hard to believe that human beings could actually commit such crimes," she says. "I devoted myself to doing what I could for these victims (many of whom were small children and some of them brutally murdered). The determination and tenacity I exhibited as a child were now assets that helped me through many cases."

It was a "work hard, play hard" environment, and Susan did both very well, frequently meeting up after work with other DAs and cops in the bar behind the courthouse. "There was a tremendous camaraderie among us and we were able to let off lots of steam over the horrific crimes we were witnessing on a daily basis."

As the years passed, the "happy hours" ended as her colleagues were settling down and having families, so she would stop at the liquor store on her way home from work. Although she never drank at work, a bottle (or two) of Chardonnay got her through the evening after a rough day on the job. And there were many rough days.

"Since I was a single woman living alone in New York City, I thought alcohol was the only thing that could take the edge off my stressful life and it had gone from a luxury to a necessity," Susan says. "And while it did not affect my job performance, it had a great effect on my personal life."

As her friends married and settled down, she tried to convince herself that she was a "career woman" who had no use for the husband, children, picket fence, and so on. But truth be told, she could not sustain a relationship, Susan says. "I had no problem meeting men, but after a few dates, it would become clear to all of them that I drank too much, and their calls would stop. That of course, did not stop me. In fact, many evenings after a few glasses of wine, I'd be dialing their numbers in the hope of 'reconciling.' I'm sure they were on the other end, listening to my slurred speech, wondering, *'How did I let this one get away?'"*

Susan had started drinking way back as a teenager and says she was "smitten from the first sip." Somewhere along the line, however, alcohol no longer worked, and instead of relieving her stress, created more. "Ultimately it was evident, even to me, that alcohol did absolutely nothing to enhance my reputation, my personality, or my appearance."

On July 15, 2001, Susan made the decision to quit drinking. In the beginning, she kept it to herself and some friends and family members, most of whom were incredibly supportive. She recalls the first time she called a dear friend and told her that she had a problem and had quit drinking. "There was a silence that I initially thought was her deciding how to end our friendship. Instead, after a few seconds (that felt like minutes) all she said was, 'Watch out, world.'"

Susan soon realized that many of the prosecutors and judges with whom she worked had seen her out at parties and/or bars when her alcoholism was on full display. "I certainly hadn't been anonymous about my alcoholism," she says. "Why would I choose to be silent on the fact that I was finally dealing with it?"

Some colleagues expressed shock and thought she was overreacting. These were primarily the ones who drank the way she had. She realizes now that she was a "functional" alcoholic. "I never drank on the job (or in the morning) and had won some really big cases during my career. And one of them resulted in a pretty nice promotion. I also prided myself on the fact that I had never gotten a DWI, although I didn't have a car in the city so that excuse was pretty flimsy."

Even though Susan was "functioning," she was not living to her full potential, and that applied across the board, whether in the courtroom or in a relationship.

"I may not have had a drink in the morning but I was usually showing up in court or at family parties with a hangover," she says. "I didn't drink before 5 p.m. but would spend a good part of most days obsessing about getting home and having a drink to take the edge off. I often woke up worried about who I called the night before or what a fool I made of myself. Those things are obviously not good for one's career or character, but for years I had resigned myself to this sort of life because I couldn't fathom the idea of not drinking."

Although Susan refuses to blame her trouble with alcohol on external factors, like office culture, it certainly played a part, as it did for me. As was the case with me, her problems started as a teenager, when she was "smitten with the first sip," well before she was a practicing attorney. But when she became a district attorney in New York City, her professional culture offered an easy excuse to keep drinking as well as a social structure that made regular drinking to relieve stress seem normal. Susan also reveals that her alcohol use was problematic not just for its potential to damage her professional reputation, it was also deeply affecting her personal life. As with me, it was these personal problems that ultimately triggered the decision to seek help.

One of her big fears was that acknowledging her problems with alcohol might be perceived by her colleagues in a way that could damage her reputation. She even worried that it might "destroy" her career. A fear of lost reputation could be a significant reason that some attorneys put off seeking help or even acknowledging they have problems in any way that might get back to their colleagues. This is borne out by the Hazelden Betty Ford survey, the two biggest barriers to attorneys seeking treatment for substance use problems were 1) Not wanting others to find out they needed help and 2) concerns regarding privacy and confidentiality.

Susan's comments remind me of some attorneys I knew. I would hear of plenty of attorneys who also had a reputation for alcohol and drug use. I would also see it for myself. We would run into each other at bars. We knew each other through mutual friends. We snorted cocaine together. Although we thought we were fooling the world with our routines designed to mask problems with drugs or alcohol, our masks were often helping us fool ourselves.

I'd sometimes see attorneys who had bright careers and the respect of the legal community, but who seemed to have no qualms about being ugly drunk at certain bars or obvious about their cocaine use. *You have the money, friend. Invest in some Visine,* I'd think. But now I understand how easy it is to get sloppy. It's easy to feel that as long as we're able to stay "high functioning" and keep our addiction world and our "respectable" world from colliding, our problems are invisible to everyone on planet respectability. Well, that's probably not often the case, and as addictions progress, it's harder and harder to keep those worlds separate.

■ July 2006

I'm at the grand opening of the Ghost Bar at the top of the W Hotel in Dallas. I'm no stranger to the Ghost Bar. There's also one in the Palms Casino and Resort in Las Vegas. I'm a regular at the Palms.

On my fortieth birthday, I took a trip on my brother's private jet to the Palms, where I had three eight-balls of cocaine delivered to my hotel room. I wasn't a big gambler but was often given VIP treatment by the casino host, "Jimmy," because of the NBA connections of the Palms owners. There was not one trip I made to the Palms prior to getting sober where cocaine and getting trashed was not the order of business. Why should the opening of the Dallas Ghost Bar be any different?

Well, there is one difference. What happens in Vegas stays in Vegas. What happens in Dallas gets around. I didn't care at this point. Addiction has a way of not caring. I show up at the event already high. The scene is amazing. The crowd is bumping. There are celebrities everywhere. Tommy Lee of Motley Crüe is spinning some bump and grind as a guest DJ. Soon I'm sitting at a table with my brother Mark, some of his friends, my father, and Jimmy. They're all chatting and joking, and I'm starting to feel impatient. After a few minutes, I head to the bathroom. I need another line. *Shit. This is a bad cocaine bathroom.* I'm practically offended. How can a bar as otherwise cool as the Ghost Bar overlook an important detail like this? Large gaps to the sides of the doors in the toilet stalls make it too easy for someone to spy what's going on in the stall. It was the same problem at the Palms. I had a friend get busted there. A plainclothes officer saw what she was doing through one of those wide stall gaps and arrested her. I know from experience that the best clubs to do coke in have stall doors that are practically hermetically sealed when you close them, one of the things I loved about the bathrooms on certain levels of the American Airlines Center when I went to Mavs games. I think: *You'll never be one of the cooler bars in Dallas until you can better accommodate people like me.* I wait until I'm sure the room is empty before I polish off my line.

Back at the table, my brother is talking to me. My father is talking to me. I feel incoherent. I'm so coked up that my body is frozen, the muscles in my face rigid. My eyes feel like they're going to leap out of my skull and start moshing at the feet of the Motley Crue guys. All I can do is stare at my brother and father and nod. *Do they see? Do they know what's happening to me?* My dad knows nothing about such things. Then my drink comes just in time to ease up the lockjaw and wild eyes. I take a sip and relax just a bit. My shirt is drenched in sweat. I reach into my pocket for cash to pay the waiter for my drink. I'm still feeling shaky, and as I pull out my cash, my baggie of blow falls out, right next to Mark's foot.

It's over. I'm done.

But no one says a word. No one looks down, or if they have seen it, they have their poker faces on. I quickly slide my foot over the baggie and drop a dollar bill on the floor as pretext to pick it up. Lesson learned. *Next time, put the baggie in the other pocket.*

Eventually, my addiction world and my "respectable" world crashed into each other. In my case, it was my personal life that took the hit. My career never exploded in any big way due to problems with addiction. But addiction certainly bled my career by a thousand cuts, and it would be no surprise to me to find out my "reputation" included gossip or rumors from other attorneys and professional contacts who knew or saw more than I'd wanted them to out in the clubs.

Still, for many facing addiction, it doesn't really matter if some people know or not. As long as we can maintain the facade and are left alone to continue using, we're comfortable. Colleagues may indeed notice there's a problem, but that doesn't necessarily mean Bar intervention is just around the corner. In fact, even in the adversarial world of some aspects of law work, collegiality is a typical part of lawyer culture. We often think we're showing respect to colleagues who might face similar pressures when we see them having a hard time and turn the other way.

Scott's story exemplifies this quality of the culture. Scott developed substance use problems early in life, and, like me carried those issues into his career. Also like me, substance and alcohol use helped eat away at his career slowly over time. But unlike my story, Scott had colleagues make it clear they noticed there was a problem, an example of how important professional community can be in empowering recovery.

Raised in northeastern Oklahoma, he lived with his father and stepmother until he was twelve years old. He then went to live with his mother and wouldn't see or speak to his father again for six years.

"My mom worked at a bar, so she was gone all night every night," he says. "I became a creature of will: I could do anything and everything better than any adult. At twelve, I cooked all my own meals, did all my own laundry, had a part-time job, and even got myself to school every day. I didn't realize until much later the effect this had on me. I began drinking and smoking weed around the same age."

Scott graduated from high school and enlisted in the Navy, where his drinking and drug use became much worse, and he began using acid and cocaine. In his third year, he went home for a week, used coke the entire time, and upon returning to the ship, was called for a random drug test. As a result, he was other than honorably discharged.

In 1999, he started college and later graduated with a bachelor's degree in business management. The drugs and alcohol remained constant. Then, in fall of 2003, he began law school at the University of Tulsa.

"The drugs and alcohol stayed, but I mostly just smoked pot," he says. "In my first semester of law school, I didn't go out socially or drink or use. I made straight A's that first semester, and the lesson I took away from my achieving excellent grades was that I could get drunk and smoke pot and still probably get by with passing grades. Thinking back, it makes me sick that I would sacrifice what being in the top 10 percent of my class could have given me for such short-term pleasure."

Upon graduation, Scott took a full-time job at the Tulsa County Public Defender's Office. After staying there a year, he went out on his own and, as he puts it, "...bounced from that to law firms and back for eight years."

In 2008, Scott married, bought his first home, bought two nice cars, and turned thirty.

"It was also when I began misusing Xanax," he says. "I was snorting my full month's prescription in a week in only the third month on them. Work was nerve racking. I was used to manual labor and had no idea how psychologically taxing law practice is. I lay awake hearing moms screaming about their children and grown men crying when faced with prison. There was absolutely no mention of this in school. I was utterly unprepared."

After a year or two, Scott realized that practicing and his family didn't mesh well with Xanax, so he began using opiates. Although he started agreeing with his wife that he had a problem, he would attend AA meetings only to keep her happy and was high most of the time.

Then his substance use eventually caught up with his ability to practice law.

"Cars began being repossessed. We had to sell our home. I couldn't take the guilt any longer and began using meth after I'd built up a tolerance to the pills. I woke up after having a week-long blackout and realized I'd separated from my wife, smoked meth in front of my kids, and driven them around while I was high."

On one occasion Scott did get brought into chambers with the Judge and the Assistant District Attorney while they were conducting a status docket, and he was getting a plea done.

"Out of the blue, the judge requested that the prosecutor and I come into chambers," Scott says. "He told me I was slurring so badly that he couldn't understand half the stuff I was saying, and he noticed a lot of my clients were noticing it, too. He sent me home. Amazingly enough, I was enraged. I began demanding a urinalysis and was upset. I can't believe I acted that way, because I'd taken three Xanax bars before court and still to this day have no memory of any of this happening. I was told by my colleague and good friend the prosecutor, who was with me in court that day."

The next day when Scott got back in court, he met his friend in chambers and expressed how grateful he was and that he probably saved Scott's career. He said, "No problem, and never speak of this again."

However, Scott continued to use and be intoxicated in court for another three years.

"I can see now that all the litigation I have done while using was sub-par due to my substance use," he says. "I would drink and take narcotics because of my anxiety and stress related to litigation, but after getting sober, I realized that they only made the stress and anxiety worse."

He entered a treatment center in 2015 and has been in recovery ever since. In his career, he has tried hundreds of criminal jury trials, everything from misdemeanor DUI to murder in the first, he says, and only now does he actually feel he is doing well.

He attends an AA meeting daily over the lunch hour and rarely misses because most of the courts and attorneys with which he works are aware of how important the meeting is to Scott. He also sees a therapist once a week. "I have found that in sobriety there are a lot of feelings and emotions I'm not used to dealing with, and it really helps to discuss them with someone who give me some pointers on how to go about dealing with them," he says. "My faith is also important in my recovery."

Scott takes as many drug- and alcohol-related cases pro bono or at cut rates as possible. "I have a higher power, a creator, that I don't understand but that I am learning more and more every day to trust," he says. "I don't worry or stress as much. I don't play into drama or hate. My life is most definitely not perfect, but I'm happier than I have been in a long time."

In Scott's story, his wife, a judge, and even the attorney on the other side of a criminal case all express concern for his behavior, yet he suffers no hard consequences for his actions, other than the risks he incurs for his family and clients. Fortunately for Scott, he was able to get help and ultimately recover his career and his life. Of course, not every professional who has his or her life touched by addiction is as fortunate.

In the next chapter, I'll take a look at some of the consequences of addiction, which can threaten some legal careers with a bang and others with a whimper. The risk is real: State Bar associations take professional misbehavior very seriously. Drug and alcohol addiction are often part and parcel to such issues. Law students may think that such worries are needless, and they are simply doing what students do. That is also a risk. I wonder how many standing before a state Bar grievance panel, facing loss of profession, family, and possibly freedom, wish they had told someone, or anyone, during the law-school years.

But the good news is that for those who are willing to confront their problems and seek help, most state bar associations have programs available to save and rehabilitate careers. Schools have mental-health and peer-assistance support programs, both formal and informal, that were virtually non-existent in my day. And beyond that, even if lawyers or other professionals are facing the end of their careers partly due to addiction, it's important to remember that the end of a career is not in any way the same as the end of a life. One lesson I take from all the lawyers I've met who have faced addiction is that a second life beyond law is always possible and can come more quickly than we expect.

14

When Bars Collide

YOU MAY BE wondering, so let's push the elephant out of the room—I've never been disciplined by a state Bar for issues that often arise out of alcohol or drug use. No official complaints or sanctions for stealing of client funds, co-mingling of funds, case neglect—any misdeed from the long list of mortal sins an attorney can commit. I don't say that as a badge of honor. There's no question in my mind that I did not represent clients to the best of my abilities. There were times I could have had grievances filed against me, and it would be related to alcohol and drug use affecting my ability to competently practice law.

As all lawyers should know, and law students will learn in their ethics classes, there is a duty before the Bar of providing "competent and zealous representation" for clients. All states have Rules of Professional Conduct governing the practice of law. I won't recap them all here. But for those who are curious, I'll boil it down to three basic mandates: be competent, work as hard and as smart as you can, and don't steal.

No matter your background, it's probably the same at anyone's place of work, and we can all agree that getting high on the job and stealing money to purchase drugs, or even just being less effective at work because of drug use, are not ideal behaviors. While I never stole from clients in the traditional sense, there were many times I was regularly too hungover and tired from being up all night party-ing to function properly. It was also not uncommon for me to be doing lines of coke throughout the day to counteract lack of sleep and a hangover. Many in the profession may argue that this is a form of stealing from clients when they pay for competent performance and receive less. I would have to agree.

Though I escaped discipline from the Bar, not every lawyer with substance use or alcohol use issues gets off so easily. Attorneys like Marsha who have shared their stories in this book have suffered sanctions for their actions. Some careers recover from Bar sanc-tions. Some do not.

■ Summer 2013

It's a muggy, hot morning headed over the 100-degree mark, not unusual for a Dallas summer. This morning I'm taking my usual drive to my favorite Starbucks in Dallas.

I drive past the same bus stop every day. To the average commu-ter, the bus stop had nothing to set it off from any other. Just one more city hub with people waiting to go to different parts of their lives: jobs, family, shopping. This particular bus stop always catches my attention, because to me it symbolizes more. I know it as a way-station for those in various stages of drug and alcohol recovery. The apartment complex across the street houses many recovering addicts. It's cheap (by Dallas standards) and within walking distance of a local twelve-step group. My home group. The bus line also takes people close to several sober-living homes. Different stories from all walks of life confirm that addiction does not discriminate.

This morning, I see one such story with whom I'm intimately familiar standing at the bus stop. It's my old colleague Gary, wait-ing for the bus. Also a lawyer, Gary has an undergraduate degree from Boston College, Summa Cum Laude, near the top of his class at Antioch School of Law, and then on to a great sports-related job with NBC in New York City. He wasn't just a lawyer; he was a distinguished lawyer.

I'd met Gary in 2003 when we both worked of-counsel to a local Dallas firm. At the time, I was trying to hold my life together between addiction and an eating disorder. Being "high-functioning" was a blessing and a curse. In my mind, I needed no help. I showed up to court sober. I did cocaine only in the bathroom of the firm or on my office desk with the door closed when I had no appointments. It provided just the pickup I needed sometimes, and it all made perfect sense to me. I viewed my law firm bathroom/coke breaks as almost a performance enhancer that would allow me to do my job better. Of course my performance was already substantially impaired from using cocaine and drinking the night before.

I tried a case with Gary—a bench trial contract matter. It was the last time I'd appear in court to litigate a case. Sober and brilliant, Gary ran the show. I admired but didn't envy him. Being in the courtroom made me sick to my stomach. I couldn't wait to be done with the trial. But Gary was truly talented, and he knew exactly what he was doing. We had a good result.

Then Gary disappeared. He'd done so sporadically over the years since I first met him. I knew what that meant. Gary would go through stretches of stellar representation of his clients, and then there'd be periods of complaints of neglect, and even rumors that he'd show up to client meetings apparently high. Gary's story was generally known among the local attorneys in recovery.

After he'd landed a job at NBC Sports, he hit the NYC nightlife pretty hard, and partying with sports stars was a way of life. It was also known that he had a family history of significant alcohol use. These were the sorts of things lawyers might know *about* each other but were hesitant to address *with* each other. There was too much stigma involved, and perhaps we all respected each other's needs to at least maintain facades. But Gary and I had often shared our addiction struggles over coffee at Starbucks. He'd gone to twelve-step meetings with me at my home group.

On this day, Gary doesn't see me drive by him at the bus stop. He's staring at the ground, just waiting. I've called him recently and noticed that his voicemail was full. I know what that means. I suspect many addicts and their families know what that means. Gary has "gone out." He's not sober.

I pull a U-turn so I can drive up alongside and offer him a ride. He gets in. He's been to a twelve-step meeting and is headed down to the transitional living home where he's a resident. The home offers housing for up to eighteen months for men and women who are recovering from drug and alcohol addiction, and it also provides them with other support and services.

After he gets in the car, Gary asks if I know he's been disbarred. I'd seen it in the local legal periodical. As often happens with lawyers and addiction, some money due to his clients never made it to them. State Bars take a dim view of stealing from clients, and addiction is no excuse. It's a surprisingly common story, and there's an unsurprisingly common explanation from Gary. It's all a big mistake, he claims. He's lost everything, but he's still in denial, still trying to cling to a reputation that was far in the past long before news of his disbarment broke in the legal periodicals. I don't say anything in response to Gary's excuses. I understand. I was once full of them.

On the way to the transitional home, we stop at a diner, and I buy Gary lunch. We talk about nothing in particular. Then, as I drop him off, he makes a request. Just a few bucks, he says, "until I get back on my feet."

For a few months, it becomes our routine. The bus stop. The drive. The excuses. The money. I just listen to what Gary has to say.

Then one day, he's gone again. I give him a call, and his voicemail is full. I worry. Then I check with the sober house, and he's no longer there. He's tested dirty and has been kicked out.

■ July 2013

My cell phone rings. A 516 area code—Long Island, where some of Gary's family lives. It's Gary. He's moved back home. Maybe he's thinking that returning to family and roots will save him. I'd had the same experience, if only instinctively, when I moved from Pittsburgh to Dallas to live with my brothers. If recovery were only that simple.

He also tells me he's sober and working as an attorney—he's licensed in New York. I bite my tongue. Am I ethically bound to say something about his disbarment in Texas to the state Bar of New York? I struggle with the conflict between my view as a lawyer and as a person in recovery. It's not my recovery. It's his. I congratulate Gary on the progress he's made.

■ November 2013

I recently appeared on the *Katie Show*, a now off-the-air talk show featuring Katie Couric, to talk about my battle with body dysmorphic disorder, and of course that includes my recovery from addiction. I'm now preparing for a "watch party" at a local restaurant.

I get a Facebook message from Gary. The message is cheerful and includes a photo of a plane ticket to Dallas for the watch party.

It's the last time I hear from him.

The message comes from his ex-wife, and the Google explosion of his name tells the story. At age fifty-four, Gary has been fatally struck by a tractor trailer. He was walking along the middle of the highway when it happened. It's unknown whether he'd been drinking, but it doesn't matter. He's gone. He never "got it" in recovery. It's not that he didn't want it. He tried. I miss him and wish he had gotten it. Gary's struggles with drugs and alcohol did not define who he was. He was a lawyer, a friend, a husband, a sibling. In his passing, he also helped me. I know my recovery is only as good as today.

Gary is just one friend or acquaintance in the law profession who I've watched battle addiction. Some of my peers have had lifetimes to either deal with issues, succumb to them, beat them, or try to live with them. Some now have children. Grandchildren. Some are law partners, and some have long-standing private practices. Some may have left the practice of law. Married, divorced, gone into long-term recovery, overdosed, lost to alcoholism and depression. Sometimes we face immediate and dramatic consequences for our actions. Sometimes we do not. Obviously, Gary suffered greatly, both professionally and personally, due to his addiction. Called before the Bar. Disbarred. Substance use playing a key role in the decisions that led to those consequences. He's gone now, and he no longer has the chance to move beyond addiction and fully reclaim his life. I miss him.

I know several lawyers who have been disciplined with drugs, alcohol, and other mental-health issues playing a direct role in their problems brought before the Bar. Gary's story is one example. Yes, it's possible that the consequences of drug or alcohol use can include disciplinary action through the Bar and even the end of legal careers. But as we've seen from some of the stories already shared by attorneys in this book, sometimes even significant consequences can be a springboard to positive change. To better understand the risks and consequences of alcohol and drug use on legal careers, I reached out to someone who has extensive experience in this area and has seen both the devastation and redemption firsthand.

I first "met" Brian Tannebaum through social media, much the same as I met my law school application expert Ann Levine. Though we got to know each other through Twitter, eventually Brian and I met in person and became good friends. I contacted him because he's a highly respected attorney who has experience defending attorneys who've been called before the Bar for disciplinary issues, including those who have ties to drug and alcohol use. Brian is also the author of the Amazon bestselling book, *The Practice*. I think his answers are illuminating regardless of one's profession.

In your experience, what are the three biggest mistakes lawyers make with regards to substance use that put their licenses at risk?

The three biggest mistakes lawyers make with regards to substance use that puts their licenses at risk are:

1. The Obvious, Not Seeking Help

Lawyers have egos. Lawyers like to show the world that "things are good," "business is great," "all is wonderful." The truth is often quite the opposite. For someone like me who represents lawyers in disciplinary matters, I'm no longer shocked when that successful-looking lawyer is actually addicted to cocaine, or the one in the paper all the time for the large verdicts is actually drinking in her office every day.

Admitting there is a problem is the last thing Type A personality lawyers want to do, but it is the first thing they should do. Seeking help is not the same as taking out an ad in the local paper. A lawyer should first investigate what programs exist through his or her state Bar to allow them to have a confidential drug or alcohol evaluation. In Florida, where I practice, we have Florida Lawyers Assistance, Inc. They evaluate lawyers and provide counseling and treatment, if necessary—and it's all confidential. Getting treatment before a judge, a colleague, or worse, a police officer takes note of the problem and can save a lawyer's license and life.

Oftentimes, though, lawyers don't trust the confidentiality of these types of services (although they should). In that case, the lawyer should tell a friend. If the lawyer is concerned about confidentiality, tell another lawyer and seek advice from that lawyer. The stress of thinking about telling someone will be quickly quelled by the reaction received—but the lawyer has to be willing to accept help.

2. Trying to Hide the Problem by Lying to Clients, Courts, Their Colleagues, and Opposing Counsel

It's not always easy to figure out that a lawyer has a substance use problem. Lawyers always seek more time to prepare and file pleadings, ask for continuances of hearings, seek to reschedule hearings, and in one word, try to *delay* the inevitable. These types of responses from lawyers wouldn't indicate a problem. How can you tell? It's subtle.

Deadlines pass without any response. The lawyer said you would have the documents yesterday. Three days have gone by with no communication. Emails and other forms of communication come at odd times—in the middle of the night. The lawyer will contend that they didn't understand the response requested, or (falsely) claim that something terrible has happened. The terrible thing will be general in nature—"I had a problem with my kid..." After a series of excuses and unusual behaviors, it becomes a point of concern, and possibly a time to confront the lawyer.

The worst part of this is that when the problem is discovered, it creates a lack of trust from supervising partners, opposing counsel, judges, and clients. While there may be some initial sympathy and understanding, those who have been lied to will question their future relationship with the lawyer. I've dealt with multiple cases of the pain-pill addicted lawyer whose problems started with an opiate prescription after a surgery.

There is a difference between not disclosing the addiction and lying. Addicts, for understandable reasons, lie. The hardest thing is convincing someone struggling with addiction that telling the truth is their best choice.

3. Bringing the Addiction into the Courtroom or Office

I have had clients so deep into their addictions that they have had drugs sent to their law firms by mail. And when I say clients, plural, I mean to say this has happened more than once. I have smelled alcohol on lawyers while standing behind them in court. Secretaries have told me of their former bosses drinking every day in the office.

Once the addiction is brought into the office or the courtroom—or both—the profession, and the Bar, become less sympathetic. A lawyer who is battling addiction and who seeks treatment prior to affecting clients will receive every benefit the profession and the Bar can offer. Once the lawyer misses court, disrupts a court proceeding by being under the influence, or otherwise causes harm to a client, it elevates the situation to a point where the lawyer's addiction may not save them from serious discipline.

Brian's advice for lawyers with a history of alcohol or substance use is not all that different from Ann Levine's advice for prospective law students with addiction histories—a lack of honesty leads to greater risks.

For better or worse, however, those risks don't always lead to immediate consequences. For many of us who engage in behavior that imperils our careers, our freedom, our relationships, and even our lives, we learn from our near scrapes—but not the right lessons. Instead of learning that we need to change our behaviors, we learn that we can get away with them. Instead of learning that we need to be honest with ourselves, our colleagues, and our families, we learn that we have a chance to maintain those relationships by concealing our problems.

15

Hollywood Nights and Hungover Days

■ **June 1991**

I'VE GOT A litigation mediation in Los Angeles coming up for a major trucking accident case about to go to trial. Though the trial is serious business, traveling to a place like LA is one of the enjoyable parts of being a litigation manager with Transport Insurance. It means I can get some sun on the beach, eat some great food, and party. First, I have to make my plans. The defense counsel is a nice guy with a great office in Burbank. I'll fly there instead of the mess that is LAX and the spaghetti knot of freeways around it. I'll get in Thursday, do the mediation Friday morning, stay over through Saturday night, and head back to Dallas on Sunday. Leave just enough time to get in a long run on the beach if I'm not too hungover.

All my plans are set, except the most important one to me: I need to call my friend Trevor. He's in the film business but works behind the camera, despite being a ridiculously good-looking guy. With long blond hair and a little stubble, he's the spitting image of Patrick Swayze's surfer bandit character in *Point Break*. He loves to tell the story of also being confused with actor Peter Horton of

Thirtysomething fame and asked on a date by actress Marlee Matlin. *Yes, I get it Trevor, you can date Marlee; I can't. Story of my life.* But that's OK because I'm happy to learn at the feet of the master. Trevor used to live in Dallas, and I love hanging with him there because he always has drugs, and he always has good-looking girls hanging around. I reach Trent on the phone, and soon we're getting down to brass tacks. I make it clear as I can that I'd love to hit the clubs with him and our mutual friend (an 8-ball of coke, of course), and he lets me know that can be arranged.

I make it into Burbank Airport without incident. I'm close enough to my hotel and the meeting, which will be ten o'clock the next morning. But what am I supposed to do, study my case files and go to sleep at a reasonable hour? I think not. I've made plans—no reason to wait for Friday night when my work is done. Trent's place in Venice Beach is much closer to LAX. *Oh well,* I think. *I'll brave LA traffic for this.*

I promise myself I won't party *too* hard. But I know moderation isn't always my strong suit. While driving down to Trevor's, I briefly flash back to the weeks before I got my job at Transport Insurance. I knew they were going to do a drug test. I gave up coke cold turkey and spent seemingly endless days drinking gallons of water, ingesting every detox potion and magic elixir that other addicts promised would purify my system, and running to "sweat it out." Giving all that up for a few days was like going to live in a monastery to me, but it was worth it. I passed that test without any alarms going off over possible coke, weed, or other illicit substances in my system. *Now that I've made it through the gates,* I think, *I'm free. As long as I don't get caught with the Tony Montana mountain of coke on my desk at work, I'll be fine.*

Sure, I could wait until my work was done to party. But why? I'm young, single (OK, recently divorced), finally have some money to spend, and I'm in freaking LA. Besides, the hearing should be a breeze: the settlement range is set, and the defense counsel is ready to try the case. Being at the top of my game Friday morning is not required. But if I'm going to be able to hang with Trevor, then I definitely need to be on the top of my "game." And I'm feeling ready. I'm driving through terrible traffic in a rare Southern California rainstorm, but I'm focused. *Neither rain, nor snow, nor heat, nor gloom of night will keep me from my appointed rounds of tequila and blow.*

One and a half hours later, I'm at Trevor's door. We hug like two guys might who haven't seen each other in a while, and whose entire friendship was based around one-hitters, cut straws, mini strainers, and white powder. In other words, it's a little awkward. I'm impatient.

"So you got it?"

"Follow me." Trevor leads me back to his bedroom.

He's exceeded my expectations. On his dresser is a happy mountain of blow.

"Trevor, thanks man!" I'm practically jumping up and down like a child at Christmas.

"Of course, Brian! Hey, what are friends for?" We just stare at the pile for a moment, then he puts his hand on my shoulder. "I'll just need $200 from you."

"Two hundred dollars! Damn, you left that part out on the phone! What happened to the hospitality of friends?"

He can't believe my response and laughs at me. "Brian, the hospitality of friends is that I got it for you. I told you I'd take care of you, and I did. Friendship doesn't apply to paying for this shit."

I sigh. "OK, man. Let's go find an ATM, and I'll pay you."

"Cool. I also don't really feel like hitting the clubs tonight. Hey, let's just stay here and party. I'll make some calls and get some of my girlfriends over. Maybe we can get them to play some strip poker." He laughs a conspiratorial laugh and goes to get his shoes.

Wait. Strip poker? Is that a joke?

"I even know some girls who love to play strip Trivial Pursuit," he calls down the hall. *That's a thing?* Doesn't matter. It's all the same to me. I'm not taking my clothes off for a group unless I am about to be operated on by a team of top surgeons, and only then if it's to prevent imminent death. Then the light bulb goes on. The solution to my confidence problem is right in front of me. A pile of cocaine that could make me feel self-assured enough to do a strip-tease across the letters of the Hollywood sign. Okay, maybe not quite that confident. Trevor comes back and offers up a hit of a joint. I look at him, perplexed. *Not the feeling I'm chasing, dude.* I hover over the pile and then dive in.

It's midnight. The cocaine mountain is now more of a cocaine hill, and the bottle Jack Daniel's is spent. Still, no women have shown up. Trevor puts on a Doors record. "LA Woman" has been going through my head all day. Now it's playing in a bungalow in Venice Beach. The cheesiness of the whole thing escapes me, as have the LA women themselves. I don't care.

Finally, a knock at the door. At last, an LA woman. One. We all chat for a minute, but it's late, and there's no more talk of games. Trevor leans over the pile of cocaine, splits it down the middle with a credit card, and retires to his room with the female visitor. I breathe a huge sigh of relief. It doesn't matter that I've spent hours sitting alone in a living room with a guy I don't know that well making awkward small talk about movies. *I partied in LA! I'm a rock star. I'm free.* I finish my pile, and it's now almost six o'clock on Friday morning. My mediation is at 10 a.m. Trevor's asleep with his LA woman, so I leave quietly to start the long drive back.

No more songs going through my head. My heart starts racing from the cocaine come-down. I'm sweating and smell awful. Depressed. A very familiar feeling. The knowledge that nothing has changed. Cocaine and booze didn't change me into a new person. What they did was wear off, leaving a pit of seeming bottomless despair deep in my gut for as long as I'm sober. The despair of failure in career and in life. Going into a situation looking for the high. Leaving unable to bear the low.

I'm suddenly angry at what I've done and will probably do again. A rare moment of self-awareness. *A dull night, and an expensive one too*, I think. Then I remember: I never gave Trevor his two-hundred bucks. *Hey, he should have told me over the phone how much he was buying. Now I still have money to party later tonight.*

As I walked into the mediation in LA, my mind drifted to a line from the movie *Less Than Zero*. The character played by Andrew McCarthy says to his girlfriend, "You're fucked up, you look like shit, but all you need is a better cut of cocaine." Reeking of alcohol, unable to breathe from all the cocaine I snorted, I probably looked as if I'd spent the night on Skid Row, but I felt that as long as I could sit there and nod along, I'd be fine. It never occurred to me that getting fired for not showing up might not be the only consequence I had to fear. My reputation was at stake as well, but that wasn't something I cared much about. That professional colleagues might notice I showed up to morning meetings reeking of Jack Daniels and with bloodshot eyes bugging out of my head wasn't an issue to me. That those same colleagues might talk to other colleagues about my appearance and inability to concentrate during an important mediation was a worry that never crossed my mind. I'd fooled the Bar. I'd fooled the drug tests. I'd snuck by the police. I simply didn't believe in consequences.

Those consequences did come, though. A year after my trip to LA, I ended up in the back of a police cruiser in Dallas for suspicion of DWI. I remember the feeling of relief a couple of days later when I admitted to my boss what had happened, and he didn't fire me on the spot. I remember acting like it was a one-time slip and out of character for me. My boss didn't say anything to contradict my illusion that I had things under control. But there's no doubt my reputation as unreliable was growing by the day, whether it was the DWI, showing up for mediations coked up and disheveled, not getting to the sites of accidents on time because I was too drunk or high, or just not turning in good work. I figured as long as my career didn't end in a bang, I was fine. I was never bothered by the fear that it might end in a whimper. And when my boss finally called me into his office in 1993 to tell me he was disappointed in my performance, I was ready to resign on the spot. The truth was, I'd rather start over than have to explain (if it wasn't obvious already) why my performance had lagged.

I had my priorities set by addiction, and career advancement wasn't near the top. Out of necessity, I started my private practice, and that allowed me to make my own hours without fear of being exposed to my boss. But I couldn't work and hide from the world completely. I still needed clients to pay the bills, and so for years I managed to cobble together a series of soft-tissue injury cases, of-counsel assignments, and even a short stint back at an insurance place. I was only unhappy with my career trajectory when I didn't have the income to support my habits. Otherwise, I was glad to not have the scrutiny of long-standing colleagues to contend with. When my stint with the insurance company ended, I was once more looking for ways to survive. I'd long given up on personal injury work, which had dried up. Once again, my brother Mark would come to the rescue.

■ December 28, 1999

I'm working out at the Premier Club, the local place-to-be-seen singles oriented health club in Dallas. It also happens to be the place where I meet my cocaine dealer in the darkness of the underground parking garage, or buy my ecstasy from one of the personal trainers in a quick "between sets" hand-to-hand exchange. In fact, I have an appointment with the coke dealer later in the underground garage.

My brother Mark also works out at the Premier. He loves to play pickup basketball. I see him occasionally, and when I do, we chit-chat about family and what's going on in each other's lives. I always chuckle when people assume we talk about the Xs and Os of NBA basketball, the latest tech public offering, or a possible presidential bid. Nope, we do what my father stressed so many years ago. We make sure the other brother is doing OK, the kids are happy and OK. It's all about family. Today, I don't have anything great to report if I run into my brother. I'm not happy. I'm not OK. My life is in chaos.

Eight months earlier, I'd been living in a hotel in Pittsburgh as Mark's point man in trying to negotiate his buying an interest in the local NHL hockey franchise, the Pittsburgh Penguins. That ended when Mark decided not to do the deal, which was a disappointment to me. I'd envisioned moving back to Pittsburgh and playing a part in the franchise. I'd be the fat "dumb bunny" high school and law school reject returning as the conquering hero in helping to prevent the bankrupt Penguins from leaving the city. I'd be coming home just like Sandy Frink (played by Alan Cumming) had in *Romy And Michelle's High School Reunion*. Everyone I ever knew in Pittsburgh would see me coming in my helicopter: "Hey everyone, Brian Cuban's landing! C'mon!" Of course unlike the character Sandy Frink, who had made a fortune inventing a special kind of rubber used in tennis shoes, I'd done nothing impressive to deserve that kind of homecoming. I'd accomplished nothing other than sharing a name with someone who was becoming famous.

After the Pittsburgh Penguins bid fell through, I'd taken a job as a claims manager with a local non-standard auto insurance company (insurance for high-risk drivers, including specialized vehicles and those drivers who have been in numerous accidents). I was kind of "running home to mama" with work I knew I could do. I hated that type of non-standard auto work, but I needed a job, since my private practice had stalled. And hey, I made a little more than I'd ever made as a solo practitioner, not that it was very much. Unfortunately, shortly after I took the position, the company went bankrupt amidst allegations of securities violations and ultimately went into receivership. I'd been without a regular income for months.

Now I'm unemployed, scared, and looking for a lifeline. Without work, the only healthy outlet I have is exercise, so this is one of many trips to the Premier. My credit cards are just about maxed out, and I'm terrified of having no more funds for my *unhealthy* outlets. As I'm standing there with a towel around my neck, staring blankly at the row of lockers and trying to decide if my dealer will trade coke for unsolicited legal advice, I feel a hand on my shoulder. It's Mark.

"Hey Bri, how's it going? I'm glad I ran into you." He has a big smile on his face, and I suddenly have the feeling he'll come to the rescue, as he has so many times before.

"Everything's good." I shrug. "Still trying to find a job." Well, that's partly true, anyway. Not much is good in my life at the moment. But neither my brother nor the rest of my family knows anything about my descent into addiction or my eating disorder. As long as I can maintain that illusion, things are good enough.

"Listen, Brian, I have some big news, but it hasn't been made public yet so you have to keep it a secret." Mark is a guy who often has big news, but I can tell this is going to be a whopper from the look on his face. He leans in close. "I just bought the Dallas Mavericks. It'll be announced in a few days." He's amped. I've spent time with Mark at Mavericks games and know all about his enthusiasm for the team, so I know how much this means to him.

"Mark, that's awesome, congratulations!"

"And listen, Brian, if you haven't found a job yet, you can come work for me." I breathe a deep sigh of relief. I tell him I'll "think about it," but there's nothing to think about. I've just been tossed my lifeline. I am "somebody" again.

■ **January 6, 2000**

Time for my doctor's appointment. It turns out I have an irregular heartbeat. Up until now, I didn't know there was such a thing as atrial fibrillation. My mind races. *Maybe I should cut back on the coke? Or is this a gift from decades of binging and purging? Couldn't have anything to do with all the exercise, right?* Doctor McNulty does not know about any of my habits. I won't be checking those boxes in the questionnaire. I'm feeling low as I fill out additional paper-work. The receptionist looks at my questionnaire. She looks at me and then down at it again.

"Are you related to Mark Cuban, the new owner of the Mavericks?"

"Yes, I'm his brother."

"Wow! We're so happy that you and your brother bought the team. Can I have your autograph?" She blushes a little and looks at me like she's just met a movie star. My mood picks up a bit.

The announcement of Mark buying the Dallas Mavericks is only a few days old, and I've already had my own business cards printed up with the Dallas Mavericks logo on them. The card reads, "Brian Cuban, Corporate Counsel." OK, I hadn't really been given that position, but let's just say I was eager to experiment with new possi-bilities. I sheepishly brought out one of those cards and signed the back. The wheels of shame started turning. *Someone wants my auto-graph? She thinks I'm a co-owner of the team with Mark?* No reason to tell her otherwise. *Someone's interested in me. Someone cares about me!* It's only name fame, but it's *my* last name too, and I like it.

As my illegible signature takes form, I feel a sudden high. It's almost the same feeling as that first hit of coke way back at the Cres-cent Hotel. A little like the feeling of running for hours and getting away from all my problems. It's almost like a feeling of acceptance, like the fantasy of returning home in a helicopter come true. For a moment, I'm no longer ashamed. I'm no longer a thirteen-year-old, fat, bullied little boy. I'm a Cuban. Someone special.

After my brother bought the Mavericks, I was no longer just Brian. I was Brian *Cuban,* someone with a name that needed to be reckoned with. Now I could journey into the social and nightlife world of Dallas with my new identity and false sense of self-worth. Free drinks. Free cocaine. No waiting in nightclub lines. Coke wasn't something I had to save up for and purchase furtively in a dank gym garage. It was just another daily perk of being me. Girls, who in my mind, would not give the real Brian the time of day, suddenly couldn't wait to talk to me. I started cycling through relationships just as fast as I could hand out my fake business card. Frankly, my identity as "Mark's brother" made me suddenly one of the biggest knuckleheads on the Dallas social scene. Part of me was very ashamed because I knew I was a fraud. I wanted so badly to just be who I really was, but was terrified that everyone would see exactly what I saw in the mirror. Then I'd be totally alone.

Suddenly, I had a self-imposed burden to manage that I'd never had before: the burden of a public reputation. Sure, I had a social circle. I knew plenty of people in Dallas, and they'd known me. But as a lawyer, I could barely force myself to care about the impression my work and behavior might make on clients and colleagues. If they spoke of me out of earshot, I couldn't care less. But this was different. Everything I had now, everything new and exciting that was coming my way, was all because of the reputation afforded by my name.

My sudden name fame not only provided more opportunity for me to feed my drug and alcohol use, but it was also an obstacle to confronting my problems and seeking help. In this way, I understand attorneys who risk so much out of fear of the damage admitting addiction might do to their reputations. Of course it's irrational; we're all much more likely to wreck our lives by allowing addiction to progress than in confronting it. There is a saying, "No one ever ruined their life by getting sober." But when your whole sense of who you are is mixed up with your standing in the community, when you feel the pressure of so many expecting so much from you, it's easy to view seeking help as a risk.

None of that was Mark's or anyone else's fault. Many in this world have someone in their family who has achieved various levels of fame and dealt with it in a healthy manner. My self-image has been and will always be my responsibility, and my reputation has always been that of my own making. My recovery has always been and will always be my responsibility. It took me years of sobriety and therapy to realize that.

But back in 2000, I had no sense that I was damaging my reputation to the point where my career was unlikely to recover any time soon. I saw myself as still climbing to the top. Shortly after purchasing the Mavericks, Mark entrusted me as his point person for the construction of the soon-to-be-opened American Airlines Center (AAC), which would be the new home of the Mavericks, and in which Mark had an equity interest. My responsibilities entailed sitting in on construction meetings, taking notes, and reporting back to Mark with anything I thought he should know. It was a high-profile position sitting in with high-profile people also involved in the construction of the new arena.

It was important work that should have pushed me to excel and open up new doors to my professional future. Unfortunately, as often happens when addiction meets work life, the Peter Principle came into play. My level of competence and caring was limited, causing me to work up to only my very low expectations and not worry about anyone else's.

I'd often show up hungover after partying all night. Sometimes I was still a little tipsy. More than a few times, I had not showered in days and smelled like a cologne factory. There were very few days when I offered anything to the process other than body odor and booze vapors coming from my corner of the conference table.

Soon, Mark moved me off the arena project. He had a new venture that he wanted my help with: HDnet (now AXS TV). HDnet was a cable television network that would use high-definition technology. In my new role, I would not be asked for legal advice. I was asked to roll up my sleeves and do whatever was needed to be done to keep a small new company growing. This was Mark's philosophy as an ultra-successful entrepreneur. Job titles do not build companies. Hardworking people do. It could have been like a career rebirth. It was not. As was the case when I packed boxes at Micro Solutions, I was more concerned with surviving in my present than looking at the big picture of my future. The present involved drinking, drugs, clubs, and ego. The present was simply repeating self-destructive cycles.

At first, my job at HDnet was to deliver state-of-the-art (at the time) high-definition television sets that we sold at a discount to those who signed up for the HDnet service. My brother Jeff and I would deliver the sets ourselves to the various bars around Dallas. We'd set them up, just like the Best Buy people. I knew nothing about HD televisions, cable connections, and other types of video tech stuff that was part of hooking up the televisions, but Jeff and I learned fast and became pretty adept at it. I could probably make a house call and set up your television if you needed me to.

My strongest memory from that time was on September 11, 2001. Every generation has those moments when you remember exactly where you were when a national tragedy occurred. On September 11 at 8:45 a.m., I was driving down Central Expressway in Dallas on my way to work for HDnet when the news came over the radio. HDnet was five days old at the time. After we watched the events unfold in horror in the office, Mark instructed my brother and me to grab a high-definition video camera and cover whatever press conferences were announced in Dallas. The first one would be the FBI conference the next day.

Jeff and I drove to the FBI building with a complex shoulder-mounted camera that neither of us really knew how to use. We dealt with our own shock and grief and talked about the surreal vision of the lack of airplanes in the sky due to the nationwide flight ban. We were such video novices that a legitimate camera operator there to cover the event for a local news station had to show us how to use our own equipment. I mounted the camera on my shoulder with my press pass hanging around my neck and pressed RECORD. On that day I felt important. I didn't care about my job description. I'd have worn that press pass around town all day if I could. I was doing something worthy. But it was only one day. I eventually left HDnet and transitioned back into private practice—a replay of my time working at Micro Solutions. I saw myself as a lawyer. I didn't want to ship videotapes and deliver televisions. With Mark there were no job titles. There were only entrepreneurial types working for the greater good of the company, doing whatever needed to be done whether it was boxing up computers or installing televisions. However, there was not one entrepreneurial gene in my body. Whichever parent he got that from, it completely bypassed me. I had no interest and was more about the assumed status of being a lawyer.

As the years went on, I'd continue to work, take some legal cases, but my career, and my professional reputation, were in shambles. It happened slowly, imperceptibly, but the consequences had finally caught up with me.

The very first step is admitting to ourselves that there's a problem. It's often the hardest step. The most frightening. But after that, the professionals such as attorneys may feel that resolving their addiction problems while maintaining their careers is like walking a tightrope. Get caught concealing the truth from others, and our integrity is at stake. Open up about our problems, and our employers or colleagues might wonder if we're stable and competent enough to handle our jobs. But should fear of exposing our vulnerabilities guide our actions? To better understand what attorneys should do once they've resolved to face their issues, I reached out once again to Brian Tannebaum.

Based on your experience, what are the three most important things a lawyer who is struggling can do to put himself/herself in the best position to continue practicing law, even if there are temporary consequences?

There may always be temporary consequences, but there are three steps worth taking for lawyers struggling with addiction and hoping to hold onto their jobs:

Tell Someone, and Be Open to Help

As I said before, the first step is to tell *someone*. Tell someone at the Bar's drug and alcohol arm, or a fellow lawyer, your spouse, a priest, rabbi—*someone*. So much of my counseling of clients involves how or when or even whether they are going to tell someone other than me. I understand the struggle of admitting the addiction, but I also have seen the sheer relief after the admission. "They were so welcoming," "understanding," "he told me he had a problem a while back." I've never heard that the reaction was criticism, or judgment, or anger. I'm not saying there are not those out there that are not equipped to understand addiction, but in my experience, the response has been, "Let me help you" in almost every case.

But it's not just making the admission. The lawyer has to be willing to address the problem. I can't stress enough the importance of addressing the problem before it starts to affect the practice. Harming clients by negligent legal work, or stealing trust funds, or worse, placing the addiction at the whim of the public through an arrest, results in sometimes irreparable destruction.

Addressing the problem starts with one of two things, depending on the severity of the addiction—detox or an evaluation. Sometimes if the lawyer is not ready for an evaluation or questions the value of one (mostly due to denial) an AA or NA meeting is a good start. Many state Bars have lawyer-only AA or NA meetings. That may not be something the lawyer wants to attend, so in that case a general AA or NA meeting is fine.

Understand that State Bars Are Open to Helping a Lawyer Whose Ethical Lapses Are Tied to Some Type of Recognized Problem Such as Drug and Alcohol Addiction

I often tell clients that state Bars have long stopped being organizations to help lawyers. They are now consumer protection agencies designed to protect clients, with large amounts of resources going to discipline. Bars will, however, still offer assistance to lawyers in a few ways, and one such way is helping those with substance problems. There are limits, though. If the substance problem results in significant harm to a client, it may be too late, or if help is available it often comes with discipline.

While tying an ethical lapse to a substance problem can mitigate level of discipline in some cases, the lawyer is always in a worse position if the substance-abuse problem comes to the Bar's attention by way of a complaint from a client, judge, or an arrest.

Know That Temporary Consequences Are Always Better Than Permanent Consequences—Such as Disbarment, Divorce, or Death

Addiction can cause the loss of a job, marriage, savings, liberty, and life. When a lawyer is addicted, the license is always in play, but there is much more that goes through the mind of an addicted lawyer. Lawyers often identify their existence with their profession. I have had lawyers tell me that "There's nothing else I can do if I lose my license." Although this isn't true, as plenty of people with law degrees go on to do other professions, perception is reality.

This is not to say that the addicted lawyer is more important than anyone else, but when a professional license is in jeopardy, the risks of addiction for the attorney include the loss of a career, reputation, identity, and everything that comes with it. While a twenty-year partner at a law firm may make $500,000 a year, when the next job is as a $50,000-a-year paralegal role due to addiction and disbarment, life changes in more ways than just a different job title.

What I frequently see, though, are lawyers resistant to any form of sanctions for their ethical lapses due to addiction or substance use problems. Although there is an obvious answer to "What would you rather have—disbarment, or a short suspension?" often lawyers are so resistant to admit a problem that they believe there is a legitimate fight to be mounted against the confirmation of an ethical lapse where there is proof of professional problems due to drug or alcohol use. The reason is simple. Agreeing to a sanction is a confession of a problem, or that the problem has resulted in real harm.

My goal is always to surround the lawyer with good and respected advice. This is often difficult because not only does the lawyer often not want others to know, but the lawyer representing the lawyer is bound by the attorney-client privilege. I attempt to make my lawyer-clients understand that surrounding themselves with trusted friends, trusted colleagues, and caring family members is a positive. If they can achieve this, then when it's time to discuss sanctions, the lawyer and lawyer-client can discuss this in a "big-tent" type atmosphere. Oftentimes the addicted lawyer will listen to the advice of their lawyer, but seek decision-making advice from others. If everyone is talking to each other, answering each other's questions, the lawyer-client has a wealth of resources from which to make a decision of how to address the Bar.

In Florida where you practice, what power does the Bar have to force a lawyer into treatment/counseling? What power might Florida or other Bars have to compel counseling of a prospective lawyer before issuing a license if he/she has passed the Bar?[17]

For admitted lawyers, if the lawyer is under investigation for anything and drugs or alcohol is part of the issue, the Bar can request an evaluation, and if the lawyer agrees, then the lawyer also has to agree to accept any recommendations of the evaluation (counseling, AA, other treatment). The Bar cannot force an evaluation, but if the lawyer refuses, the Bar could seek an interim suspension if it determines the lawyer is a danger to himself/herself or others.

As for applicants, the rights are different. You don't have a license yet, so the Board of Bar Examiners can order you to enter into a contract with Florida Lawyers Assistance for a period of up to five years. It's called "conditional admission." If you refuse, you are entitled to seek a hearing on that recommendation, but that is terribly risky.

This is all great advice for those who have come to realize they have a problem that needs addressing. But as discussed above, it can be easy to avoid admitting a problem exists, especially in the absence of some single, life-altering crisis. Sometimes that crisis might come through work, such as an employer realizing that an attorney is mismanaging funds. But for me, and for perhaps many others, that moment comes not through work, but through our personal lives. It can be hardest to admit our problems to those who truly love us, but in many ways, the consequences can be more dire than the loss of a career when we're not honest with those who love and support us.

16

Many Women, One Love:
Rock Bottom Is Relational

■ Summer 2005

I'M AT A strip joint—the Dallas Men's Club. I'm trying to figure out why. I look at the couple next to me, "friends" I've met out partying after a Mavs game at the American Airlines Center's Jack Daniel's Club. It's not uncommon for me to close the club down to celebrate a Mavs victory. Or to mourn a loss. Whatever the outcome, it's always a good occasion to party. My new friends are getting a lap dance and having a great time. They brought me to the club, telling me how much they loved strip clubs. I don't love strip clubs. I find them depressing. Strippers make me remember all the pretty girls who scorned me when I was young. In the back of my mind, I'm always afraid that if I don't give them money, the dancers might reveal their true feelings about me. They'll laugh and shout out loud that I'm ugly, just like one pretty brown-haired girl did my freshman year at Penn State. Core anxieties are triggered for me at these places.

But I didn't say no to my new friends. As always, I want to prove I'm capable of having a good time.

This was certainly not the first time I've been to a strip club. I'd gone occasionally, especially with other lawyers. *Why do male lawyers love strip-clubs?* I'd hear it all from my colleagues. "Well, I have to entertain the clients. That's where they want to go." *Yeah right...* "They have a great lunch buffet." *So does Golden Corral.* (Yes, I admit I love Golden Corral.) "I'm networking!" *The Bar Association does not have enough networking groups for you?* The reasons are as varied and long as the nighttime hours spent and the dollars stuffed.

I've no judgments of the employees or participants. I'm the last person who should cast stones, due to the extreme fragility of my own glass house. I'm only sitting there wondering because I can't figure out why I keep ending up at these places. I always spend most of my time staring awkwardly at the floor.

"Do you want a lap dance?" A woman's feet have come into my field of vision.

I can only respond with a blank stare. *Where should my eyes be? What's most polite in this situation?*

"Twenty dollars for a dance."

My eyes are focused on the mystery stain on the floor in front of me. I notice the smell of perfume, alcohol, drunks. The sound of the crowd noise and the blaring dubstep. I won't look her in the eye. I can't. It's a mirror into my shame. Not shame at what she is doing. It's my shame in being here despite not enjoying it. Deeper than that, it's the shame of knowing that I'm lying to myself, telling myself that I'm outgoing, the life of the party, a desirable man. When I'm really high, I can pretend that a beautiful woman offering me a lap dance is because I'm wanted. The cocaine helps me do that, but the cocaine isn't enough tonight. I can't pretend I'm having fun.

I feel my head swaying back and forth. I can't speak, only shake my head to tell her I'm not interested. That mystery stain on the strip club carpet is suddenly like my best friend. It's like my reflection. The feet move out of my field of vision. She's moved on to another guy.

I try to think back to the last time I had a lap dance. Can't even remember. That's not why I come. *So why am I here?* I'd rather be drunk and high at my tiny apartment, alone.

I suddenly remember the first time I went to a strip club, my first lap dance, and I lose myself in memories. The bachelor party for my first marriage. I remember how embarrassed I was that day. I was unable to look the young lady in the eye as my friends showered her with dollar bills to give me lap dances. Like this moment, my eyes were fixed on the carpeted floor. Nothing had changed in eighteen years. Even if she didn't know me, to look into the eyes of the woman would be to expose myself in the most vulnerable of ways. To allow her to see right through me. The ugliness. The self-loathing. Even the rational thoughts from a legally trained mind would not penetrate the ugliness I saw in myself.

Suddenly I realize that my actual romantic relationships follow the same pattern. I pretend to be the life of the party, but ultimately I won't let my partners truly look into my eyes. I'm afraid of what they'll see.

As I look back on my time at strip clubs and nightclubs, my time there was the epitome of what psychologists call "narcissistic object choice." Basically, seeking companions that offer the most flattering "mirror" into our lives. When I was younger, I sought out relationships that would confirm the story I liked to tell about myself—that I was successful, that I was fun, that I was the life of the party. This went far beyond visiting strip clubs for validation or trying to pick up women at the bars. Even in long-term relationships, I sought out women who wouldn't challenge the fragile narrative I'd constructed that I was a healthy, successful guy who just liked to have a good time. Of course, those relationships were based on keeping my real feelings and insecurities secret, and perhaps it's no surprise that none of them lasted.

■ **December 1990**

Driving home from work. Listening to music. The Righteous Brothers "Unchained Melody" starts playing. The song is on the radio a bunch these days thanks to the movie *Ghost*, which was released a few months earlier. I now know the words by heart. I am softly singing along. Once again, the tears start. I'm bawling, and soon I have to pull over. I start screaming at the top of my lungs. "I'm sorry! I am so sorry! Don't leave!"

It doesn't matter. She's gone. We're still in the same house, but she's gone. Divorce is imminent, but I can't accept it. I've never known so much pain. I've never known such intense grief. The grief of failure. The grief of loss. Divorce is loss. The confusion of not understanding why she didn't love me anymore. I'd never told anyone I loved them before. She was the first woman I'd dated who had ever said she loved me. *"I love you."* Magic words to me. The words of acceptance. The words that told me someone saw more than I saw in myself. The most important words in the world to me. As I let go of everything on the side of the road, those words seemed like ages ago. Like they never happened.

We'd met at a bar a little over a year after I got to Dallas. My favorite hangout, Fast and Cool. I was drunk and high when we met—cocaine was giving me all sorts of new confidence with women. Cocaine had become part of my social survival kit, along with my fake diamond earring. Whatever look I was trying to pull off, it seemed to work with her. She told me I looked like Bruce Springsteen. She liked that I walked her to her car and asked permission to kiss her. I loved her West Texas accent. A sharp contrast to my Yankee Pittsburgh accent, and having her interested in me made me feel like I belonged in Dallas. When I gave her an alcohol-aided goodnight kiss, she was only the third woman I'd kissed romantically in my life.

We were married in 1988. We hadn't been dating long. Sure, we could have waited longer and gotten to know each other better, but for me at least, that wasn't necessarily a desirable outcome. When she looked into my eyes, I could tell she was looking at someone she admired. That meant the world to me. I wasn't going to blow that by letting her get close enough to see who I really was. I hid my coke use from her. I hid my eating disorder from her. I never told her what it was like for me to look in the mirror. All that would only complicate the one important truth of our relationship: *She actually likes me.*

Our early marriage was a continuation of our first date in many ways. We'd go out drinking together. But perhaps for both of us, young as we were, and as little as we'd actually come to know each other, the "going out" part was far more important than the "together" part. She had more and more girls' nights out at the country bars. Not my thing. I was having more and more guys' nights out at the coke clubs. She didn't know what I was doing. I thought that was for the best. I'd never learned how to allow myself to be loved. Not only did I want to protect my secrets, I wanted to protect myself from knowing what my own wife thought of me, of our relationship. In my mind, if I ever opened up to her or sought to talk about feelings, she'd reveal the truth of who I was—a fat, ugly little boy.

■ February 1991

The last time we're together as a married couple. We're in her car in the parking lot of the Blue Goose Cantina. We've been separated since January. I moved in with my brother Mark, who once again is there for me. Our meeting at the Blue Goose is about finally having a talk about how we really feel. There's so much I could say, so much I should say if I want to keep her, but she speaks first. She pulls out a handwritten note. "Brian, I've made a list of the pros and cons of our marriage. I miss the comfort of being with you. I miss the security. I, however, don't miss you. I want a divorce."

Days later, the moment I've been dreading. She's coming to my office at Transport Insurance with the papers. The office phone rings. It rings again. I almost let it go to voicemail. It doesn't matter anymore. Avoidance won't bring her back. She's at the front reception desk with her mother. The fifty-foot walk to the reception area seems like three football fields. My legs feel like they are encased in lead. They don't want to move. Look at the floor—one foot in front of the other. I don't want to do it in the lobby. I don't want to cry in the lobby. I don't want my failure to be in the lobby. We walk out to the car. I sign the papers. I don't want to, but I believe that if I am agreeable, she will reconsider. She's crying. In sixty days, it'll be over. I walk back to my office and shut my door. I think of the Righteous Brothers again. I start to cry. I'm convinced no one will ever love me again.

If there was an upside to my first divorce, it was that it was the first time I'd ever thought about the possibility of therapy, even if my motives were a little misguided. Through the tears and pain, I hatched a plan to get her back. I'd go to marital counseling. If I showed her I was trying to be a better husband, she'd join me in counseling, and we'd reconcile before the divorce was final.

I was broke but I did have health insurance, so I scoured the providers available for those providing marital counseling. It was slim pickings. I finally found a Christian-based counselor. Because I was Jewish, he was not the ideal choice for me, but was better than nothing and would serve the purpose of showing my awareness of the error of my ways. My wife was in the Church of Christ, so I thought that the religious element would be a plus in getting her to join me.

I drove the twenty miles to the counselor in Duncanville, Texas, projecting out the fantasy I needed to hang onto. I continued to see the counselor for about three weeks until it became clear that my wife wasn't interested in reconciliation on any terms. I later found out that she'd met someone before we were divorced and had moved on. My plan had failed.

But as with my personal relationships, I revealed nothing of my drug and alcohol issues to the therapist. As far as he was concerned, it was situational depression. I cried a lot, and he gave me a lot of tissue. As with "frank" discussions in my personal relationships, seeing a therapist was more about patching up the story I wanted to tell myself about my life than exploring any problems. Soon I gave up therapy all together and delved deeper into the Dallas nightlife to find someone who would lift me up again.

Over the years, I'd occasionally see therapists, and I'd also get antidepressant prescriptions. (I started those after my *second* divorce.) But just like failed relationship after failed relationship, therapy wasn't ever going to help sustain me because I continued to conceal what was really going on in my life. I got used to only revealing a little of myself to my therapists, just as I'd reveal just enough to my girlfriends—or wives—so they'd think they knew something about me. My biggest secrets were keeping me from love, and from self-understanding.

Relationships are hard enough, but when substance use is added to the mix, and recovery is not a part of the picture, not many survive. I was no exception. I was no exception three times over, in fact. I often think of the movie *Glengarry Glen Ross*. The character played by Alec Baldwin is trying to "motivate" a group of down-and-out salespeople with a sales contest he's come up with: "As you all know, first prize is a Cadillac Eldorado. Anyone want to see second prize? Second prize is a set of steak knives. Third prize is you're fired." If third prize in a sales contest earns you a pink slip, what does three failed marriages earn you? I've long since blown past earning my set of steak knives. I figure one more failed marriage and I'm dismissed from the dating pool.

In reality, none of my divorces were funny, and each in its own way was just as painful as the others. Loss is painful. Failure is painful. My first divorce was a link in a chain of denial that kept me from having successful relationships. In all three of my marriages (as well as other relationships), I refused to address or reveal two essential facts of who I was: my underlying mental health issues stemming from childhood, and my substance use issues. I was in denial, and more than that, I did whatever was necessary to conceal those truths from the women with whom I shared my life. Without honesty about those fundamental issues, how could I expect help from those who loved me?

Even in moments of relative clarity, I figured that if I revealed my weakness or vulnerability, I'd be unlovable. My wife or girlfriend would leave me. And not just the wife—I'd lose my friends. I'd lose my job. My family would give up on me. I'd lose it all. Maintaining the brick wall seemed easier in the moment.

Of course, it's much harder to hide substance use or mental health problems from a spouse or loved one than it is to hide those issues from work colleagues. But there are similarities—our destructive actions can damage trust with our loved ones even when they have no idea about the source of those destructive acts. For me, my personal relationships often ended the same way my jobs ended— not with having my problems revealed in some dramatic way, but with the slow degradation of trust. Those lost relationships hurt much more than the lost jobs, however, and ultimately led to my deepest, most dangerous crises.

■ July 22, 2005

A dark room. Table, desk, chairs. I'm with a staff psychiatrist of the Green Oaks Hospital. I've heard of Green Oaks—it isn't far from my home in Dallas. Now, in the room with the psychiatrist and psychiatric nurse, scenes of Jack Nicolson in *One Flew Over the Cuckoo's Nest* go through my muddled mind. *I am in the middle of a crisis, and I'm thinking about movies.* My brothers sit at the table across from me. As I sit and listen to the doctor's questions, I have a vague recollection of my younger brother rousing me from my bed and then having an angry confrontation. My .45 automatic had been lying on my nightstand. Then shock and confusion on the drive to the treatment center.

The residuals of cocaine, Xanax, and Jack Daniel's are still coursing through my veins, but the fog is lifting slightly. Raging anger is settling in its place. Battle lines are being drawn in my mind. *They want to take me prisoner. It's war. I'll lead the inmate rebellion.*

Questions from the shrink pierce my anger like tracer rounds. What drugs have you taken? How are you feeling? *Are you nuts! I'm angry! Do I want to hurt myself? Yes! Maybe! Not sure.* Not sure of anything. The anger is too powerful. I believe if I died, it would teach everyone a lesson. My family. The kids who ripped my pants off. My mother. Myself, for being unable to fix the distorted reflection I see in the mirror each day. *I can't tell him that! What answer will get me out of here?* In the back of my mind, what's left of the internal lawyer takes over. I know that my family can't commit me, but he can. *Proceed with caution.*

"If I wanted to hurt myself there would have been bullets in the gun."

I don't mention the fact that the person I had asked for bullets had ratted me out to my brothers. And I don't mention that I had been "practicing" sticking the barrel of the gun in my mouth and dry-firing it. I drift away, thinking about that night with the gun, the barrel in my mouth, my confused beagle, Peanut, watching from the doorway.

Ripped back to reality, I hear voices in the room. The doctor is talking to me again. When was the last time I used cocaine? *I'm pretty sure it has been recently, since it was all over the room when my brother showed up.* I had become the consummate liar in hiding the obvious cocaine habit from my family. It's that damn persistent cold that used to appear mysteriously every weekend. Now it's a daily occurrence. No one in this room is buying it.

Yelling. Accusations. All coming from me. I am angry at my brothers. *I hate you! I want your attention! Now I have it!* I am an eleven-year-old child, lashing out at my mother, who is a thousand miles away. *They've taken away my control.* What control? *I'm out of control.* Anyone in my line of sight is fair game. I'm blaming my brothers for everything that has gone wrong in my life. *Why are they trying to hold me back? When I'm on drugs, I'm their equal.* I can't even look at them. If I did, I would see nothing but love and concern. I look at the table. I look at my shoes. I find that fixed point on the floor that provides me comfort. *I wish that shrink would stop asking me questions!* The shrink is my enemy. My brothers have betrayed me. They're calm, trying to make sure I am still above ground tomorrow.

I notice the room is not really dark. Sunlight pours through the windows, but I am in the darkest of places. I remember seeking a release of everything in me. *Need those bullets! Too coked up and Xanaxed down to go out and buy some. Who do I know that can help?*

More questions. Do I think I need help? Will I go to rehab? *Sure, whatever will get me out of here?* I lash out again. *They have no right to do this.*

I yell across the table, "You have no right to control my life! I am an adult! Mind your own business!"

They quietly let me rant, allowing me to release the pain and loneliness of my reflection.

Blaming them for the darkness is so much easier than seeing the light. The doctor is asking calm, focused questions to ascertain whether I am a danger to myself. At times, I am calm in my answers. At times, I am crying, angry at him, then at my brothers. *Quit asking the same questions! I know your game! Quit treating me like an idiot!*

So alone. More and more I start to feel like the shy, introverted boy I once was. I'm no longer the sophisticated, in-shape, cover model I created in my imagination—the myth that drugs and alcohol helped to forge.

Up until now, each day has been a battle to see someone different when I looked in the mirror. But in this room, there is no reflection. I'm unshaven. Unkempt. I reek of booze and days of neglected hygiene. I'm as raw and vulnerable as I could possibly be.

I'm exposed. And I can no longer escape the stark reality of how I was getting by day by day.

An hour has passed. The room is getting brighter. The love and calm of my brothers soothes, quiets me, softens my edges. Their support has always been there, but I wasn't present enough to sense it. I was thinking only of myself: My next high. My next drink. *Without the drugs, what am I going to see in the mirror each morning?* The thought terrifies me. My brothers calm me, and I begin to focus on my love for my family. Arms are around me, holding me. I begin to feel the love penetrating my shell. They are not the enemy. There is a pinhole of real light, and it's beginning to expand. Should I go to rehab? What about twelve-step? I'm still on the defensive, but at least for the moment, I can listen. Have to grab those moments. They don't come often.

After the one-hour psych evaluation, I was taken home from Green Oaks, wondering how I had brought myself to the brink of death so quickly. In reality, it was not quick. It was a gradual lifelong descent with just enough good moments to blind me to the reality of the slide. Even in addiction and body dysmorphia there were good moments in my life.

It was decided that an out-of-state facility, away from my crowd of coke addicts and alcoholics would be the most beneficial. But ultimately I would not go.

✳   ✳   ✳

The journey that led me to Green Oaks was decades in the making, but the decision to go had been made just that very morning. Early on that summer day, I was roused out of a Xanax/alcohol/cocaine stupor by the sound of my younger brother Jeff's voice asking me if I was OK. He had used a key I had given him to enter my house. I had no memory of sending emails to my older brother hinting that I was going to kill myself. I don't remember emailing one of my close friends to obtain bullets for the Spanish Star Single Action .45

automatic he had given me as a gift a few years before. I have never been a fan of guns, but you don't have to be a fan to know what to do with one. I wanted those bullets. I was suddenly a gun person.

Then my brother spotted the gun on my nightstand, within my reach. Still unloaded, but he didn't know that. He asked me what I was going to do with the gun, and then he demanded it.

"Give it to me, Brian!"

I angrily pushed it in his direction. "Take it! It's not loaded." I wished it were. I wanted it to be. I was angry. Angry that he wanted my gun. Angry when he hinted he would confiscate my drugs, but too intoxicated to confront him. I passed out again.

Sometime later, Mark showed up. He had been out of town but flew home immediately. They made a call to an in-patient psychiatric facility in Florida that had a bed clear for me if I could get down there for screening. I did not push back, but I was angry at the prospect of leaving my home to go anywhere that was not my choice. The loss of control I had always agonized over when I looked in the mirror had become a stark reality, in the worst possible scenario. In the short term, they decided to take me to Green Oaks. I didn't resist. I felt like I was at rock bottom. I was also still in a half-drugged haze of confusion. If a friend had come to my house instead of my brother, I probably would have pushed back and told him to leave me alone. But the shame of knowing my brothers— who I loved with all my heart—had seen my situation was enough to get me to go.

As we left the house, my brother Jeff commented on the huge collection of bottles of alcohol in my bar, and the full scope of my problems started to become obvious. He said, "We should get Brian into rehab." Mark replied, "He is depressed, we need to deal with that." They were both right. I was keeping the liquor store within walking distance from me in business. I had also gotten into the habit of chugging whiskey as a sleep aid if I had no Xanax or sleeping pills to bring me down from a cocaine high.

My brothers would take my supply, but I wasn't ready to be helped, so getting rid of the alcohol and drugs was a very short-term fix. It is virtually useless to take the alcohol from an alcoholic or the drugs from the drug addict, if they haven't surrendered to the need for help. It's only a delay until they can hit the liquor store again or call the dealer. It simply breeds resentment at the removal of independence and self-determination. Addicts can benefit from the right support, but only we can save ourselves. We are the only ones who can say no.

As I slowly came out of my coke-and-Xanax stupor, we pulled into the Green Oaks parking lot. As my brothers spoke with the nurse, I filled out the intake form. The embarrassment and shame were overwhelming. I was a worthless stain on the Cuban name. I really did want to kill myself. Was this going to be in the next edition of the *Dallas Morning News*? The feeling was worse than when I stood on the side of the North Dallas tollway handcuffed in the DWI arrest back in 1991. At least then I was only an embarrassment to myself. It was well before Mark's successes had made our family name well known in Dallas. Back then, I was just another drunk. My thoughts in the waiting room were of ego, not of recovery. On reflection, this was a red flag that there would be no recovery at that moment in my life.

In talking with my brothers on the drive home from Green Oaks, I strongly resisted the suggestion of rehab. As an alternative, they suggested that I confine myself to my house for a while and stay away from the Dallas party scene. To make the point, they took my car keys from me. I should have been in detox, then rehab, but there was nothing anyone could do if I was not ready to admit defeat.

Once home and without access to my car, I was angry all over again. I felt outrage at my family for trying to control my life as I defined it, so I took a cab to the auto dealership and bought a new set of keys. I was a good boy for a couple of weeks. I did not call my coke dealer. I did not drink. *I'm cured*, I thought.

But sitting alone at home, I had nothing to think about except my old problems. Jeff had taken the gun, but my mind returned again and again to that night of "target practice." Sticking the barrel as far back in my throat as I could and counting the seconds in my head from pressure on the trigger to the click of the simulated firing. How many seconds to live. *Click*...Pull back the slide. One more time... *Click*...Just once more. I'm ready to release the pain...*Click*. The calm, warm, resigned feeling coursed from my stomach to my head when I played the game with the .45. Then I thought of my rescue dog, Peanut. *Who will take care of her, and my cat, Useless?* Tears. I was bawling, and I noticed Peanut was at the door watching. She was lying full length with her head extended out in her submissive position. *Does she sense my pain? What is she thinking? Will she miss me? I will miss her.* The thought of the only creatures on this earth who touched my soul and gave me unconditional acceptance caused me to consider the true meaning of what I was about to do. I hugged Peanut and had no idea what would happen to me next.

Being home alone with just memories was excruciating. About two weeks after I had declared myself cured of cocaine, alcohol, and the club scene, I had had enough self-imposed isolation. Historical revisionism set in. *I did not have a problem. I had simply gone through a bad time,* I told myself. The solution was simple. I would not party during the week. I would use more cocaine and less alcohol to avoid chemical depression. If I could find the right balance for feeling good, everything would be OK. I would also be a responsible addict and always take cabs or have someone to drive me when I went out on the town. Problem solved.

As far as hard consequences go, that was the closest that addiction had brought me to death. By the time I'd reached middle age, suicidal thoughts were no strangers during depressive episodes, but I'd never acted on them in any way. The feeling of wanting it all to end often felt like background noise during my darker moments, but they came to the foreground that year. So what had changed by 2005?

I wish I could give an accurate account of my life and my state of mind then, but much of my memory of that time is shrouded in the fog of clinical depression and a drug and alcohol haze. I do believe that the word "selfish" meant something different to me at that time. Frankly, I thought it would be selfish of me to keep on living. It would be selfish of me to continue to burden my family with my existence. I didn't want to be selfish. The lawyer in me saw the decision as coldly logical, the best outcome for all concerned parties. And I can also remember that the decision came on fast. Maybe only someone who has experienced the descent can explains just how fast. Family and friends might all be there for support, but it only takes that one moment of isolation and self-certainty to make the decision.

The truth is, family and friends simply can't be there every moment. But their support does matter. It did to me. I'm alive, in part, because my support system saved me. And perhaps I can thank a bit of luck as well.

I don't remember it happening. But apparently, I emailed a friend asking for bullets for the Spanish Star .45 automatic he'd given me years before as a gift. I'd also sent emails to my brother Jeff that suggested I might hurt myself. The email I don't remember, but I remember dry-firing the gun in a manner that would end my life if loaded in the days leading up to that.

Whatever I said in the email was enough of a red flag that my friend called my brother Jeff about it. The next morning, after all my digital SOSs had been received, my brothers showed up at my house, put me in the back of Mark's car and drove me to Green Oaks. The only thought in my mind was, *How dare they meddle in my business. I don't have a problem. Leave me alone!*

I was panicking, but not over the grave danger I'd put myself in. I was panicking because regardless of what my family actually knew at that time, my secret life was front and center. My worlds had collided. I was ashamed, and had misplaced anger at my brothers for making me feel that shame, for seeing it for themselves. I wasn't worried for my life as I should have been—I was worried that my trip to a psych facility would end up in the *Dallas Morning News*. My instinct for preserving reputation above all else was in the forefront.

What was going on in my life in July of 2005? What I have determined, as is often the case, is there was no one thing, but a combination of factors. My social circles were almost completely limited to those who did cocaine and went to the clubs every night, and I'd begun to distance myself from family to maintain that lifestyle. My "relationships" were all formed around the common love of drugs and alcohol and were for the most part with women significantly younger than I. You might read this and say "Good for you!" But my need to engage in narcissistic object choice with younger women in my relationships was far from healthy. It was my belief that if a pretty woman, sometimes less than half my age my age was interested in me, then I must have value as a person and was someone to be respected. Exactly the mindset of the shy, lonely sixteen-year-old desperate to be wanted. I was sixteen at forty-four. That's not good.

In reality, the only strong connection I truly had day in and day out was with my dog Peanut who loved me and was waiting for me at the front door every day, even if I was drunk and high. The only relationship I had free from my imagined judgment when I sobered up.

In 2005, I'd been seeing a therapist, but decided that my depression was "cured" and without telling my shrink, I'd stopped using my anti-depressants, which I'd been taking on and off since my second divorce in 1998. I'd been diagnosed with depression after my first divorce but had not heard the term clinical depression until my second divorce. I went to a psychiatrist at that time recommended by a guy who lived in my apartment complex. She put me on Wellbutrin, which is also approved for helping people stop smoking. I remember her telling me that it was contraindicated for people with problems using cocaine because it could cause seizures. I didn't reveal my cocaine problem and, after about a month, stopped seeing her and taking the Wellbutrin because I'd rather do the cocaine than have a seizure. Dealing with my depression on an on-going basis was not yet part of the equation.

I was simply not ready for recovery or treatment of my depression at that time, but there was one point of self-discovery in that two-month period. I realized that I'd been clinically depressed since at least my early teens. I just didn't know what that meant in terms of my self-image, my body dysmorphic disorder, or my drug or alcohol use.

During that time, I experienced cycles of compliance and noncompliance with my medication, the same cycle often repeating. That involved thinking I was cured or simply abandoning usage because I saw no improvement, although that could have very well been because of the prescription's interaction with the alcohol and un-prescribed drugs I was taking. I had unconsciously set myself up for failure each time and blamed everyone and everything around me when the train wrecks occurred. The mask of respectability would disappear. The real Brian was ultimately revealed. Depression. Addiction. Worlds colliding.

My two lives had coming crashing together in 2005 with my near suicide and first trip to Green Oaks, but I was still not ready for recovery. I went right back out and tried to re-create the buffer zone between the Brian with drug and alcohol addiction and the "respectable" Brian. I convinced myself that since alcohol was a depressant, if I just drank a little less, I'd be able to avoid depression. Of course, that didn't work, and I was behaving as recklessly as ever.

By this point, most people who had known me for any length of time knew that I was both Jekyll and Hyde. Most people, but not everyone.

In 2006, I met someone new. Amanda, also a lawyer. She admired me, trusted me, and what seemed best of all to me at the time, was someone who didn't know the real me. Being with her was like a fresh start for my fake life.

Not that she didn't have her suspicions (as I'd find out much later). She knew something wasn't right but couldn't put her finger on it. Maybe it was the time I was driving to a family gathering with her in the passenger seat, and I was so tranced out I nearly rear ended a couple of cars at stoplights. She didn't know I was zonked on black market Xanax at the time, but she knew I wasn't acting normal. I remember telling her and my brother Mark (who also noticed I was acting strangely at the dinner) that it was the effects of antidepressants I was taking. They had no experience with antidepressants (or black market benzos, for that matter), so they didn't question my explanation. But that doesn't mean either Mark or Amanda completely bought my explanation, either. In general, though, I was careful. I held it together around Amanda, and I presented myself as this important player in the Cuban empire. I showed her my most serious side and did my best to hide the party life. In fact, I found I could generally stay clean and sober when she was around. But it was silly to think I could hide my true self for much longer.

■ April 7, 2007

Eyes open. What day is it? Lying in bed. Last I remember is walking into a nightclub Friday night. It now feels like the middle of the day. Sunlight is in my eyes.

That's when I sense a presence in the room. I know I'm not alone. Startled, I sit up. Amanda is by the bed looking down at me, confused, worried, angry.

This is her home now too. She took a little convincing, but I was able to persuade her to move in with me. I thought that having her around would help me stop my drug use, because I would not do them when she was around. That seemed perfectly logical to me. Like the Marines. Like family. Like literally running from my problems. Now I was counting on Amanda to fix me. *But she's not supposed to be fixing me today. Today, she's supposed to be on a business trip in Houston.*

"Brian?"

I glance at my clock and see it's Sunday afternoon. Then my eyes focus on the cocaine laid out on the dresser table. Then I look down at the bottles strewn on the floor. Next to a tequila bottle is a condom. *Oh no. Who was I with?* I'm confused, afraid, and my first thought is how I might manipulate myself out of the situation. *I'm a lawyer. I can come up with something that she'll believe.* Amanda is also a lawyer.

"Amanda...That's nothing. There was no one here. I was using the rubber as a water balloon." (Yes, I really said that. Yes, I really believed she would buy it.)

"Brian. Seriously?"

"Amanda, I think I need to go to Green Oaks. I've been there before."

"What? What's Green Oaks?"

"A psychiatric facility."

"You've been to a psychiatric facility? How come you've never told me that before?"

"Yes. I'll explain. But now, I need to go."

Somehow, she agrees to take me. Into the car, I'm silent. She's crying and angry. The familiar drive. The familiar parking lot. The familiar walk through the double doors to intake. This time my brothers aren't there. They don't know yet. I can't look at Amanda, and instead I look down at the floor in shame and fear as I give my name to the intake nurse. She's kind. Her voice is soft. It calms me a little. She's seen many Brians at that window. Then she's on the phone. I need air. I won't look at Amanda. I walk back into the parking lot. Fixating on the black concrete. Thinking.

I'm still in denial, insisting there was no other woman in my bedroom. I know there had been. I can't remember her face, name, or how she got there, but the rubber didn't lie. There were no water balloons. After this, there is nobody left to believe me. No one left who believes in pretend Brian.

I accept that Amanda will leave me. I'd leave if I were her. There's no reason for her to stay. I've betrayed her trust on every level. I have nowhere to go now but the truth. I'm beaten. I've let down everyone. I think of my father. I think of my two brothers. In the few moments of what seems like an eternity, I think of a little boy and his brothers in our father's arms. Crawling over him on the floor as we tried to pin him down pretending we were wrestlers. His laughter. The love. The bond.

I know in that parking lot, I'm on the verge of so much loss. I'll lose my girlfriend. And I feel close to losing the gift my father instilled in each of us decades before. Sure, families grow apart in some ways. My brothers had wives. They had children. That did not mean I had lost their love, but they'd realized they could not make me better. That was up to me. had to.

The thoughts of disappointing my father, one of the last people who knew nothing about my struggles with addiction, was more than I could bear. Once my family was gone, I'd have nothing. I was afraid. Fear had been holding me back from seeking help, but now fear was my motivator. It was time for an honest step forward. I didn't know what that step would be, or who I would have to help me. At the moment, Amanda was by my side, and that was something to be grateful for. And there was something else, too. In the midst of that fear, shame, and humiliation, I, for the first time, felt something that had eluded me for decades—hope.

■ March 13, 2015

Moving toward my eighth year in sobriety. The Dallas Mavericks are playing the Los Angeles Clippers. Amanda and I are in attendance, as well as my brother Jeff, my father, Mark's children, and members of his wife Tiffany's family. It's not an unusual occurrence. Mark has a suite for family, and we often all gather for games. This game, however, is not about basketball for me. I have a secret. Maybe that isn't unusual either. I was once great at keeping the secrets of addiction and other mental health issues from everyone sitting in that room. I'd leave at halftime to do cocaine in the bathroom. Then I'd return and talk about the allergies I couldn't shake as I sniffled from the cocaine. Today, just as in the past, I slip out to the bathroom at halftime. But tonight, what comes out of my pocket isn't cocaine. It's an engagement ring. I go back to the suite, and with everyone watching, I drop to one knee and propose to Amanda.

We've come far from that day in April 2007 when I was sure she was gone. We've spent more than nine years together, during which time I've worked on myself, learned to reach out to others, attended twelve-step, therapy, and worked hard to rebuild the trust I lost with Amanda that day. This moment is a big payoff, but I didn't work toward recovery just so I could get married one more time. It's about rebuilding a new life in sobriety, one step and day at time. I know without sobriety, everything is lost—Amanda, family, career, self-respect. I know always trying to do the next right thing is the only way to hold onto the love I've found. She says yes. No steak knives necessary.

17

Sick Is Not Weak:
Where to Turn

■ **April 8, 2007**

I CALL MY brother Mark.

"Mark, Amanda and I are breaking up. I've slipped. It was bad."

"Well, what's your plan to get better? It's on you, not her."

"I don't know."

"Well, let me know when you know."

Short and sweet. He'd seen and heard it two years earlier. He'd be there if I was ready for recovery, but there would be no more enabling. It was all on me, as it should be. The call to Jeff was pretty much the same conversation. He was pushing hard for me to go to rehab, but I was right there with Amy Winehouse on the subject— no, no, no. *I can't go to rehab. I'm a lawyer! Like, there are no lawyers in rehab, right? Who will handle my cases? What will my friends think?* I had only two cases. I was working of-counsel for a local PI firm on an office sharing relationship. I was doing cocaine in their bathroom every morning to start my day. Not like my legal career was setting the world on fire. *People will talk about me!* They were already talking about me. I just didn't want to know about it. That would have meant facing my present. Fear and ego overpowered rational thought about recovery.

I'd been seeing a shrink for a few years. I'd go faithfully every Tuesday morning. Sometimes hungover. I'd sit on his comfy sofa, and he'd sit in his comfy chair in his cardigan. We'd stare at each other, and then I'd tell him how depressed I was. He was there for the end of my third marriage. My ex had even come to one of the sessions, but it was over by then. The anger in the room was thicker than a Seattle fog. My view on how to handle my therapy hadn't changed. Admit nothing. Talk about nothing, especially my past. Wear the mask. Get my antidepressant prescription.

I sometimes get asked, "Why would you lie to your shrink? Why would you even go if you didn't want help? You're paying the guy!" I wanted help but was not in a position to accept help. I was not in a position to face my past. I was ashamed. Shame knows no hourly rate.

This day would be different. I'd thought about not going, but I knew that I had to do something or the pressure would increase to go to rehab. I was also hanging on to my slim hope that Amanda wouldn't leave me. If I didn't show some outward willingness to change my life, she certainly would leave me. Some step forward had to be taken. I wanted to take it but I was also terrified. I'd never experienced such fear. Fear of losing my girlfriend and family. Fear of a life without drugs, alcohol, and bulimia. Fear of rigorous honesty—something I'd never been a fan of. Fear of dying.

I finally got honest. At least partially honest. I didn't talk about the eating disorder or the issues with body image I had been battling for decades. The stigma of body dysmorphia and eating disorder for me was exponentially greater than the stigma of addiction. But that day I finally unloaded the burden of my own feelings about my addiction. The shame, the guilt, the fear, the drugs, the failure. My therapist asked me what I wanted to do. I was blunt: I wanted to live. I wanted to keep my girlfriend and family. I wanted to have a life not defined by alcohol, white powder, and surviving day to day. I wanted a future.

Rehab came up. Same as when my brothers suggested it, I said no. So my therapist suggested something else.

"Have you considered twelve-step? There is a group that meets right next door to this office."

I looked at him skeptically. "Yeah, I drive by there, next to the deli. They all look like homeless people and sterno bums." My ego taking center stage. My mind flashing back to the "20 Questions" pamphlet I had enthusiastically tossed in a trash bin after answering "yes" to many of the questions decades before.

"No, Brian, there are all kinds of people that attend twelve-step. If you're adamant about not going to rehab, I think it's a good place to start. If it doesn't take, then we can revisit in-patient treatment. There's actually a meeting starting in a little bit. Let's end the session, and you can go over there and check it out."

Once again, I was resistant. I brought up my "law practice." *I'm a lawyer. I have clients who need attending to. I'm a busy guy. I'm above such things as twelve-step in grimy, smoke-filled rooms of despair.* I remember my shrink's response as if it were yesterday. "Brian, yes, you have a law degree. Yes, you sometimes go through some of the motions of what being a lawyer looks like. But you are *not* a lawyer in this room. You have an addiction. And this is a good first step for many addicts. I don't know if it'll work for you. But for now, it costs nothing but a walk over there and an hour to just listen."

As he was giving me the dose of reality, my wheels were turning with the fantasy. What I heard was, "You don't have to go away to treatment. You can stay in Dallas." *It's anonymous. Nobody will know.* I could take the smallest of steps and stay in my comfort zone. What I didn't know then was that even the smallest of steps into recovery are OK. In reality, even a small step can be life-changing.

I walk up to the door of the building where the local twelve-step meetings are held. My shrink feels that a trip here is the first step to recovery. If this doesn't hold, then I'll have to go to rehab. Lucky for me, the twelve-step building is right next to my shrink's office. If it hadn't been convenient, I might have just made excuses to not go at all. For an addict, excuses are often more plentiful than reasons for recovery. The present is more important than the future—the present of the high.

After pacing around outside the door for a long time, I finally peer in, down the long hallway to where people are gathering. I'm afraid of being recognized. My ego is still paramount in my worries. I'm ready for change but not ready to give up my pride. I pace outside the door of the building for another ten minutes, sometimes opening the door a bit but never going in. For a time, I sit listlessly in a nearby sandwich shop.

When I finally work up the courage to walk into the building, each step into the unknown seems harder and harder. Who are the people I'll meet in twelve-step? My mind flashes back to one of my favorite childhood movies, *Willy Wonka & the Chocolate Factory*. I suddenly imagine that as soon as I enter the twelve-step meeting room, I'll be carried away by a team of chanting Oompa Loompas determined to punish me for my bad habits. I have no desire to meet the Oompa Loompas on the other side of that door. I again consider rehab, but I'm even more embarrassed about the idea of my friends, other lawyers, and everyone who knows my family name finding out I'm going to in-patient rehab than I am about a small group of strangers scrutinizing my deepest flaws.

I finally make it to the door of the meeting room, and I can smell the fumes of stale cigarette smoke and day-old coffee. My eyes lock onto the 1950s-era tile floor, ingrained with the dirt of countless feet. There are other people milling around in the hall. Are these the people with whom I am supposed to share my darkest secrets? Will I be made fun of, teased, bullied, insulted? Who are these people? Skid row bums? That's my perception of twelve-step. I think of Nicolas Cage's character, Ben, living in the sleazy "no-tell motel" as he drinks himself to death in *Leaving Las Vegas*, and Dick Van Dyke's character, Charlie, drunk, alone on the beach with no future in *The Morning After*.

Still not ready, I walk back to my car, and I sit there with the key in the ignition. I even start the engine. But I don't go anywhere. Instead, I think about my next move. It's all on me. I could drive on home and check out my bathroom mirror. Go through all my routines. I might get through the next day and the next. But any comfort would be temporary. I would certainly restart the cycle of destruction. My shrink couldn't save me. Therapists can only do good work if their patients are honest, a quality rarely found among addicts or sufferers of BDD. This is the biggest decision I've faced yet.

As I sit paralyzed in my car, I think of another recurring dream. The dream begins as I walk out the door of my house. I have no girl-friend or wife, no friends, no family. No one who loves me. I feel hollow and empty, as if I'm experiencing a kind of starvation. I start walking. I feel I have to begin a new journey. Somewhere. Anywhere. But I can't walk past my driveway. My legs just won't carry me—it's like being in quicksand. So I grab my bike, the one my father bought me as a child, but the tires are flat. I manage to get the bike to a shop, where they replace both tires. But those are also flat. As I leave the bike shop, I try walking again, but now the sidewalks are icy and slippery—I can barely move. But I must go. I must go somewhere far away. Northern Canada seems a good destination. I need to walk until I reach a place of total isolation, to be away from everyone who knows me and who can see through me. I know leaving will hurt my family. I want them to see how much I hurt. I'll run away. I'll show them. I keep walking. Now my feet are moving as fast as I can lift them, but I am going nowhere. I am completely stuck in place.

I shut off the engine and take the keys out of the ignition. There's no way to escape my problems. I have to face them. I go back to the front door of the meeting room. Deep breath. Don't look around.

Eyes down at the floor. That fixed point. Watch the feet move forward. One baby step at a time. It's the way I'm able to accomplish things in life. It's how I was able to finish eight marathons. Facing any difficult task, my best self is that part of me that can place one foot in front of the other until a goal is accomplished. Don't look left. Don't look right. Don't think about the finish line. Watch your feet, one in front of the other. Again. One in front of the other, back down the long hallway. Now open the glass door. People are looking at you. Don't look at them. Fixed point. Open it.

I do. And I go in.

My blue short-sleeve shirt was soaked with sweat. I sat in the corner and listened. I raised my hand when the call went out for who was in for the first time. Two others were also attending their first meeting. They raised their hands, gave their first names, and said, simply, "I'm an alcoholic." My turn came. "My name is Brian." That's it. I was sobbing. I was too embarrassed to take the chip at first call. I cried in that corner for a few reasons. I instinctively knew I was beaten. I was ashamed to be there. I was ashamed of what I was. I was ashamed of the decades I couldn't look at my reflection in the mirror. I heard my story over and over again in others' mouths. Not the same facts exactly, but the same pain. The same fears. The same shame. I heard those with long-term recovery talking about their first time through the doors, what they'd learned. I heard hope. For the first time in my life, I was beginning to see what recovery looked like.

Even though I wasn't entirely comfortable yet in that room, I felt I'd found the support of a group who understood. Who didn't judge. Who told me I was not alone and would never be alone in my recovery. The first day of one-day-at-a-time had begun.

I often think back to my first weeks of sobriety. I kept a diary. I hadn't looked at it again until I wrote this book. I share a little here because I think those words capture some of the hope and the trepidation of starting a treatment program:

April 14, 2007: Maybe there is a "grand plan" to life. A higher power. My relationship with my father was deteriorating over the last year. A great source of depression. I've been living with him since my alcohol blackout. Our relationship has strengthened, and we have a renewed bond. Absent this incident, it may not have happened. I hope Amanda and I are stronger although I still expect her to walk.

April 11, 2007: It was so hard for me to walk through the doors of AA. Pride. Shame. Still detoxing. Fear. Abandonment. Feeling them all at once. I dreamed last night that the city of Boston was burning, and I walked through it. I realized today that in almost every single stupid decision I've made, alcohol has played a factor.

April 14, 2007: Quiet day in group. Amanda spent the night. I love feeling her warmth and love up against me. Today I realized that when I'm not depressed, I can drink socially without getting drunk. Without doing drugs. But I can't see depression coming. It blindsides me. It becomes a freight train. That's why I can't take that first drink.

April 17, 2007: Today I was rocked by fear. For some reason, I got it in my head Amanda was going to leave me. It was overwhelming. Maybe because I'm back home for the first time after living with Dad. I emailed her to see if everything was OK. It was. I spent the night at her place. I'm so insecure. Maybe I just need reassurance now and then. It's hard dealing with these feelings. I destroyed her trust. I went to a 2nd AA meeting today, and felt better.

Looking back on those entries, it's clear I was terrified. Terrified of losing my girlfriend. Terrified of being alone. Terrified of the future. But more than anything during that time, my fear was based on feeling like there was no solid ground under me. All my habits and

THE ADDICTED LAWYER   193

routines had to change, and what was left over was a lot of scary questions about who I was. And without drugs and alcohol, I didn't have my usual distractions from those questions.

In my encounters with many who are actively confronting addiction, it seems that a feeling of not being grounded often leads to a search for spiritual wellbeing as part of recovery, even in those who may not have previously embraced spirituality in their lives.

Here is a revelation that may very well anger some in twelve-step (even though it shouldn't, because we all have our own journey that should proceed without judgment). I've never worked the steps as a "sponsored" sobriety plan, and never made it past "We Agnostics" in the Big Book.[18] I don't reveal that as a badge of honor or as a suggestion to anyone that they should approach AA as I did. It's simply the hard truth of my journey. I found it an absolutely archaic, brutal read. Books need to engage me, even in recovery. It did not engage me. If I were to look for real life corollaries to the steps in how I live my life in sobriety, I suspect some things would match up. Maybe one day I will revisit that, and I do keep going back. That said, the mutual aid, connection-based therapy inherent in AA has helped me tremendously. The "god" aspects, not as much.

AA was originally founded around explicitly spiritual/religious concepts and goals. Partly for that reason, I get asked on a regular basis what part faith and spirituality played in my recovery. It's a complicated and fluid answer, but an important issue for many in recovery. Especially in twelve-step. During the nuts and bolts time of building initial sobriety, my answer would be "not much at all." To be clear, I'm not an atheist. I do not reject the notion that "god" or some type of "higher power" in the universe exists. I always considered myself more an unquestioning agnostic. My true answer to the question of whether god exists would be, "I don't know—I'll find out when the time comes." My overall belief can best be summed up by author Kurt Vonnegut and something I learned in twelve-step. "I am a *humanist*, which means, in part, that I have tried to behave decently without any expectation of rewards or punishments after I'm dead."

Translated into recovery terms, I always try to get to the "next right thing" in my daily life. Of course, I often don't know what the right thing is, and there are often choices that, like the multiple-choice questions on the LSAT or the Bar exam, all seem like they may be the right answer.

But I've learned in seeking help and in watching others seek help that part of that "next right thing" is not trying to tell anyone what their "next right thing" is. And as I talk about my path to recovery and those that others have shared with me, I want to make it clear that I'm not advocating choice A, B, C, or D. I only want to show that recovery is possible, even if we have to work through setbacks, and that there are many paths to breaking addiction and making peace with our pasts.

What about my past? Why am I so resistant to the "spiritual" aspects of twelve-step? When I talk or write about it, I will inevitably get a few "just keep going back (to AA) and you'll get it" comments. I'm always perplexed at those statements from those who know nothing about my religious upbringing. I'm not a square peg to be placed in the square hole of the twelve-step. I'm a person with feelings and beliefs that have been incubated over five decades. Incubated long before I began drinking and using drugs. Beliefs that have to be understood in the context of my parents' beliefs. Their grandparents' beliefs. Or how these things were handed down through generations.

First, I'm not critical of the concept of finding what AA literature famously refers to as a "higher power," or spirituality in general. AA has been good to me—developing new connections with those in sobriety and having those people's support was and is critical to my recovery. I couldn't do it myself. I see no need to call it my "higher power," but many do, and that's fine. I am, however, critical of what I believe is intellectual dishonesty in some AA advocates claiming that recovery requires a belief in "god," and that belief is one and the same as simple "spirituality." I know anecdotally that pressure to believe has driven people out of the group.

My own spiritual upbringing has clashed at times with elements sometimes present in AA. I'm Jewish. I consider myself a "cultural Jew" in that I do not actively practice the religion. I dropped out of Hebrew school in the second year, and as I write this book, have probably been to a total of three High Holiday services in the last thirty years. I am considered an "Ashkenazi Jew." That basically means my Jewish ancestors originated in Eastern Europe. Both sides immigrated to the United States through Ellis Island in the early 1900s, a common scenario for many Jews living in the United States.

Like many of the Jewish ancestry, my family has been touched by the Holocaust. My mother's family lost my great aunt, her husband, and their two children. For the majority of my life, that history was unknown. As an adult in recovery, my journey to identify my relatives who had been murdered was critical self-exploration for me. Learning what being Jewish means to me in my day-to-day life has also been critical, and a journey I consider a spiritual one. However, that is not the same to me as developing a faith in a particular god or "higher power."

My mother lit Friday night candles for the Shabbat. On Rosh Hashanah and Yom Kippur, we went to an orthodox synagogue. My parents seemed to be following a ritual and nothing more as I saw it.

On my mother's side, there was very little in the way of religious beliefs handed down, or as she puts it, "the minimal amount." I reached out to her about our religious and cultural upbringing, and she responded by describing some of what she remembers of a spiritual tradition passed down to her.

My mom went to a Jewish School from the fourth through seventh grade. At one point, she wanted to be a woman Rabbi. After seventh grade, she transferred to a public school, stopped buying kosher food, and beyond the holiday routine with her parents, lost interest in the religious aspects of Judaism.

My father is in his nineties as I write this, so I spoke with his younger brother Larry to get a perspective on the religious tradition on his side.

> While I do not remember observing Shabbats on Friday night, we did observe Rosh Hashanah, Passover, Purim, and Succoth mostly by my mom doing the special dishes for dinner for those holidays. I remember, for example, helping my mother make gefilte fish for Passover by hand-turning a grinder.
>
> My father (Brian's grandfather) was the one who kept closest to Jewish rituals—in Squirrel Hill he joined Shaare Torah, an Orthodox synagogue, and I remember that I and occasionally your dad would come sit with him while he was there for Rosh Hashanah and Yom Kippur.
>
> Neither your dad nor Marty (the oldest brother of my father and Larry) were bar mitzvahed, as I recall. Times were hard for the family economically when both were thirteen with the Great Depression, moving to Pittsburgh, and the family on welfare. As I came along later, the economy had improved, and Father earned enough income, so I did attend Hebrew school at the Hebrew Institute in Squirrel Hill and had my Bar Mitzvah in 1947.

When I was about twelve, my parents did join a synagogue. My mom felt that they owed it to us to provide a religious education and to be bar mitzvahed. According to my mom:

> The rabbi, on a Friday night service, spoke about children being taught religion and then living in a non-religious family as being very confusing for the child. That made me think that we would be better off without religious school. The synagogue leaned toward orthodoxy, so I quit. I didn't keep a kosher home, and the extent of my involvement in religion might be at the most a yearly observance on the high holidays. I truly didn't have religious commitments.

What I take from this, and what jives with my memory, is that the pressure to adopt a religious belief or participate in religious rituals was not forced upon me as it was not forced upon my parents. I wasn't bar mitzvahed as a teen, nor were my two brothers.

The feelings stirred in me by these revelations take me back to a shy boy sitting in Hebrew school in Temple Emmanuel in Mt. Lebanon, PA, not wanting to be there, feeling as if he did not fit in. Eventually, I just stopped going. I don't think I initially even told my parents that I stopped showing up. While there have been times in my life that I've wanted to explore more of my religion by reading and even explore wrapping Tefillin,[19] I've never had the desire to commit to the religious aspects of my heritage. No religious faith has replaced my belief that if I continue to do the next right thing, whatever happens when I die, or nothing at all, it'll be fine. None of it has caused me to have any desire to embrace "god" either in my daily life or as a higher power in twelve-step. It's not who I am, and I see no need to put on an act in recovery to be something I'm not just to fit in. I am however always mindful that my great aunt Freda, her husband Menashe, and their two children were murdered because of their religion. It's that memory which in part, keeps me sober as I continue to be involved with remembering the Holocaust. Maybe their memory is my higher power.

Of course, recovery and the faith of others can be tricky to navigate. When someone has passionately embraced faith that is an integral part of their sobriety, they might feel certain that faith in the higher power they believe in is the only true path to recovery and spiritual well-being. It certainly was tricky for me early on dealing with competing views of what was needed in twelve-step to achieve long term sobriety. It was something that at times caused me great anxiety, and even anger, in the context of my upbringing.

■ June 2007

Two months into my sobriety. Sitting at a table at the normal Sunday morning gathering at the Corner Bakery, which is near my home twelve-step group. The Sunday morning group makes it a regular event after the meeting. I'm angry. Agitated. Combative. Worried. I have no interest in the spiritual aspect of twelve-step, which feels like it suffocates me in every meeting. The Lord's Prayer. Talk of God. Talk of the "god of my understanding." Is there a difference? *Read the Big Book. Work the Steps. It will all become clear to you.* It sounds like jargon to me. I have to remember that even in twelve-step, people are still people. There are competing views of what spirituality means. There's talk from a few about how no one can get sober if they don't believe in God. Talk of how the chapter in the Big Book entitled "We Agnostics" will make everything clear when I get to that part. Many recite the Lord's Prayer or the Serenity Prayer to close the meetings.

I don't want to be told about any "god of my understanding" as a necessity to getting sober. It makes me feel sometimes as if twelve-step isn't right for me. But I have to look at the upside, and the upside is that I am two months sober. I can't remember the last time I strung together two months without a drink. I try to focus on that. I focus on the support of my family and girlfriend who had stuck with me despite the brutal betrayal of her trust, not only by hiding my addiction from her but also through my infidelity. And I have to focus on the support of the group itself, of people who have been through some of the same things I've been through, and who have the power to make me feel less alone in that respect.

The coffee is ordered. I'm sitting with two old timers. Let's call them Zed and Emma. They have well over fifty years of sobriety between them. Zed also happens to be an attorney and retired judge with a very long and successful career. As I start to dig into my vegetarian omelet, Zed walks over to me and says in a near whisper, "Brian, Emma and I would like to speak to you privately."

"Sure, let's sit over here away from the group."

Emma says, "Brian, if you want to stay sober, you need to accept god into your life."

Cue the hair on the back of my neck standing on end. My body temperature rises, my temples pulse. The room is cool, but all of a sudden I'm sweating as if I've just done a couple of lines of blow.

"I'm not going to say that, Emma. It's not what I believe. I've made that very clear in group."

Zed says, "Brian, yes you have, but you need to read and study the Big Book. Read the chapter entitled 'We Agnostics.' Brian, you're a lawyer correct? So am I. Let's approach this from a legal standpoint."

"What does my being an attorney have to do with my belief or lack of belief in god? It's no one's business but mine."

"Brian, you understand how to logically approach things, and I'm telling you logically you need to acknowledge a god, any god. Just pick something, anything, and then say, '. . . otherwise known as god.'"

I swivel my head side to side to see if anyone else is catching this and wonder if I'm on some type of hidden camera reality show.

"I'll consider it. Please feel free to finish my breakfast. Have a good day."

There are certain moments in the trajectory of my addiction descent and recovery that I'll always remember. The moment the bullies physically assaulted me because of my heavy weight and tore my pants off. I can show you exactly where that happened in Mt. Lebanon, Pennsylvania, all these decades later. That moment in the parking lot of Green Oaks when I decided that I was probably going to die and was going to lose my family if I did not take that first step toward recovery. The moment when two people who truly insisted that a belief in god was necessary to have long-term sobriety tried to shove religion down my throat as a prerequisite to recovery. It was a moment that felt like a threat to my whole plan of recovery, since twelve-step was seeming like maybe an imperfect fit. But it was an important moment, because I pressed on anyway. Finding the right path to recovery wasn't about finding a program that felt tailored exactly to my desires and personality. It was about finding a path that simply worked, that allowed me to move forward.

To be clear, that story is a criticism of the approach of two people, not twelve-step. Recovery programs are programs of people, and when you're interacting in recovery groups, regardless of type, there will be all kinds of personalities and agendas beyond just getting sober. Sides of the street become blurred, and some cross over to tell others what your recovery should be without being asked, instead of working their own side of the street.

I get setbacks, and I understand dropping out from recovery programs. Whether it's some self-righteous person in the twelve-step group, the twelve-step philosophy and mantra, family discord, stress, trauma, there is always a reason to not stay sober. It's what happened in that moment when I could have used it as a reason to quit that defined me. I don't go to that group anymore, but I did keep going back.

Of course, there are those whose religious faith is of extreme importance in their recovery, in and out of twelve-step. I found contributor Todd's story interesting because his reasons for not embracing the twelve-step process were not lack of faith but his pronounced faith.

✳   ✳   ✳

"I sometimes wish I could blame my substance use on a genetic predisposition," Todd says. "I cannot. Although alcohol fascinated me throughout my preadolescent and adolescent years, for religious reasons, my family did not drink."

When Todd went off to college, he discovered that he liked beer. A lot. "I was also 'blessed' with a physical constitution that allowed me to consume tremendous quantities of alcohol without suffering the debilitating effects of the next morning's hangover," he says.

Alcohol played a big, but lesser, role during law school. Because he was living at home during law school, his drinking options were limited, he says. "Alcohol was not allowed in my family's home. I honored that rule until Bar review time." Then, he discovered how easy it was to sneak alcohol into his room. "The stress of the Bar review classes and the impending exam were numbed by my old friend," he says.

During law school, he cut back his partying to a relatively subdued pace, relegated to the weekends. He clerked for a small P.I. firm. "One year, we all went to a Christmas party with an open bar," he says. "I was in heaven! I remember having drink after drink of as many different types of alcohol as possible."

The next time he went to work, his boss (one of the partners and the man who had driven him home from the party) was waiting for him. The partner was livid.

Todd says, "Apparently, I took the opportunity to share with him my best 'dead baby' jokes. The partner and his wife were expecting their first child. He told me how furious he had been."

Fortunately, the partner was also a compassionate man. He told Todd he needed time to cool off, and that he'd decided not to report him to the state Bar. "I didn't know he could even do that," Todd says. "I was ultimately able to keep my job, but I never drank in front of that group again."

Todd passed the Bar and was ready to start his life as a hard-working, hard-partying young lawyer.

"I had five jobs over the course of my first seventeen years of practice, including two short stints as a sole practitioner," he says. "I never drank on the job, but the prospect of nightly bashes was never far from the forefront of my mind. Lack of sleep and a foggy brain caused me daily concern; however, I found I could alleviate the symptoms and my concerns with more alcohol."

In the mid-2000s, Todd was approached by a sole practitioner who suggested Todd contact him if he was ever looking to make a move. A few years later, he reached out and was offered a job. "At some point in late 2008 or early 2009, I had the brilliant idea to try having a few drinks at the office," Todd says. "Success! Not only could I party at night, but I could keep the buzz going, slightly, at first, until I got through the work day."

By this point, the party had long since stopped being a social affair. Alcohol was too personal and too important to share the experience with other people. While it appeared that he was able to successfully drink and work, there was a price, he says. "I lived in constant fear of being caught and disbarred or arrested for D.U.I. or losing my family and/or my home. Buying alcohol had become much more important than paying bills."

Through all of this, he was still functioning at a high level. "I never drank before going to court or before meeting with clients," he says. "I chalk this up to the amazing ability many alcoholics have for creativity, whether it be in manipulation, time management, fund-raising, etc."

By mid-2009, Todd was drinking at least a half-pint of vodka for breakfast. "Usually in one big chug because I really liked the rush that method of consumption gave me," he says. Some days, he would have finished a fifth by lunch time. Neither his boss nor his paralegal ever noticed.

His boss told him that on one or two occasions, he thought he smelled alcohol on his breath, but since Todd never drank in public, his boss assumed he was mistaken.

"One of the last straws involved me hiding a partial fifth of vodka in our home," he says. "My then four-year old son was able to find it. Fortunately, my wife found him walking down the hall with it before he was able to get it open."

On February 19, 2010, he went into inpatient treatment. "For the first time in years, I had not had a drop of alcohol for an extended period," he says. "It has now been six years plus, and I feel better every day."

Early in his recovery, Todd attended AA meetings on a regular basis. He got a temporary sponsor prior to leaving treatment and stuck with him for a short period of time. Todd, however, quickly became disillusioned with AA.

He says, "Let's be honest: AA is a spiritually-based program. That it's been tweaked so that it doesn't offend the atheists or the agnostics in recovery is fine, if that is what works best for them. I, however, know there is a real higher power. I have witnessed His authority plenty of times as I have grown up, and even as a seasoned drinker. I know what He can do for me and what 'that chair over there' cannot. I phased out of AA and phased into reestablishing my relationship with my Creator. For me, it was the best choice I could have made."

Todd points out that his method of remaining sober hasn't been easy all of the time. "There have been times, such as on a hot summer day, when I have thought, 'Boy, a beer sounds good right about now.' Those moments are fewer and farther between as time goes by."

Since Todd become sober, his career has advanced by leaps and bounds. He is now in a partnership with the attorney for whom he had been working. Todd says, "He was remarkably understanding, albeit a little scared, when I went into treatment." Todd is the president of the local drug court board of directors. He is an active participant in the local Bar association. He teaches and has taken the Illinois Lawyer's Assistance Program volunteer training course so that he can help other attorneys who are walking a self-destructive path.

Today Todd limits his practice to matters of family law, some estate planning, and residential real estate. "I think that my recovery experience has made me a better lawyer," he says. "I am now clear-headed. More important, I've learned to be more compassionate and more understanding of the difficulties we all experience as we go through life."

✱   ✱   ✱

Of course, as I've mentioned, twelve-step is one route to recovery. It has been helpful in my recovery, but far from the only tool I've used. As I have previously written, medication and traditional therapy, including mindfulness, have been vital parts of my recovery as well as family support. Simply put, there are other ways to get there, and there are other ways to connect again to loved ones, to fellow travelers, and to purposeful pursuits and careers.

For instance, some in recovery to whom I've spoken have pursued a program called SMART Recovery. Like AA, SMART Recovery (Self-Management and Recovery Training) is a program that allows people struggling with addiction to meet and discuss their stories and hopes for the future. But proponents of SMART Recovery view it as more of a "self-help" than "support" group, in that it's more about helping individuals find their own paths to recovery rather than advocating a particular set of actions and beliefs. SMART Recovery has no particular religious or spiritual component, though it makes room for personal religious beliefs. It draws more on language from the world of therapy such as Cognitive Behavior Therapy (which has been very important in my recovery) rather than language from the world of spirituality. Some may indeed feel more comfortable with a program such as SMART Recovery or an even more explicitly Christian, faith-intensive program such as "Celebrate Recovery," while many remain steadfast advocates of twelve-step based programs. I advocate neither. I simply point out that there are options.

I only mention these to illustrate that unlike in 1939, when Bill W. and Henry Parkhurst wrote the Big Book, there are numerous treatment options and paths to long-term recovery.[20] Whichever choice you make, it should be an informed one based on your personal situation and life experience. We are not all square pegs for square holes.

I believe that, at least for me, the framing of the program isn't as important as the connections made with others within the program. It is the connections that have helped me stay sober while working on the underlying psychological and childhood issues that took me to that moment at Green Oaks.

If you're a lawyer, law student, judge, or family member of someone in the legal profession, there may be free, confidential recovery resources in your state tailored especially for you. Most every lawyer and law student in the U.S. has access to what are known as Lawyer Assistance Programs (LAPs). These programs offer free counseling and assessments to Bar members and their families who are struggling with mental health and addiction challenges. The nature of LAPs may be a bit different from state to state and program to program, but generally they grant confidentiality to everyone who reaches out to them for help.[21]

To better understand what these programs are and how those connected to state Bars can use them, I reached out to Michael Cohen, executive director of the Florida Lawyers Assistance program. As a side note, to again show how valuable social media can be, I connected with Michael through contributor Brian Tannebaum, whom I met on Twitter. I asked Michael questions similar to those I asked Brian about lawyers facing crises related to addiction. Michael responded with some great information and advice. As with Brian's advice, much of Michael Cohen's response is relevant even to those outside the law profession.

In your experience, what are the three biggest mistakes lawyers make with regards to substance use that puts their license at risk?

Refusing to admit to themselves that there's a problem, believing they can handle it by themselves, and refusing or postponing asking for help, even if they know help is available. Let's take a look at these three responses one at a time.

1. Refusing to Admit to Themselves that There's a Problem

Alcoholic or addicted lawyers don't start out by sleeping under a bridge or mainlining heroin. As with most substance use issues, early behavior is likely no different than colleagues in undergraduate or law school and, unfortunately, there's no way to predict who will wind up dealing with the consequences of this disease. The progression of a substance use disorder can take years, during which time the lawyer will often blame other factors for consequences of their substance use (*my partners/the judge were too harsh, my spouse doesn't understand the pressure I'm under, I was late to court because of the damn traffic*). Unfortunately, it's often not until the consequences are undeniable (arrest, bar complaint, report from a judge) that the lawyer may admit there's a problem with their use of substances.

2. I Can Handle This Myself

We are taught from day one in law school that we should be able to out-think, out-argue, and out-reason any problem. After all, we're the advice givers, not the advice takers. This attitude when applied to a substance use disorder is disastrous. We have no frame of reference for dealing with a deadly medical condition—it would be like saying, "Yup, I have this lump growing in my chest, but I should be able to use my legal skills to deal with it." I don't know any lawyer that would say that with reference to cancer, or diabetes, or hepatitis, but it is almost always the thought process that takes place when a lawyer finally acknowledges they may be dealing with a drug or alcohol addiction. Part of this is clearly the stigma that still exists regarding addiction, part is the fear of being taken advantage of by admitting a "weakness," and part is the belief that addiction is an issue of willpower that can be overcome by our legal acumen. Clearly, this approach does not work for most lawyers dealing with addiction.

3. Refusing or Postponing Asking for Help

For the reasons above (stigma, fear, belief in their own abilities), most lawyers will not reach out for help, even after they've acknowledged there's a problem. Almost every state now has a lawyer assistance program (LAP) that provides free, confidential help to legal professionals dealing with substance use or mental health problems. Every LAP devotes a great deal of time to getting the word out that they exist and that they're there to help, but lawyers often refuse to seek that help until it is forced on them by a referral to the LAP by law enforcement or the Bar disciplinary agency. Sometimes, this refusal to seek help is based on the belief of lawyers that they can handle the problem themselves, but it is often the belief that by contacting the LAP, they will be exposing their situation to the Bar and other lawyers, which is not the case.

Every LAP safeguards confidentiality as the cornerstone of its existence, and most are staffed by recovering attorneys and volunteers who have dealt with their own problems. In some jurisdictions, like Florida, confidentiality is protected by Bar rule and by state law *unless* the lawyer is referred to the LAP by the Bar disciplinary agency or Bar admission agency. Obviously, contacting the LAP or a treatment program before the substance use disorder comes to the Bar's attention can save an attorney's license, family, and possibly life, but unfortunately the combination of fear and ego often prevents this.

Based on your experience, in general, what are the three most important things a lawyer who is struggling can do as soon as possible to put himself/herself in the best position to continue practicing law even if there are temporary consequences?

Find out what resources are available and use them, engage in the appropriate level of treatment, and stick with the program.

1. Find Out What Resources Are Available and Use Them

Once the lawyer has acknowledged that a problem exists, the question is "what now?" Many lawyers "choose" to avoid seeking help out of fear that exposing themselves will result in disciplinary sanctions, loss of license, or loss of esteem because of the stigma still associated with addiction. As noted previously, we're a profession that tells ourselves we can handle any problem by using our big brains. Combating addiction is not something that can be done without help, but there are a number of resources available to an attorney who wants to recover. A good first step is to contact the state's lawyer assistance program. Some LAPs are part of state Bar associations, others operate independently but cooperatively with state Bars, while others have no connection to the Bar association. In all cases, however, the primary concern of the LAP is confidentiality. A lawyer can approach the LAP, be candid about what's going on in his or her life, and know that the information will be kept inviolate. Most states have Bar rules that prevent the LAP from disclosing any information, and some states (such as Florida) have both Bar rules and state laws protecting information.

In addition to the state LAP, large firm lawyers may have access to a confidential employee assistance program (EAP) which, like the LAP, can assess the problem and recommend treatment options. Unfortunately, the fear associated with seeking help more often than not prevents the lawyer from asking for help while the problem is still manageable. Sadly, it often takes an outside force such as an arrest or Bar complaint to push the lawyer into getting help.

2. Engage in the Appropriate Level of Treatment

Once the lawyer has worked up the courage (or hit the level of desperation) to ask for help from a LAP or EAP, it is likely that recommendations will be made about how to best address the issue. These recommendations may range from attendance at twelve-step meetings, to individual or group therapy, to outpatient or inpatient treatment. Very often a lawyer confronted with a recommendation, especially for inpatient or outpatient treatment, will respond with, "I have a practice to run. I can't possibly disappear for 30 or 60 days." or "I have a family. I can't go to outpatient treatment three nights a week for the next few months." What the lawyer needs to understand is that if the treatment recommendation is not followed, it's very possible there will eventually not be a practice or family to worry about. Treatment may be a life or career-saving opportunity, and disregarding a recommendation made after an appropriate evaluation often leads to further progression of the addiction and more serious consequences.

3. Stick with the Program

After having the courage to ask for help and engaging in the appropriate level of treatment, the lawyer's task is to use the tools they've been given to remain in recovery. All too often, the lawyer's (or more accurately, the addiction's) thought process after completing treatment and putting together six or eight months of abstinence is, *Well, I've got this thing beat. I know what my problem was and won't make the same mistakes again. There should be no harm in having a beer or two.* This is a natural reaction to feeling healthier, patching up things at home, business picking up, and life in general getting better. However, discontinuing the measures that got the lawyer there (twelve-step meetings, therapy, and so on) will all too often allow the disease to reassert itself and start the long slide back into active addiction. The correct reaction to life getting better is to continue doing the things that turned life around, one day at a time.

It's important to also recognize that LAPs are open to law students where available, and that it's never too early to begin confronting problematic alcohol and substance use. These days the treatment options are myriad, and many address the special concerns of the young, including undergraduates.

Recovery has taken on a meaning well beyond twelve-step and traditional treatment over the years. One of the stories that embodies this is that of Robert Ashford. I first met Robert when he came to hear me speak at a conference. He then invited me to speak at the University of North Texas and gave me my first "Party Sober" T-shirt! Robert is one of the pioneers in the concept of "peer recovery" in the collegiate setting. He is not a law student or lawyer, but his concepts and philosophy transcend choice of career. Those concepts have helped countless numbers of students feel less stigmatized with getting help during school and with their recovery moving forward. Robert is a true pioneer in this area.

His résumé is impressive for such a young man. Born in north Texas and raised in northeastern Pennsylvania, Robert is a certified Peer Recovery Support Specialist, and an advocate for all individuals seeking long-term recovery. He was the Founding Program Director of the University of North Texas Collegiate Recovery Program. Robert holds a Bachelor's in Social Work, and a Bachelor's of Science in Psychology, and is currently pursuing a Master's of Social Work from the University of Pennsylvania. He's been the recipient of many prestigious awards, most notably NADAAC's Young Emerging Leader Award (2014), Young People in Recovery's Advocate of the Year (2014), and the University of North Texas Founders' Award (2015). Robert also serves on multiple nonprofit organizations' board of directors, the Council for Advising and Planning for the Texas Department of State Health Services, and is a current national planning partner for the Substance Abuse and Mental Health Services Administration (SAMHSA).

He is also in long-term recovery. He says, "For me, that means I no longer utilize mind-altering substances to change the way that I manage and cope with my life." But for ten years, Robert did just that. Throughout those ten years, he also self-medicated generalized anxiety disorder, major depressive disorder, and a bipolar diagnosis.

"I was a highly functional individual even throughout this time, and found my way into college," he says. "But unfortunately, as I am sure you can surmise, that wasn't very successful (at least not the first five times around!)." Eventually, he found himself out of college, and into the general workforce, where it was much easier to engage in drug use. He says, being in the service industry, "My substance use was largely celebrated."

This, however, isn't the story of Robert's time spent in active drug use, but rather a story of how collegiate recovery helped him get back on track.

Robert says, "After ten years with an active substance use disorder, I found myself at a crossroads." By that point he had received three DUIs. "I take responsibility for my decisions," he says. "After ten years and those three DUIs, I was finally graced with the awareness that I would need help to overcome my substance use disorder."

Robert couldn't do it alone however. He sought help and was allowed to seek inpatient treatment at a state-run treatment center in Fort Worth, Texas.

Robert knew that he would also need long-term support and services to continue his recovery, he says. "I wanted to go back to school, to finish what I had started so many years ago. So off I went to Denton, Texas, to one of the most highly recommended recovery residences that I had been referred to, and one that would require me to pay my own way, and either get a job or be enrolled full-time in school. At fifty-eight days in recovery, I began the process of enrolling full-time at the University of North Texas."

Robert was of course nervous starting the process. Walk in any direction on campus and you could hear discussion of smoking marijuana, finding Adderall for studying all-night, or spot the neon lights of the row of bars that every college and university has within blocks of the main campus. "I remember wondering to myself how was there any possibility, that knowing what I had accomplished the last time I was on a college campus (which was a tremendous amount of nothing), how was I ever going to maintain my recovery AND get a college degree," he says. "Nothing had seemingly changed about college—it was still in large part the gigantic party scene I remembered from years ago."

Still to this day, he gets many looks of "Huh?" when he lets people know that he is in long-term recovery. He says, "I remember telling this to the first person on campus after I had been accepted, and the response was something akin to, "So you don't drink, like, ever? How can you deal with your classes and all the drama?"

For the first few weeks during that first semester, Robert felt like an outsider on campus. He was overwhelmed. Though he had successfully made it back into college and what he considered a strong program of recovery, he was in an environment that was a threat to that recovery. "If I had continued on campus in isolation, I can say that it was only a matter of time before one of two things happened," he says. "I would either fall into the party life once again, or I would leave the university to save myself and my recovery."

Luckily, neither of these things would have to happen. In his fourth week back in school, he found a number of like-minded students and a staff member who understood what is was like being in recovery and being on a college campus. "Being around this group of peers in recovery saved my college career," he says.

Banded together with these new peers, he no longer felt like an outsider. Stress from homework, mid-terms, and finals were now more manageable because he had found a support network of students with whom he had the opportunity to meet multiple times a week in a safe space on campus. "For the first time outside of the treatment center and program, I felt like I was part of something bigger than myself" he says. "In that environment, this new community was potentially lifesaving."

During Robert's first attempts at making it through college, he thought the college experience meant hitting the best parties, blacking out at tailgates, and mainly having the time of his life for a few short years. At North Texas, however, he was learning that the college experience, can be about self-exploration, taking part in large spirit-filled events like homecoming and bowl games, building a network of friends and professionals, and expanding his mind in a field of his choosing. "It's amazing the ability you find within yourself to experience all facets of life when you have a program that provides resources, services, and support so that you can seek love and care," he says.

Robert graduated with two bachelor's degrees, and is now attending graduate school at an Ivy League institution. He says the only reason he is able to do that today is because of his recovery and because of the resources he had at the University of North Texas.

I asked Robert what advice he would give to either an incoming or current law student seeking support for addiction or other mental health issues. He says:

"As with any rigorous endeavor in recovery, law school is going to be a trying time that will push you to your limits. As a student in recovery, these limits can have dire consequences if self-care doesn't become a priority. Unfortunately, I've learned over the last few years (as I consulted with a Fort Worth Law School) that it was near impossible to disclose recovery status on a law school campus. Fear of being put into a box, shamed, and forever given a 'scarlet letter' was too great to speak out in need of support. Coupled with the rigors of any law school program, this is a system designed for failure for any individual with a substance use disorder, mental health concern, or any other quality of life disorder—and this only speaks to those who make it into recovery!"

Robert aptly points out that there currently is no collegiate recovery community on any law campus. It is therefore paramount that the student finds a way to support his/her mental health and recovery status with external supports such as mutual aid meetings, counseling, or social support networks.

"For that student who needs help, the best piece of advice I can give is to immediately go seek out professional guidance from a licensed addiction specialist or mental health professional. They can help you determine the severity and likely treatment regimen that will be most helpful, and you will have the facts and information you need when making a decision of whether to seek a medical discharge, or leave of absence from school.

"The worst thing I have seen happen with students who seek help, or ultimately take a leave of absence or medical discharge to receive care, is not returning to their studies. One of the most empowering things for any individual is finding and working toward a goal, which in this case is higher education. Whether it is an undergraduate degree, a master's degree, or a JD, education empowers those of us emerging and living in recovery. A momentary pause in your education does not make you a failure. It makes you human."

Robert suggests a number of available paths for young people including law students who are ready to seek help and maintain both recovery and a developing career. Ideally, increased awareness about the problems of drug and alcohol use among the law community will continue to transform the ways law schools, law practices, and other legal institutions such as state Bars accommodate recovery. While state Bars and some law practices have begun considering the roles they can play in supporting lawyers in recovery, it seems more can be done within law schools to acknowledge and support students who may be struggling with substance or alcohol use and the stigma students often fear when seeking help.

18

Recovery Is No
Yellow Brick Road

■ **August 2010**

I'M CRYING FOR hours, non-stop. Can't get out of bed. I'd been getting along pretty well—in recovery for over three years, going to twelve-step meetings, slowly but surely working on repairing the loss of trust with my girlfriend that awful day in April. Then all of a sudden, the bottom drops out. I feel worthless. I don't have any urges to drink or do blow, but I'm definitely restless and discontented. An all-consuming depression cuts deep to the bone. Suicidal ideation returns, which had not knocked at my door since that trip to Green Oaks in 2005. I feel as if three years of sobriety never happened. The ashamed, fat, teenage Brian has come back to visit. What happened? What *is* happening? Like that day in 2005 lying in bed with a weapon on my nightstand, I see only a bottomless abyss in my future. There is no point in going on. The signs running up to that moment were there. I've been unable to find any enjoyment in life. Lying in bed all day. No strength to even walk or play with my dog. Frequent temper outbursts, with the frustration of being unable to vocalize what was wrong. I. Will. Never. Leave. This. Bed. My old friend, depressive disorder, is back front and center.

At the moment, my brother Mark is making a bid to buy the baseball team the Texas Rangers. The owner of the Rangers, Tom Hicks, has put the team in bankruptcy. Mark is bidding against a group led by baseball Hall of Famer Nolan Ryan. For a time, it appears Mark is going to win the bidding. The more it seems a reality, the more depressed I get. Instead of measuring myself against the reality of my ongoing recovery from eating disorders, drugs, and alcohol, and taking the mindful joy in how far I have come in my life and the changes I have made, all of a sudden, I take a step backward. I'm feeling sorry for myself, and my measuring stick is Mark's success. It's an impossible measuring stick from a financial and entrepreneurial standpoint. I'll never be Mark. What do I want? I want to do more than exist in sobriety. I want personal and professional achievement beyond that. I want to leave that little boy completely in the rearview mirror and look at myself with pride. I'm not there yet. Lots of work to do. Have to start with pulling myself out of this bottomless pit of depression over something I should be happy about: the success of my brother whom I love dearly. Instead it makes me feel empty. I cry. My dog Peanut senses my sadness. She's licking the tears from my face. She would do anything to ease my pain. *What do I want?*

I no longer want to practice law on any level, and even if I've been successful in maintaining sobriety. I see no way forward in my career. I might have sobriety and a supportive family, but what do I have that's going to make me want to get out of bed every morning? I began sobbing uncontrollably.

I've been missing my psychiatric appointments. I sleep all day. The hopelessness of my future consumes me. My family sees it, and they are worried. My girlfriend Amanda sees it. She's also frustrated and worried. I want to tell her what's wrong, but I'm embarrassed and ashamed that it seems so trivial yet is so consuming.

As I listen to the progress of the bidding for the team on the radio, I head to my computer and compose an email to Mark. I ask him to please take me back into his company. Any position, I'll sweep floors. I'll sell tickets. I don't care. I just want a stability I don't currently feel. I want to feel included. I want to feel loved. I stare at the email for what seems like hours. Finger just above the key, ready to send it. I don't send it. I'm not sure why. Maybe I'm afraid of the answer, although I know Mark will be supportive as he always has been. Maybe I don't want him to say yes, because that ultimately will be a step backward in forming my own personal and professional identity. Instead of sending the email, I go to sleep.

The next morning, I get a call from my psychiatrist, who is concerned that I've been missing sessions without explanation. It's not like me. We talk about my state of despair. He asks what's changed in my life, other than the Texas Rangers issue. Well, one minor thing. I had been feeling well and thought I did not need my antidepressants anymore. I've stopped taking them.

"You've stopped taking the medication. Well, Brian, you think that might be an issue here?" He states the all too obvious that was a mystery to me.

"Well yes, doctor, I guess that could be playing a part."

"Get back on your medication and come on in. Let's talk about why your family's success made you feel like a failure in that moment."

I did, and I did. I realized at that point that clinical depression would always be trying to fool me into thinking I'm cured. I needed to stay present in my recovery, and I needed to stay on my medication. I still have that email to Mark saved in my drafts folder. It's a reminder that I need to be my own person, and the only standard for my success and recovery is what I create. And it's a reminder that recovery and feeling like I've created a whole life are constant works in progress, and that just because I've maintained sobriety doesn't mean I've got everything figured out. In recovery, as in life, there will be steps forward and backward. I've never been very good at the cha-cha, but in recovery, I know that missing a step occasionally is only a brief pause in my journey and not the journey itself.

For those of us in recovery, potential setbacks come in all shapes and sizes. Obviously slipping back into active substance or alcohol use or other self-defeating behaviors is the setback everyone fears who is actively seeking recovery. But that's not the only challenge we face. None of us is able to hit the pause button on the rest of our lives while we figure out the routines that help keep us sober. We still have the stress of work (or finding new work and ways to support ourselves), we have personal relationships to maintain or repair, and we all have a past that sometimes surfaces in our present. Any of these other aspects of our lives can tempt us to turn to old habits for refuge or relief. It is often tempting to give up on the discipline of treatment programs, support groups, self-help groups, medication, or therapy that helps us to move forward even when our lives get messy or cluttered with other obligations. Obligations and missteps in the real world create stress. Stress often creates emotional and professional challenges when it triggers destructive behaviors. There's the stress of the competitive legal profession or other work. There's the stress of maintaining relationships. And there's the stress of personal tragedy, whether it be injury, illness, or grief for lost or ill loved ones. The list of potential triggers is endless. I can't think of a better example of having to deal with these sorts of setbacks—and surviving in recovery—than our contributor Susan, who earlier described her recovery from addiction to alcohol. As she explains, she was able to maintain her recovery even as she suffered great personal tragedy and hardship.

Susan says that over the past fourteen years, there have been plenty of situations in which a glass of chardonnay would have taken the edge off. In fact, most of the hardest experiences of her life occurred after she got sober.

"I had fewer than two months of sobriety on September 11, 2001, when I watched the Twin Towers on fire from my apartment," she says. "During the early morning hours of July 4, 2002, I awoke to a strange man standing above my bed. He'd broken into my apartment and I'm not sure what would have happened if I had not screamed and caused him to run out (especially since they later found out he was involved in an unsolved homicide and rape case)."

Susan's mother's cancer was diagnosed at the same time that her father was gravely ill with emphysema. About a month into her mother's chemotherapy treatment, her father was experiencing intense difficulty breathing and wanted to go to the emergency room (which, she says, was rare for a man who avoided doctors and hospitals). Susan says that as they drove in the car, her mother, wearing a bright bandana covering her bald head, tried to lift his spirits and said, "Joe, we are so lucky" (referring to their years together). She says, he just looked at her and quietly said, "Yeah, if I could breathe, I'd be whistling."

"Even toward the end of his life, he possessed a dynamic sense of humor we all adored," she says. "My three brothers and I all flew down to North Carolina and spent precious moments with him before he died."

Life hit Susan hard again in 2007 when she was diagnosed with breast cancer. In 2008, the man she had been involved with for several years was diagnosed with bladder cancer and died six months later. In 2009, she was diagnosed again with breast cancer for the second time and had a double mastectomy.

She says, "It really didn't seem like the 'life beyond my wildest dreams' that I'd been promised in the rooms. But the reality is that when looking back, I am so grateful that I was able to get through each of these experiences sober."

Susan says that her father's death in 2005 was probably the biggest challenge she faced without using a glass of wine to dull the pain. She goes on to say, "Fortunately, I realized that alcohol would just make these 'bad' situations even worse. There was not enough wine in California that would take away the pain of losing him, so why would I even consider it? There was no escaping the pain; I just had to walk through it. It was a hard lesson, but I believe it has been a key to my sobriety."

Susan says that she has also gained a new appreciation of "tough times." She says that as she looks back at some of the hardest moments, she now can see that there was something in each and every experience that was positive. Her decision to quit drinking was the beginning of a journey in which she discovered that she had an inner strength and a joy for life that she never knew existed.

"When I look at this in a timeline, it all makes perfect sense," she says. "That is the magical thing about life—you must live going forward, yet it only makes sense looking backward. I now know that getting sober prepared me for my fight with cancer."

Susan says that she also met a fellow sober breast cancer survivor who lamented that she didn't get sober for the cancer to happen.

Susan suggested to her that perhaps she did.

She says, "I cannot even imagine how I would have handled this if I were still drinking. And if I had been, I doubt I would have even had the courage to push for more answers. Sobriety has given me tools to deal with life on life's terms. It has given me healthier ways to relax, which include praying and meditating. These tools have brought me tremendous peace—although admittedly my meditation sometimes merely consists of me obsessing with my eyes shut. But it is far better than picking up a drink."

Sobriety also taught Susan to look at things from a perspective of gratitude.

"Had I still been drinking when I was diagnosed, I would be wallowing in self-pity," she says. "Instead, I relied on my faith and prayed for the strength to do what I had to do. And through sobriety, I found that the strength was deep inside the whole time. Of course, there have been moments of doubt, but overall instead of asking 'why me?' I am now able to say, 'I was able to save my own life—two times!'"

This tremendous shift in Susan's perspective has helped her cope with the double mastectomy as well. She says that she finally realized that the "external" things (including parts of her body) have nothing to do with who she is. For years, she was self-conscious about her body and would try every gym club and exercise machine imaginable to change it.

"Initially I thought that 'losing' my breasts would be devastating, but ironically I feel more comfortable with myself than I ever have before. Today, I believe that my heart and soul define who I really am, and they are also what saved my life. I still don't like my thighs, but I love my spirit. Perhaps that has been one of my greatest lessons of all—the power of the human spirit. And I give thanks every day to the woman who first nurtured that spirit, my grandmother, Adele."

In 2003, Susan followed her dreams and moved to Washington, D.C. She is currently an Associate Research Professor at Georgetown University. Her work centers around improving responses within the juvenile and criminal justice systems to the addiction crisis currently plaguing our country.

"I am very open about the fact that I am sober because I want others to know that recovery is real and it is transformative," she says. "And I am not just referring to those who find themselves facing charges, but also to others within my professional community. I hope to serve as an example for those who still may be 'functioning' and let them know that if they are struggling with an addiction, there is a solution."

Susan goes on to say, "Recovery has given me the chance to become the woman that I always dreamed of becoming as a little girl. A sober lawyer in Washington, D.C.—yes they were right—it certainly is a life beyond my wildest dreams."

19

A Leap of Faith

■ **August 27, 2004**

MY COUSIN IS getting married. I am flying out to Seattle on Saturday morning on my brother's plane, then boarding a puddle-jumper to Orca Island for the wedding. It will be a happy day for my cousin and the entire extended Cuban family. Wheels up at 7 a.m.

At one in the morning, I still have an hour until last call. A group of cocaine buddies and I are closing down the local bar that doubles as a boutique hotel. It's one of my favorite places to party. The club has a "safe" bathroom—one that has stalls with solid closing doors. Addicts can never be too careful.

Now it's just before closing. Have to get that last sniffy in. Back to the bathroom. No dollar bill. Left my keys on the table. Snort it off the back of my hand. Ready to rock. More Jack and Diet Cokes! We go back to my place. Now it's close to four in the morning. Incoherent jabber, watching *Scarface*. We recite our favorite line from the movie before each line of cocaine. "Say hello to my little friend!" We are one with Scarface. The thought that I have to be on a plane in a few hours vaguely penetrates the back of my cocaine brain. No sleep? No problem! A couple of black market Xanax will do the trick, and then I can sleep on the long flight to Seattle.

Just in time, I head to the airport, get on the plane—loaded with lots of close Cuban relatives—I pass out. The next thing I know it's wheels down in Seattle. I wake up with a raging Xanax, cocaine, and whiskey hangover, and I'm pissed off that I didn't bring a baggie of coke with me for a quick recovery. Still have to take the puddle-jumper to Orca. That will be fun! I'm determined to not puke in the puddle-jumper and thus announce my disrespect for my family, my cousin, her family, and last of all, myself. There's a minimum code of conduct for drug addicts.

I survive the flight to Orca Island—barely. I'm in one of those tiny twin-engine planes that gets bumped around by every wind. I don't know how I keep from puking all over the plane. When we get to our rooms at the wedding site, I head straight to the toilet and upchuck. I am suddenly very uncomfortable being around so much family. Leaving my insular world of addicts and joining responsible, happy people who lead productive lives is always risky.

The wedding itself was unlike anything I had experienced before. It was set on a beautiful lake in the wilderness of Washington State. The sky over the green mountains was just a bit cloudy, and the air was alive with birdsong. The extended families of the bride and groom had come from around the world, and some folks were meeting for the first time.

I rarely looked anyone in the eye the entire trip. I was afraid they would see the addict within me, and I would sense their disappointment. I felt it regardless. Not because it was verbally expressed, but because I knew that my brothers knew. I knew they were disappointed in me. And I knew that my father didn't know; it would break his heart. I knew that my extended relatives did not know save for my aunt, the mother of the bride. She was a clinical social worker, and I would sometimes reach out to her. Starting in 1990, after my first divorce, we would occasionally discuss my depression and feelings of unworthiness. But how could I possibly impose my misery on this joyful occasion?

During the wedding dinner, I was sitting at a long banquet table. One by one, family members stood up and toasted the bride and groom, and the entire time I stared directly at my plate of food. For some reason fixating on a single point somewhere near my salmon and thinking about nothing but the plate gave me comfort and allowed me to listen to what was being said. If I looked at anyone, my mind would immediately start processing projected thoughts. Being able to focus on a fixed point and listen gave a normalcy to everything. No past, no future, only that moment. This would be my modus operandi for family events at the apex of my addiction.

As I watched my cousin being carried around in a chair to the song "Hava Nagila," a Jewish tradition, it occurred to me that the happier people were around me, the more miserable and depressed I became. I seemed to be in an almost hallucinatory state, even hearing little whispers: "Brian looks unhappy." "What's wrong with Brian?" I felt an urge to slip away into the Washington wilderness, never to be heard from again.

Really, I only wanted to get back to Dallas, to my safe haven of addiction and isolation. I wanted to be with other addicts and experience those increasingly rare moments when I could bask in the lie I had worked so hard to create. By 2004, drugs and alcohol offered less and less relief. And when they didn't work their temporary magic, I was overcome by raging depression.

I couldn't help remembering this wedding and desperate state I was in, when in 2016, Amanda and I married, a sober marriage this time for me, a different life, maybe even a leap of faith for both of us.

And now, I'm thinking back to when I'm sixteen years old, and I'm on a trip to Niagara Falls with my family. The sound of the water rushing over the falls is like a tornado. I try to walk closer to the handrail protecting me and everyone else from falling in, but with each step closer, my legs become weaker, and my heartbeat quickens. I look out at the violent force of uncontrolled nature. I can't take another step forward. I'm terrified. I have no sense of balance. The falls begin to spin. I drop to my hands and knees. The feeling of the concrete on my hands giving me some sense of protection. As long as I can feel it, I won't fall in. I look back for my mom. She's gone. Had she been next to me at all? Who will save me from falling over the ledge and being swallowed by the falls? I switch to sitting on my butt and using my hands to propel myself forward feet first, inch by inch. I finally make it to the railing and grab hold. I'm safe. I allow my feet to dangle over the side. Suddenly the concrete gives way. I grab hold of the railing, but I'm a fat child, I'm a weak child. I'm a stupid child. My mom has told me so. The other kids have told me so. I can't hold on. I drop.

I wake up sweating. My fiancée tells me I was screaming in my sleep.

■ May 20, 2016

I'm fifty-five years old. I'm not dreaming, although part of me is hoping I am. I want to wake up safe in bed, ready to head to Starbucks to work on my book. Instead, I'm confronting a great fear, let's say it's the *third* greatest fear in life: my fear of heights. I'm not standing at the precipice of Niagara Falls, 176 feet high with a guardrail to protect me, but one that's even higher. I'm on the observation deck of Reunion Tower in Dallas, Texas, fifty stories (541 feet) high. There's a gaping hole in the mesh protecting tourists from a free fall worthy of a parachute. I will be taking my 6'2" frame of 220 pounds through that opening. High above the ground, the image of a plane decompressing and being sucked through a tiny window into a thirty-thousand-foot freefall briefly invades my consciousness. In my mind, I'm also revisiting Niagara Falls.

And more than that, I'm revisiting that day on April 8, 2007, when I was terrified of sobriety but took that step forward in taking my desire chip. It's time to take another step in my recovery. In being able to trust. In facing my greatest fears. This time, it's my fear of heights. It's one of the great tricks of my recovery—to always find ways to challenge my comfort and sense of security with myself.

I learned early that recovery for me was going to be about facing fears. When I walked into twelve-step for the first time, there were so many fears I had to confront. The fear of having to be "me" in sobriety. The fear of failure (relapse). The fear of trusting others and having them trust me. The fear of being rejected by those closest to me if I relapsed. The fear of being alone in my sobriety. The fear of professional consequences.

In recovery I confronted each one of those fears and came to realize that at least for me, fear was a projection into the future based on emotion rather than facts. Fear allowed the fiction I told myself to cope to shape my reality. I was protecting and nurturing my worries, not protecting myself.

So what was I doing fifty stories above the ground looking out into an open sky with no hope of survival if I fell? I have to go back a year to explain.

In 2015, a gentleman by the name of Gary Mendell reached out to me to have lunch and talk about his addiction advocacy initiative, Shatterproof. I'd never heard of it before. There are lots of advocacy organizations out there, and a lot of different agendas. Anyone involved with mental health advocacy knows you can't be all things to all people, and you must pick where you can make the most impact. Most of my advocacy had been in the eating disorder realm. Being a guy in eating disorder recovery, I felt that was where I could do the most good. As I write this book, there are simply not that many guys out there sharing their stories publicly as compared to women. The stigma for men is very strong. But I felt something was lacking in both my advocacy and recovery. Addiction to both drugs and alcohol are integral parts of my story, and I wanted to do more to connect to others about those topics.

I met Gary for lunch to discuss Shatterproof. Within the first minute of conversation, he stated that they put on rappelling events all over the city to raise both money and awareness for their addiction advocacy work. In addition to discussing involvement with the organization overall, he asked if I would rappel at one of their events, and that there would be one in Dallas at some point. All I knew about rappelling was that people dropped from very high places, seemingly holding on to nothing but a slim rope, and if their grip failed, certain death was to follow. I jokingly thanked Gary for contributing to the new nightmares I would have, replacing my dreams of Niagara Falls. I cited a recent hip replacement and declined to participate on that level.

In reality, I was terrified. I would bow to fear instead of facing it. It never occurred to me sitting there that from a purely selfish perspective, it was the perfect opportunity to advance my recovery while advancing my advocacy. Here was another deep-seated fear I could confront. I got involved but declined just then to rappel. I successfully deflected my fears and life went on.

Then I heard from Gary again. The Shatterproof Rappel Challenge was coming to Dallas. Would I be interested in participating? It would involve another thing I had a fear of, asking people for money. Down the list of my fears in life is cold-calling and soliciting funds. Integral to those activities is the fear of rejection. From girls. From my mom. From friends. A fear that infected everything I did as I survived day to day time passing but not advancing in my development as a person. I simply hated asking for anything that if someone said no, I would see it as a reflection on me versus the reality that it had nothing to do with me.

I decided that I would face my fears. I would be doing something I had never done before, from a height that I would have needed to get drunk first or do some blow in order to agree to do it, and then accomplish it before I sobered up. I said I would rappel from Reunion Tower and ask people for money as part of the jump. After getting clearance from both my hip surgeon and my fiancée, I began the next step in my recovery.

In the two-week lead-up to the jump, I watched videos of other people rappelling, other Shatterproof jumps, and came to the conclusion that it was best to compartmentalize my fear. I gave no more thought to the act of rappelling, the height, or how it would be done. I had to rely on one of the gifts recovery had given me. Trust. Trust in the process. Trust in the people there to support me. Trust in the ropes that would guide me down the fifty stories. If you're in recovery, does that sound familiar?

"Jump" day comes. Compartmentalizing has worked great. I've given no thought to the process or the reality of having to do the hardest thing I have done since getting sober. Trust that I would not become a chalk drawing fifty stories down. In reality, it would boil down to just a few seconds. Those seconds of moving myself through where the wire mesh had been removed and allow the ropes, pulleys, and the people helping me who were all experts in rappelling to do their job. The split second where it would be a "free fall" while the ropes tightened and supported my weight. As the elevator rose slowly to the top of Reunion Tower and it started to become real to me, I could not get that split second out of my mind. I could not get Niagara Falls out of my mind. I could feel the weakness in my knees. Walking out of the elevator and onto the observation deck my instinct was once again to drop to my butt and inch my way over to the rappelling area. I'd already been "geared up" and was ready to rappel as was my partner who was rappelling for her son "Bubba," who she lost to heroin addiction earlier in the year. We were both thrilled that we'd been the top team fundraiser for the event, but I could see the fear in her eyes as clearly as I could feel my feet in quicksand. We went through about five minutes of training and the explanation of the process and how to control our descent. It was time. I stepped sideways up a ladder and put my butt on the ledge facing backwards and was helped to slowly guide myself off the precipice into the realm of recovery and trust.

"Oh my god, Oh my god." The words came out of my mouth as I felt that split second of weightlessness. Funny words from a guy who considered himself a humanist. I had found a foxhole in those seconds. The ropes tightened.

"I'm alive! "I'm alive!" came out of my mouth as the tension released from my body. That split second of fear evaporated into calm and the knowledge that fear will always be there in life. It's how I face it and react to it that matters. As I controlled my descent to meet the people who loved and supported me, I realized that the step off the edge was just another step forward in the process. That's my journey. No better, no worse than any other in this book. We all take our unique path. That is recovery.

Addiction and recovery can take us down many different paths academically and professionally. It may end up being the same path we started on. It may entail numerous exits and reentries, U-turns, and returns to the starting point. The highway of recovery is often full of turns and obstacles. Take my story. I didn't want to be a lawyer but ended up in law school in part because of how I dealt with untreated addiction and mental health issues. Like some of the stories in this book, I eventually left the practice of law. Others stick with it and become accomplished in their professions, and recovery is something that makes them better at what they are passionate about, getting the best grades possible, the best job possible in the chosen profession. You have followed your passion and your effort in the law or decided to put the effort somewhere else.

I remember the moment I decided I had enough and was ready to finally let go of the practice of law, something that was never a passion. It was a negative experience, but one of clarity and truth that came from confronting my fears.

In 2008, I was a year into recovery but a lost soul. I was feeling sorry for myself in that I did not feel I was doing anything of worth. I was doing a lot of First Amendment blogging, which was satisfying from a legal standpoint, but the ultimate purpose of my future was unseen to me. I was empty in professional drive and personal spirit, I considered a drastic career change and interviewed at Sears for a position with one of their corporate branches in Dallas. After three interviews, I didn't get an offer. Once again I was feeling inadequate on numerous levels.

My twitter bio read that I was an attorney with Mark Cuban companies. I was not doing any legal work for him, however. I was doing work with his Charitable Foundation, the Fallen Patriot Fund, which was very fulfilling work providing support to seriously injured veterans from Operation Iraqi Freedom, something I still do today. I still wanted more. I was feeling like Fredo from *The Godfather* or Billy Carter and his "Billy Beer."[22] The goofy brother, hanging on his brother's coattails but accomplishing nothing in life.

One day, I tweeted what I thought was a clever joke about the AT&T mobile phone service. At the time, they were running commercials with Luke Wilson about being able to surf the web while also taking a phone call, a big deal back then. My joke was something to the effect of "Surf the web between your fifteen dropped phone calls." That evening I received an angry email from Mark. I had not considered that Mark had an interest in the American Airlines Center and part of that was "AT&T Plaza."

Oops! He was rightfully angry. I had his name, therefore his brand, on my Twitter profile. I had potentially damaged that brand with a derogatory tweet. He told me that if I wanted to tweet without accountability, I immediately had to stop saying I work for him. I had to stop using my Dallas Mavericks email address. I had to cleanse all of social media of any implication that I was putting out content under his umbrella.

It was a big moment for me. But after thinking it through, I realized it was an important one. Being a Cuban had been a big part of how I was perceived for a long time. Being a lawyer was also part of my public perception. Sure, it was basically just changing a few sentences on my Twitter, Facebook, and LinkedIn accounts and picking up a new email account. I vividly remember Mark telling me that while I might be upset at him for the moment, it was a positive change for me, and I would thank him for pushing me to be my own person. He was right. Thank you, Mark.

It felt good to abandon my lawyer's sense of caution. I could be a smart ass when I wanted. I could be honest about my opinions. I soon realized it was what I'd wanted for a long time. I realized that for me, one of the great pleasures that I came to later in life was the pleasure of candor. In recovery, I can be myself.

Ever since giving up the façade, I don't have to pose anymore. I don't have to pretend. Of course, many attorneys are not in a position by profession or by temperament to sharing the details of their lives (or their candid opinions) with others. I get it. I'm by nature an introvert, and I've been an attorney, so I know how important putting up those walls can be sometimes. I still believe that if you or anyone you know is experiencing addiction or mental health concerns, the most important step is to reach out. Make a connection. Share a vulnerability. It's not always easy, but I've learned how lives can be touched by simply sharing stories.

The toughest audience I ever had was the first time I spoke publicly about my struggles with eating disorders, addiction, and recovery. It was to a local Rotary Club group in Dallas. Rotary Clubs are great for aspiring public speakers, because if you make mistakes, it's not a reputation killer, and if you mess up completely, hey, at least you get a free lunch. It's good practice. It can, however, also be a difficult room for certain types of subject matter. Speaking about eating disorders to a group of primarily older men who had little understanding that guys also suffered from eating disorders was nerve-wracking. When I got to the part about dealing with alcohol, drug addiction, and depression, I saw more nods of understanding.

The second toughest audience I have spoken to, though, are lawyers. My first talk to that demographic was to a group of family lawyers at a lunchtime event in Fort Worth, Texas. When the event was over, there was polite applause, but as busy lawyers do, no one stuck around to ask me questions or engage in the usual dialogue that I get with many other groups. In my mind, I had failed in getting my message of experience, strength and hope and love of family recovery across.

Dejected at my perceived failure, I headed home and began the process of figuring out how I could better connect with members of my profession (or what once was my profession). I checked in on Twitter to see what was going on in the world. There was a tweet from a previously unknown young woman to me. Her attorney father was at my lunchtime talk. Her string of tweets to me read: "You don't know me, but I want to thank you. My father was at your talk today. He reached out to me afterward. We are going to have dinner together for the first time in a year."

The moment I thought I was failing miserably, just spinning my wheels, I was actually making a connection. A connection of hope and love. One person. One life. I realized that I did not have to change the world. If one person takes just one thing from what I say, and acts on it in a positive way, I've succeeded.

Letting ourselves be vulnerable and admitting our fears is hard, especially for lawyers. As members of the legal profession, we're not super-human. We're just people. We bring genetics and the baggage of our past and present to the table like anyone else. We want acceptance. We want love. We want to be loved. We want to know that our lives have meaning. We are also our pasts. We are the shy, the bullied, the abused, the depressed. And the resilient. Traits that cut across all demographics and professions. We may bring unresolved and unacknowledged co-occurring issues to the table. Eating disorders, depressive disorders, bipolar disorders, the list goes on and on.

Earlier in this book, I stated that getting sober was the most terrifying thing I have done in my life. As I stepped from that ledge into another leg of my recovery and trust, I told the person lowering me that my fear of heights was my second biggest fear. I was wrong.

I put it at third. The second most terrifying thing I ever did in my life was to tear back all the layers in therapy to that shy, bullied little boy who did not feel loved, who did not know how to tell anyone how alone he was. Who wanted to be loved by a mother who did love him but brought the baggage of her past to her children. Taking that time machine and talking to that little boy. How many of us have talked to that child? Had conversations with that child? Being strong tells us to leave that child behind. I can tell you without hesitation that talking to that child was as important for me as getting sober. Why? It helped me stay sober. Forgiving that little boy and allowing that little boy to forgive me tells me it is OK to be vulnerable even in a profession where such a trait is considered weakness.

Talking to your younger self is just one technique. For anyone who wants to make recovery work, there are resources available. There are people out there who want to fight for you. And even if you haven't been successful in recovery in the past, the landscape is always changing. And more and more people—both advocates and the general public—have the language at hand now to understand and speak about active recovery. Stigma and fear of lost reputation will always be real, but for many of us there is less to fear now perhaps than ever before.

In 1979, deep in an eating disorder and body image issues, less than a year away from a descent into alcoholism, I was obsessively weighing myself at the Penn State campus infirmary (a common behavior with some eating disorders). One day while I was standing on the scale, I looked over and my chart was laid out. I took a peek. I noticed a line written by the campus nurse that was something to the effect of, "Brian is weighing himself multiple times a day, and it is concerning." That was it. No follow-up. No mention of a possible eating disorder. Nurses were simply not trained for that in 1979, especially to notice the signs in men. I would not go into recovery for that eating disorder until 2007.

If I were that same teen at Penn State in 2016, it would probably be different. The university now has staff specifically trained in seeing the signs of eating disorders in men and women. They have screening tools. There is much greater awareness of how eating disorders affect men. The odds are exponentially greater today that I would have been noticed and steps to empower me to choose recovery would have been taken. Times have changed. Students are more aware and more engaged. They are often willing to reach out to friends. There are awareness campaigns. There are on-campus, student-run peer-recovery support groups. Are there still stigma and stereotypes? Of course. They exist in both eating disorders and addiction. I see it every day. "Eating disorders are a choice. Just eat!" "Addiction is a choice. Just stop!" We know neither of these is true genetically, biologically, or environmentally but the stereotypes persist.

Let's advance to 1980 when I was drinking heavily, well on my way to being an alcoholic at nineteen years old. Was there a path to recovery? As I have previously written, the closest I ever came to help was reading an AA twenty-questions pamphlet and decided that I was not an alcoholic despite answering in the affirmative to many of the questions. When I speak at colleges, a student will invariably state (jokingly), "You're not an alcoholic until you graduate." No. I was one. What if I was that same student on the campus of Penn State in 2016? There are many currently in the same situation.

Once again, a different ball game. There's much more awareness today. There are screening tools and resources on many campuses, student-led recovery groups, as well as the long-standing options of AA and other self-help groups. Of course, stigma is still an obstacle. Many worry about the threats to social life and future career choices without realizing that the ultimate threat to the future is to NOT take that step into recovery. What path would nineteen-year-old Brian take in 2016? Maybe none, or maybe I would have been in recovery much earlier than waiting until my forties.

Now I am in my fifties, on a new road chosen beyond the confines of what lawyers are expected to be and what I would have ever envisioned as I struggled to survive as a law student so many years ago at the University of Pittsburgh. Am I still an "addicted lawyer" beyond my Starbucks Vente? I often hear "once an addict, always an addict." I certainly get that in the sense that I always have to be vigilant and present in my recovery, but I worry about that label, as it presupposes that people cannot change and reinvent themselves as part of that recovery. I stated at the beginning of this book that I am a person in long-term recovery. I am many other things. I am a shy teenager wanting so badly to be loved and accepted for who he was. I am that lost law student walking through the doors of Pitt Law for my first time feeling insecure, inferior and terrified of being exposed. I am a middle-aged guy standing in the parking lot of a psychiatric facility just about to take that first step. I am the Brian who was too afraid to allow himself to be helped through three marriages. All of those Brians are within me and I think about them every day. I talk to them, I comfort them. I don't want them to ever not be a part of me. That is when I stop learning. That is when I lose sight of my path forward in recovery. I become afraid of the darkness and stop trusting the process.

Is that your path? I can't say. We all bring different memories, experiences, and fears to the recovery rodeo. They certainly define our past and there is nothing we can do about that. I recall a quote from a gentleman named Christopher Paolini. It goes, "Without fear, there cannot be courage." I had so many fears. I still get afraid. I am, however, glad I found the courage to overcome them and create the Brian writing this book today. You may be afraid—afraid of not cutting it in law school. Afraid that if you seek help you will be left behind or ostracized. Afraid of losing your license and earning a living the only way you know how. Afraid of tearing back the layers of your life and talking to the young girl or boy with so many dreams and so much pain. What will you do? Will you allow the fear to define you and stay stuck where you are, or will you start the path of redemption even if that path is different than you envisioned as a young man or woman?

Talk to that youngster, ask what he or she would want for you today. I'll bet that you can still be that person, no matter how dire things seem. There's no need to wait another day. Take a step. Stop. Look around. Smell the roses or even the crap. Embrace that smell. Allow it to guide your next step. That's recovery regardless of your profession. Don't allow yourself to pre-define what recovery looks like. If you believe AA is the best route. Do that. If decide you're not the AA type, find a recovery program that is your type. If you try it and you decide it's not for you, pivot, juke, and start again. Remember that the goal is not to fit into someone else's subjective definition of what recovery looks like. It is to become a person in long-term recovery. There are many roads and often many detours. Some temporary, some permanent. As long as you are above ground, both recovery and living redemption are possible.

Epilogue

AS I WROTE this book in 2016, the process brought back many memories, including one I want to share with you here.

■ October 15, 2015

I'm back in the Green Oaks parking lot, this time alone. I have a rush of feelings and memories as I pull into the parking lot. The blackness of the asphalt. The walk through the double doors. The intake station just to my right. *Where did they take me the first time?* I can't remember the room. My brothers were in fear the first time, my girlfriend (now-fiancée) in tears the second time.

This time however, I'm not in crisis. This time, my thoughts are not of suicide. This day, instead of needing help, I'm here *to* help. My thoughts are about reaching out to others who came both before and after me at Green Oaks—those in crisis as I was. The stories will be as varied as the environment, but fear and uncertainty is a constant in these narratives. So many here describe the darkness and panic of falling into what seems like a bottomless abyss with no clear way out. I knew all those feelings.

Today I'm still about my own recovery, but I'm also about helping others with theirs. I want to share with these people my own story and let them know that in the worst possible circumstances, Green Oaks was a positive for me in getting me thinking about recovery—even though it would take two trips to understand. There is no shame in psychiatric crisis treatment. Even if it doesn't seem like it at the time, and we fight with all of our strength against it, we often find ourselves in crisis treatment when we need it most. I tell the people here, and I tell you: Let yourself be loved by those who care about you, and let yourself be helped by those trained to provide it. There is a way out, and it's with the helping hands of others. But you have to want it. It starts with self-accountability. It starts with you.

ENDNOTES

1. P.R. Krill, R. Johnson & L. Albert, *The Prevalence of Substance Use and Other Mental Health Concerns among American Attorneys,* J. Addiction Med. (Jan./Feb. 2016).

2. Though not covered here, I describe my use of anabolic steroids as part of a larger struggle with body image in my first book, *Shattered Image.*

3. "Alcohol Use Disorder" is the term used by the current *Diagnostic and Statistical Manual of Mental Disorders* (DSM-5) to describe habitual, pathological use of alcohol. Since 2013, the diagnosis of AUD has replaced the diagnoses of Alcohol Abuse or Alcohol Dependence in the DSM. AUD is diagnosed based on positive response to 2 of 11 questions. Depending on the number of questions answered positively, AUD is described as mild, moderate, or severe.

4. Lawyer's Assistance Programs (LAPs) are programs established by state Bars or independent organizations that provide free, confidential addiction and mental health services to lawyers, judges, law students, and family members of those in the law profession.

5. 2014 Survey of Law Student Well-Being was funded by the ABA Enterprise Fund and the Dave Nee Foundation.

6. *The Paper Chase* is a 1973 film about a first-year Harvard law student who learns to deal with the pressures of law school. In one of the first scenes of the movie, protagonist James Hart (played by Timothy Bottoms) is so humiliated by the professor in his first contract law course that after class he immediately runs to the bathroom and throws up.

7. The 11th Tradition of Alcoholics Anonymous (AA) states, "Our public relations policy is based on attraction rather than promotion; we need always maintain personal anonymity at the level of press, radio, and films." I acknowledge that discussing my personal AA participation in this book may run contrary to that tradition. I however, have been completely open and honest in the public realm about all aspects of my recovery since my first year of sobriety. I have received both criticism and support during that time. To suddenly change now would be disingenuous to what I believe and have always believed about

self-determination when it comes to personal anonymity and the need for public critical discussion about every mode of recovery. Your choice may be different and I have the utmost respect for that.

8. My first book, *Shattered Image*, focuses on my struggles with eating disorders, body image, and depression.

9. For more on SMART Recovery, see chapter 17, page 204.

10. All civil litigation and lawyers will know what a mediation is. If you're not one of those, maybe you've been involved with one being a party to your own divorce or you've personally sued someone, or been sued. At some point in a lawsuit, the judge orders the parties to get together and try to settle a case with a neutral mediator.

11. A term that refers to people with relatively low wages that spend their money in public like they have limitless resources.

12. Of course not all social media connections are healthy in recovery, and as in real life, limits have to be set. Sometimes the past should remain in the past. I once got a Facebook friend request from one of my former drug dealers. I had to remind him that hand-to-hand cocaine exchanges on the campus of Southern Methodist University really was not a "friendship." If he were coming to me in recovery, fine. The past is the past. But he was seeing if I was still in the market for an eight-ball. I didn't accept the request.

13. Body dysmorphic disorder is generally characterized as a disabling preoccupation with imagined or exaggerated defects of physical appearance. BDD is a clinically recognized disorder and thought to affect 1–2 percent of the U.S. population. I wrote about my struggles with body dysmorphia in my first book, *Shattered Image*.

14. I have a vivid memory of my high school English teacher telling me that that my SAT score was not very good and I would not get into a good college when I expressed happiness at scoring over 500 on the verbal part of the SAT.

15. MDMA, the active ingredient in ecstasy, is a type of amphetamine that generally causes feelings of euphoria and lowered inhibition. "Bath salts" are any of a number of chemically similar but less expensive substances such as MDPV. Effects of MDPV and other substances sold as bath salts can include delirium, paranoia, panic attacks, and even death.

16. An eight-ball is $\frac{1}{8}$ ounce of powdered cocaine.

17. Every state Bar has its own rules and regulations, including sanctions and procedures for making continued Bar membership contingent on

seeking help. Interested readers should consult their own state Bar guidelines for more details.

18. The "Big Book" is the commonly used nickname of the primary text of Alcoholics Anonymous, which was originally published in 1939. (The full name of the book is *Alcoholics Anonymous: The Story of How Many Thousands of Men and Women Have Recovered from Alcoholism.*) As many as 40 million copies of the book have been sold, and it has seen numerous new editions published. The Big Book outlines the famous 12 steps and 12 traditions of AA, among other content. The chapter entitled "We Agnostics" argues that for the alcoholic of the "hopeless variety" recovery without spirituality or the belief in a "higher power" is ineffective.

19. Small boxes containing parchment with verses from the Torah that many observant Jewish men bind to the arms or forehead during week-day morning services.

20. Henry "Hank" Parkhurst was a businessman whose testimonial about the ways alcohol use affected his career makes up chapter 10 of the Big Book, called "To Employers."

21. For a directory of LAPs by state, please visit the website of the American Bar Association: americanbar.org/colap.

22. Billy Carter was the younger brother of President Jimmy Carter. He was best known for embarrassing schemes such as playing up his own image as a hayseed to market a brand of beer bearing his name.

ABOUT THE AUTHOR

Brian Cuban, the younger brother of Dallas Mavericks owner and entrepreneur Mark Cuban, is a Dallas based attorney, author, and addiction recovery advocate. A graduate of the University of Pittsburgh School of Law, he has passed the respective bar exams of Pennsylvania (retired) and Texas. Brian has been in long-term recovery from alcohol, cocaine, and bulimia since April 2007.

His first book, *Shattered Image: My Triumph Over Body Dysmorphic Disorder*, chronicles his first-hand experiences living with, and recovering from, twenty-seven years of eating disorders and Body Dysmorphic Disorder (BDD).

Brian has spoken at colleges, universities, conferences, and non-profit events across the United States and in Canada. Brian has appeared on prestigious talks shows such as the *Katie Couric Show* as well as numerous media outlets around the country. He also writes extensively on these subjects. His columns have appeared on CNN.com, FoxNews.com, *The Huffington Post*, *Above the Law*, and in online and print newspapers around the world.